Shared Structures *Private Spaces*

Housing in Mexico

Fernanda Canales

To my parents and my sisters, Lorea and Jimena

So the house can be our world
and the world can be our home.

Contents

Foreword

Over the past years, Fernanda Canales set herself the titanic task of preparing an official record of modern Mexican architecture from different points of view and on varying scales. In previous books she traced the arc of great institutional works and the most memorable feats of Mexican modernism from innovative critical perspectives (see *Architecture in Mexico 1900-2010*, Vols. I and II); later she took on the challenge of recording the distribution typologies of 100 housing blocks in *Vivienda Colectiva en México: El derecho a la arquitectura*; and now she brings us a comprehensive new survey of residential structures, rooted in an understanding of their capacity to build cities and contribute to the education of citizens through design.[1]

All of them are systematic works, based on analysis and drawing, which have gradually compiled a kind of encyclopedia on the what, how and who of Mexico's generous modernism. Not only do they allow us to expand our knowledge and vision of the laborious modern Mexican epic, as intense and changeable as it is rich in glorious moments of abstraction and serenity, but they also give us insight into a particular method of practicing architecture, a method Fernanda uses to construct her own identity while also recording the work of others, which is at once objective in the data it offers and subjective in how those data are organized and "designed".

1 Canales, Fernanda, *Architecture in México 1900-2010. The Construction of Modernity:* Arquine - Fomento Cultural Banamex, Mexico City, 2013.
Canales, Fernanda, *Vivienda colectiva en México. El derecho a la arquitectura:* Gustavo Gili, Barcelona, 2017.

This type of action –or, perhaps more accurately, "activism"– can be understood as "documentalism", a form of architectural creation in which analysis and creativity emerge in a disjointed fashion. It is no coincidence that this description applies equally to many of today's most fascinating artistic practices in fields such as film, literature or the visual arts, at a time when Cedric Price and Rem Koolhaas –undoubtedly the most meticulous documentalists of previous generations– have become the protagonists and benchmarks of practically every relevant initiative in contemporary architecture. Documenting processes implies immersion in the floating data medium of one's choice, causing its information load to trigger a change of state in us, so to speak, that releases a burst of genuine creative energy. Documenting means stoking the system to boiling point, thus distilling a new state of matter which we might call a book or a project, or both.

Fernanda's chosen subject, Mexican material culture, is immense and incredibly beautiful, and she has distilled its alchemical creativity to produce precisely that: a greater quantity and quality of material culture, of Mexican culture. I am convinced that this is a productive effort which reveals not only the documented subject, but also the significance of analysis as a tool for contemporary architectural design.

Iñaki Ábalos

Preface

Shared Structures, Intimate Spaces

Books about Mexican architecture rarely mention the real conditions underlying construction: for example, in the capital the earth trembles, the city is built over what used to be a lake, rainwater is sent to drainage systems and causes repeated flooding, and distant rivers are drained dry to serve a population that complains about breathing polluted air and builds more parking lots than schools, hospitals, or parks. How should the buildings in a city that moves, sinks, and floods be? What sense does it make to talk about architecture when there are no plans regarding its links to services? What is the relationship between a building, the conditions of the territory, and peoples' ways of life?

As I wrote the final lines of this book, a violent earthquake in Mexico City sent me running terrified into the street, only to find out with relief that unlike the same date exactly 32 years ago –September 19, 1985– where more than 400 structures fell, this time, in 2017, only 40 buildings collapsed. That initial optimism faded as we learned of the disastrous effects in different parts of the country and the additional consequences caused by a previous earthquake that had struck just twelve days before; the strongest in one hundred years. In the capital, these earthquakes reminded its nearly 20 million inhabitants that the seemingly solid layer supporting thousands of buildings is technically still water and that seismic waves are magnified and accelerated in a ground of lacustrine origin.

The earthquakes of September 2017 revealed the distance between the reality of a place and the projects that pretend to impose themselves on that territory. They also exposed the effects of corruption in the construction industry: collapses were due primarily to irregularities such as that of a luxury residence built illegally over an elementary school where nearly thirty people died or housing structures clandestinely built over old houses. It soon became apparent that the earthquakes of September 2017 had been just as destructive as those of 1985 but in different ways. What were once small villages had become large cities lacking any urban planning or regulations. For example, Cuernavaca, until a few decades ago a paradise filled with weekend homes about an hour away from the capital, and Iztapalapa, an informal settlement on the outskirts established in the 1970s, each currently has two million inhabitants. The earthquakes were a reminder of the problems that everyone assumed had been resolved after 1985. The images of the destructions frightened a population that seemed impervious to fear. The contrasts between urban effervescence and rural abandonment revealed a country that does not know how to count its dead, protect its living, and safeguard its heritage.

After the earthquakes, the government announced reconstructions that rebuff the importance of the existing legacy and are based on demolishing everything that stands in their way: replacing thousands of traditional homes with mass produced housing projects foreign to traditional ways of life, to the local climates, and to supporting infrastructure. This is a hasty building strategy that has forgotten what I attempt to address in this book: the importance of understanding the house as the space where personal histories are interwoven with the histories of a place and a culture. While governments are making one-sided, short-term decisions, architects are trying to organize interdisciplinary teams to address the difficult issue of providing housing for thousands of distant and anonymous users. The same themes tackled by John Habraken and Christopher Alexander decades ago have once again come to the fore around the world given the shortage of decent housing options in our increasingly inhospitable cities. This led me to re-examine the housing project that Alexander built in Mexicali in the 1970s. His book, *The Production of Houses*, about this project in northwest Mexico, shows adaptable prototypes produced with the occupants; homes that relied on self-building and on materials produced on site by occupants...[1] In this book, all of the ideas that are

1 Christopher Alexander, Howard Davis, Julio Martinez, and Don Corner, *The Production of Houses* (New York/Oxford: Oxford University Press, 1985).

always brought to bare in design are addressed, yet, in today's conditions, they seem unreachable. Alexander's Mexicali project is not the large residential cluster suggested in the book but rather a small complex that currently houses a section of the Nursing School of the University of Baja California. It is also not a self-sufficient community or a new way of conceiving the city. It is just part of a city block buried among streets and houses inhabited by people who have never suspected that better housing designs could improve their lives.

Why have architectural contributions to cities been so small, when the benefits they offer to inhabitants seem so glaringly obvious? We continue building houses for a social structure that no longer exists and for abstract cities that differ greatly from reality. The rising number of *natural* disasters around the world is actually not caused by nature but rather by humans who have ignored the earth and climate's natural behavior.

Among the thousands of photographs taken of buildings destroyed by the earthquakes that shook Mexico in September 2017, one seems particularly eloquent to me: it is an image of a housing block that is still standing but has lost part of the facade, revealing a series of fractured rooms almost hanging in mid-air. That image clearly reflects the private space: a half-made bed, dresses hanging in the closet, shoes set out for the next party, a blueprint tube leaning against the closet... From afar and through the camera lens, we are able to glimpse the most personal aspects of the occupants' lives and understand their tastes, age, and many of their daily routines. There are no people in the picture and the damage caused by the collapsed facade is not visible. All we see is a frozen moment in the existence of a structure that seems as solid as it is fragile and quotidian as it is unbelievable. In the photograph of the damaged building, next to the rooms that have been left hanging over the abyss, other neighboring apartment windows appear to show a repetitive and anonymous façade. Unsurprisingly, that veiled façade shuts itself off to the city with distrust. That image clearly evokes the title of this book not only because it reveals the different layers of interconnected lives –above or beside each other, alone or crowded– that are present in the different housing, but also because it shows the responsibility of a few for the lives of many. We are dealing with structures that, whether we like it or not, we all share.

Mexico is an ideal place to find architectural examples that contrast scale, budgets, materials, and programs; a melting pot of transformations where the future between rural and urban life is played out and where questions of identity, reconciliation, and survival are addressed. This legacy, sparsely

Building in the Narvarte colony, 2017
Photography: Cuartoscuro

documented and progressively illegible in today's rapidly-changing cities, piqued in me the interest in gathering a compendium of architectural ideas and solutions that describe how some of the leading experts, in a specific country and over the last century, have sought to achieve a balance between individual aspirations and the need to create a common territory.

Given that most of the world's houses have yet to be designed and will be the cornerstones on which our societies are constructed, this book posits new approaches to collective domestic typologies that make up the urban fabric. Its intention is to reactivate theories and drawings as elements that incite us to develop new ways of living. The aim is to bring together the connections between two concepts increasingly posited as polar opposites: the house and the city, in order to establish smoother transitions between the private space, the shared infrastructures, and the territory. For that reason, I have focused my work for more than two decades on building bridges between different periods, authors, and project scales, between two-dimensional graphic representation and three-dimensional space, and between the minimum housing unit and the urban space. This analysis is part of a broader work that I have developed on the topic of housing: initially focused on low-income projects and later creating experimental prototypes and vertical housing projects and while continuously alternating between an architecture practice, teaching, and research agendas. The idea is to create tools capable of generating more open dynamics in an attempt to build less harmful environments.

Due to the privacy that a house provides, it is not easy to represent the ideals that have shaped our daily ways of dwelling. The aim of this book is precisely to provide that missing account: rethink the elements that define how we sleep, cook, construct our personal universe, and relate with others. Therefore, the book emerges from questioning the tools that we commonly use to design; the way we conceive and represent the house. The purpose is to gather the discourses of different authors in order to trace the meaning of privacy within shared structures; addressing the commitment of envisioning personal worlds for others.

Introduction

Between One House and Another

This book explores the relationship between ideas and houses, the space that exists between rooms, people, and cities; that space that is first materialized in a drawing and ultimately defines everyone's lives. The research is centered in the modern housing culture in Mexico, and consists of two parts: the first is comprised of a series of texts that address the topic of housing; starting in a global context and then focused on a local historical account. The second is an analysis of 70 collective housing projects designed in the last hundred years (between 1917 and 2017) intertwined with a collection of statements by architects involved in the issues of housing during that same period. The selection of buildings and statements reveals specific ideas which, taken together, offer valuable insight for understanding the ways through which the relationships between people and the environment have been established. The selected projects encompass thousands of houses and are represented in drawings rather than photographs to offer a uniform reading that highlights different methodologies. In this way, the modern habitat is approached on different levels, giving equal importance to ideas, drawings, and buildings.

The drawings are not to be read as passive depictions but as tools capable of influencing the decisions and inventiveness of those who build. Therefore, each project is represented by two illustrations: a floor plan at an urban scale that exemplifies how the building's shape is related to its context; and another, an axonometric view that interprets the building in its totality in order to give a general idea of its design decisions, scale, openness, and density. The projects are presented in a chronological order and are interlaced with quotes by architects in order to provide a sense of the historical moment and situate the building in the context of both the city and the prevailing ideas of its time. This format refuses to view architecture as a set of given facts and immutable decisions. The drawing serves to challenge positions and the architecture is (re)presented as something more than a built element, revealing buildings as discourses and as themes that must be revisited and that are necessary to rethink.

The axonometric drawings made for this book in collaboration with LANZA Atelier –exhibited at the Museum of Modern Art in San Francisco (SFMOMA) from March to July 2018– are a form of anti-perspectives that present the buildings as lacking periodicity or history, without a front or a back. This decontextualization does not aim to erase the surroundings but rather to let the designs express their own logic independently of their circumstances. The drawings create a common language for designs that are very different from each other and places them under the same lens; rather than seeing a photographic fragment we are offered a retrospective vision that makes the different positions tangible and forces us to lessen the focus on materials and on gestures that generally distract our gaze. In this way, the projects are approached not by analyzing their stylistic or temporal features or by using the representational techniques of each author but rather by visualizing the ideas proposed by these works and expressed in their diagrams. The formal simplification of the drawings allows us to immediately grasp a residential complex or a building with multiple facets. What is shown are attitudes. In that way, the connection between a concept, a building, and a street is revealed, and the different attempts at reinventing the house are emphasized not as isolated battles but as part of a strategy for thinking how we want to live in an increasingly individualistic, monotonous world. Consequently, the projects presented in the following pages illustrate alternatives to conventional models of living. These projects can be seen as challenges, but also as vacillations; some buildings were designed to prove theories, others as tools for discovery, and yet others to sell more square footage. All were motivated, however, by the desire to build a certain sense of community. These proposals, built or not, portray lessons on how to align the hopes and dreams of life with the real conditions of the projects.

Architecture is the setting in which we move but it is also the space that defines how and what we want to be surrounded by. As American critic Paul Goldberger wrote, "we build, in the end, because we believe in a future –nothing shows commitment to the future like architecture. And we build well because we believe in a better future."[1] Despite the relevance that housing has held to the architectural profession, the majority of the world's homes are not designed by architects and there is no way to evaluate how ideal each model is as we would do with the design of a chair and the perfection of its prototype. How, then, can the interaction between people, structures, and the world be improved?

A house, any house, defines the space that exists between what belongs to one and what belongs to everyone, and the sum of houses in the territory determines the habitability of the planet. The effects of houses have multiplied and, with them, our awareness that a society's wellbeing depends precisely on its decisions regarding the construction of dwellings. The human species is the principal agent of physical transformation in our world and that opens up new prospects for the house; the types of houses we replicate will determine whether or not we move from destruction to sustainability and from exclusion to inclusiveness. The concept of house is very broad and encompasses everything from a cell, nest, or hut to a palace, hotel, ship's cabin, or tent. Practically anything can be considered a house. No other typology has sparked so much interest or inspired so many fantastic worlds yet no other has ended up being so monotonous. Why?

Although it might seem that everyone is free to decide how to live, in reality, our social, economic, and political structures drastically condition our housing options. Before, houses were constructed according to their use, guided by an anthropological connection linked to a place and to available materials in a process of intimate correspondence; where users built their house, occupied it, and adapted it over time to suit their daily routines, their economic situation, and external conditions such as weather or views. The advent of modernity engendered a separation of these natural dynamics: the modern house emerged from a representation made by a specialist who would never occupy it and, as a general rule, had no vested interest in its future outcomes. Yet beyond this simplistic dichotomy of the old adaptable house versus the rigid modern house –which, we must remember, was invented to solve the problems of unhygienic conditions and lack of suitability to new needs posed by its predecessor– today's houses are neither adaptable spaces nor intelligent machines. The unbridled growth of cities worldwide has revealed the difficulty

1 Paul Goldberger, *Why Architecture Matters*, New Haven: Yale University Press, 2009, p. 40.

in planning for the development of cities and, as a result, the house went from being the key element for exploring the possibilities of more equitable societies to become a global, repetitive, obsolete stereotype, increasingly out of touch with the needs of its occupants, and simply a money-making mechanism for a privileged few. This model has led to greater inequality and implies that architectural contributions have no impact on cities that we can no longer control. The Modern Movement's notion of the house as a dynamic garment never managed to materialize on a large scale, not even in terms of the protective shell that gave rise to the first human constructions. Neither flexible modern tools nor comfortable skins: the majority of the human race lacks even the most basic form of safe and healthy dwellings. What other animal species is so unskilled at fitting out its basic habitat? Where in the animal kingdom can we find such dramatic contrasts between the shelters of different specimens?

While the number of homeless people grows around the world, the number of second homes that remain empty most of the year also grows. On the one hand, the housing shortage grows and spreads. On the other, more and more houses are designed not so much to be occupied but rather as investments; thousands of people without a home and thousands of homes without people. This happens at the same time that downtown areas are being drained of residential buildings and new houses are built further and further away from urban infrastructures.[2] These contrasts engender more contrasts; the impact of housing on the makeup of cities becomes increasingly visible and permanent.

Few countries present the striking contrasts found in Mexico between urban and rural, wealth and poverty, and private and public. This geographic, social, and economic diversity makes the country a prime example of the challenges inherent to meeting individual needs in an increasingly crowded world. Mexico is one of the countries with the largest number of informal settlements, of urban housing structures, and with the worst housing shortage rates while, simultaneously, having millions of abandoned houses (one-seventh of all houses are vacant).[3] It is a prime example of the ambivalent development that characterizes contemporary metropolises that are built as an amalgamation of ghettos: houses built on the outskirts of cities lacking basic services and houses built as islands in urban centers indifferent to the resulting overload on water supplies, waste management, traffic, and public space.

2 In Mexico, for example, the percentage of abandoned housing in downtown areas is as high as 40%. OECD, 2013: 134.

3 Censo de Población y Vivienda 2010 [2010 Population and Housing Census], Instituto Nacional de Estadística, Geografía e Informática (INEGI), Mexico City, 2010; available at http://www.beta.inegi.org.mx/proyectos/ccpv/2010/, accessed June 2017. Over 14% of the houses in Mexico are unoccupied and average transportation costs are equal to 30% of the inhabitants' monthly income. See Yuridia Torres, "Deshabitadas 14% de las viviendas en México", in El Economista, March 20, 2013.

Mexico was the first laboratory for gauging the urban and social repercussions of the demographic explosion, pollution, and traffic on the vast megalopolis of the 20th century. There the modern utopias envisioned in Europe and the United States were built on an unprecedented scale; there, too, Luis Barragán and Juan O'Gorman developed some of their most important lessons, while others like Hannes Meyer and Christopher Alexander conceived key projects in their careers. In few places has it made such sense to design so many housing projects intended to define the cities of the future in contexts characterized by rapid growth, low budgets, and diversity of climates, densities, and customs. This variety allows the dramatic coexistence of different dwelling programs based on diverse ways of dwelling "residential high-rises, neighborhood buildings, communal buildings (*vecindades*), standardized housing complexes, small duplexes, minimum housing prototypes, etc." that encompass concepts such as the architect-as-developer and the user-as-builder and that unleash complex relationships between mass produced, improvised building techniques, the logic of the construction industry, and everyday regulations and realities. From these contrasting conditions, diverse solutions arise that can be explained simply by looking at only two out of the 70 projects analyzed: the Izatacalco Housing Development built by Imanol Ordorika, J. Francisco Serrano and José R. Nava Requesens in 1973 as the pilot project for the newly created Instituto del Fondo Nacional de la Vivienda para los Trabajadores [Institute of the National Housing Fund for Workers (Infonavit)] and the project "Un cuarto más" (One more room) designed for the same institution almost 35 years later by Alberto Kalach, Rozana Montiel, and Francisco Pardo. The first was built to house 23,000 people in a housing development surrounded by parks, lakes, sports areas, schools and commerce in the western edge of Mexico City and the second promotes the creation of additional rooms to increase the size of existing houses in underused areas of the city that lack public services. This case exemplifies the changes in the roles that architects and the state have played in the last decades: it shows the shift from the design of new cities based on organized housing projects and communal spaces to commissions to build small interventions of private spaces; the shift of design at a macro level on a *tabula rasa* characteristic of developments of the 20th century to minimal and adaptable strategies for reusing existing structures. These changes become clearer at the moment of juxtaposing the distinct phrases collected for this volume that exemplify the priorities of different era. For instance, at the beginning of the 20th century, to talk about the house was to talk about issues of style, technology, and identity. During the revolution, the word *house* was substituted by the word *housing* and it became an issue of social justice. In the middle of the 20th century, housing was considered synonymous to urban planning, of the design of cities endowed with public services. In the final decades of the 20th century, to talk about the house was to discuss the failed proposals of incompetent governments while, at the beginning of the 21st century, it is to complain about the logic of the housing market and corruption. However, statements like the following give the theme a renewed sense: "70% of cities is made up of housing. If we improve housing, we improve the city."[4]

The progressive urbanization of the world transforms in just a few short decades the pre-existing conditions of a place and completely alters the course of our history. In less than a hundred years, we have seen our world go from empty to full, where we have built more than our ancestors did in centuries, and where we have used more energy than in the entire history of humanity.[5] What is built in the next thirty years will constitute 60% of what will be our future cities.[6] How can we improve, then, our ability to respond in the construction of a shared habitat? How can we narrow the gap that exists between what we build and what we actually want to live in? In a world where 1% of the population owns 50% of the planet's wealth, houses are a key element to redefining our modes of coexistence.[7] In this dizzyingly fast-paced present, what sense does it make to look back at the past? To rethink the house is to rethink the primary relationship that exists between an individual and society; between ourselves and the world. We have built our cities at the cost of destroying our planet. To change this implies that we must change our notion of the house as well as review the projects that have defined our habitat.

4 Carlos Zedillo, El reto de la vivienda en México, Instituto del Fondo Nacional de la Vivienda para los Trabajadores (Infonavit), México, 2016, p. 5.

5 Marina Garcés, *Filosofía inacabada*, Barcelona: Galaxia Gutenberg, 2015, pp. 28-29.

6 Augusto Barrera, lecture at Mextrópoli, Teatro Metropólitan, Mexico City, March 13, 2017.

7 Richard Ingersoll, "La mirada del marciano. Rem Koolhaas, a Reporter of Globalization", in *Arquitectura Viva*, no. 188, Madrid, October 2016, p. 24.

Toward a New Domestic Project

Warning: Please do try this at home.

Architecture is a roof but, before, it is a wall, a boundary, a series of elements made to demarcate but also to unite. Its greatest asset can be found in that duality, that ability to achieve both protection and be inviting. Architecture is the materialization of a society's desires for cohesion and isolation. Mediating between those two poles may consist of building imperceptible boundaries or, on the other hand, insurmountable divisions. Our built environments are, in fact, vestiges of the nuances that reconcile the private and the social. That dual nature –to demarcate and to articulate– which links private and public, is conspicuously concentrated in collective housing. There the intermediation between the individual and the shared is established and it is where the relationships of its occupants to each other and the world around them are determined.

The history of a country is the history of its houses. They uncover what temples conceal: the structures that house the majority –and not its icons– reveal how a population lives. Dwellings reflect aspects of everyday life; they illustrate customs, technical progress, and family roles and also express the degree of equality that exists in a society. They tell us about the level of culture and justice among their inhabitants, the wisdom with which they use their resources, the way they care for the territory or their indifference toward it.[1]

1 Four out of every ten people in the world do not have access to a latrine. See Josep Maria Montaner and Zaida Muxí, *Arquitectura y política: ensayos para mundos alternativos*, Barcelona: Gustavo Gili, 2011, p. 179.

Today, the construction of housing is the primary cause of urban expansion. However, in recent decades, cities have grown at a rate dictated not by the actual need but by the logic of the market. Usually, urban sprawl is not defined by population growth; it is merely the product of a developmentalist drive to sell more, grow more, and build more. For example, in the past thirty years, the population of Mexico grew by 210% while the rate of urban growth was 700%.[2] These absurdities can be explained thus: while a high percentage of the population is homeless, there is a surplus of abandoned dwellings. In most cities, especially in under developing countries, an unjustified territorial expansion occurs and is symptomatic of the same blindness exhibited by those who defend urban re-densification without stopping to consider the consequences of over-saturated services and territorial imbalance. In terms of efficiency, vertically grouping together several families on the same surface area where only one lived might seem like a good idea. We must also consider, however, that a densely populated city needs more land to supply energy and food for its inhabitants as well as much more space to get rid of its waste.[3] Cities, where most of the people in the world live, occupy just under 2% of the earth's surface but they consume nearly 70% of total generated energy and produce 80% of the world´s pollution.[4]

When density rises, what grows is not only the square footage of built-up area and the number of inhabitants but supply problems and instances of marginalization.[5] These re-densification dynamics polarize the existing disparities between the urban centers and the peripheries and between regions that produce and those that consume.[6] It is no coincidence that some of the most densely populated cities in the world –Manila, Cairo, Lagos, and Macao– are also some of the poorest.[7] They are also the ones that have some of the worst mass transit systems and high crime rates; trapping them in an endless spiral of inequality.[8] Shanghai exemplifies this disparity: half of the population lives

2 Sergio Trejo, "En 70 años creció 700 veces la mancha urbana", in *La Razón*, July 6, 2013; available at www.razón.com.mx, accessed September 2, 2015.

3 Alejandro Hernández Gálvez, ed., *Densidades* (Mexico: Arquine, 2015), p. 9.

4 José Fariña Tojo, "Una ciudad más próxima: el futuro de las ciudades", in *El País*, June 28, 2015, p. 2. See also Pablo Linde, "Los alcaldes de las grandes ciudades piden más peso en la escena mundial", in *El País*, October 18, 2016, p. 7.

5 A. Hernández Gálvez, ed., op. cit., p. 9.

6 See Ricky Burdett, *Diseñando la democracia urbana: densidades*, Mexico City: Arquine, 2015, p. 23.

7 The largest cities are more segregated. See Joel Kotkin, "Megacities and the Density Delusion: Why More People Doesn't Equal More Wealth", in *Forbes*, April 16, 2013; available at http://www.forbes.com/sites/joelkotkin/2013/04/16/megacities-and-the-density-delusion/, accessed April 2016.

8 Justin McGuirk, "Understanding The Numbers", in Ricky Burdett and Deyan Sudjic (eds.), *Living in the Endless City: The Urban Age Project by The London School of Economics and Deutsche Bank's Alfred Herrhausen Society*, London: Phaidon, 2011, p. 297.

on less than 5% of the city's surface area, while the other half has the rest of the land to themselves.[9] On average, each person has sixty-four square feet in which to live.[10] But how do you fit a bed and bathroom into an eight-by-eight foot space and still have room to stretch? And not only that: if this is the average, what about those who have even less space? The worst part of this is that the problems are not limited to homes: inequality affects everyone. In the last few years, commuting time for the residents of Shanghai has increased by 70%.[11]

Part of the problem is the single-family housing model linked to personal car ownership. The ideal of the free-stranding single-family house has become translated into a larger number of people who spend more time commuting. This is not only a waste of time but also a waste of space and of resources. In Mexico, where single-family homes account for 90% of the housing stock, the number of cars has doubled in the last eight years.[12] In the capital city, known as the world's most traffic-congested city, more parking lots were built in recent years than anything else.[13] The fact that cities are growing to make room for cars rather than people underscores the absurdity of this trend. Even in a city like Barcelona, known for its urban balance, cars take up 70% of the public space but only transport 17% of its residents.[14]

The housing problem is not only about mobility, the shortage of homes, their density, or the height of buildings, but rather about the ideas behind the projects. When new buildings turn out to be useless, it's obvious that the concept of housing is flawed from its very core. In the words of the chairman of one of Mexico's biggest housing developers, which operated in as many as 35 different cities, the current situation can be summed up by the following statement: "We realized that we could use the same prototypes we had for

9 Ibid., p. 485.

10 Ricky Burdett and Philipp Rode, "The Urban Age Project", in Ricky Burdett and Deyan Sudjic (eds.), *The Endless City: The Urban Age Project by The London School of Economics and Deutsche Bank's Alfred Herrhausen Society*, London: Phaidon, 2011, p. 19.

11 Ibid., p. 110.

12 See *OECD Urban Policy Reviews: Mexico, Transforming Urban Policy and Housing Finance*, Organization for Economic Cooperation and Development (OECD), Paris, 2015; available at http://www.oecd.org/publications/oecd-urban-policy-reviews-mexico-2015-9789264227293-en.htm; Spanish version: *Estudios de políticas urbanas de la OCDE: México, transformando la política urbana y el financiamiento de la vivienda*, Censo de Población y Vivienda 2014, Instituto Nacional de Estadística, Geografía e Informática (INEGI), Mexico City, 2014, p. 8; available at http://www.oecd.org/gov/sintesis-del-estudio-mexico.pdf, accessed April 2016.

13 See Andrés Señudo Gavaldon, "Garantia de estacionamiento: ¿beneficio público?", in *Nexos*, November 1, 2015; available at http://www.nexos.com.mx/?p=26753, accessed November 30, 2015. In Mexico City, 42% of property development projects built between 2009 and 2013 were parking facilities. See http://imco.org.mx/competitividad/el-peso-de-los-estacionamientos/, accessed June 27, 2017.

14 Josep Bohigas, lecture for the Master's in Housing program at Centro (Center for Design, Film and Television), Mexico City, March 2, 2016.

building houses to build prisons."[15] It is ultimately in the way that the concept of dwelling is promoted that the type of society being built is developed.

Why do historic achievements in housing now seem like utopias? Many groundbreaking designs, endlessly replicated in the hands of others, shattered the ideals of modernization and called into question the reforming nature of architecture itself. The phenomenon is the same around the world: minimal houses have become even smaller and large houses have grown even larger. The gap between miserable and lavish homes is getting wider and wider. In the United States (excluding the wealthiest 10% of the population), the annual income has risen by 10% since the 1970s yet the average price of a home has doubled.[16] Today, a person working the same hours could only buy a fraction of what was once a whole house which, it goes without saying, would probably be located hours away from the original one. The price of housing and the cost of getting to and from it affect the wellbeing not only of a person or a family but also of the entire city.

Generally speaking, a house's flaws are not visible from the outside yet when those internal problems remain unsolved they ultimately surpass the walls and flow out into the city. Yet urban environments cannot make up for the shortcomings of its houses. After all, it is not a question of how many parks, recreational or leisure spaces a city has to offer: places for living must strike a balance between services and needs. Thinking of residential complexes as isolated entities is the same mistake as regarding the house as an individual unit reserved for one client and limited to a specific lot. This way of thinking has created a lopsided correlation between houses, services, and transportation that affects the dynamics of everyone's daily lives.

The verb "to dwell" implies more than just having a roof over a certain number of square feet: it means having a little world of one's own which, at the same time, is connected to the world of others. The disparity that exists between the home we want and the home we can afford explains the separation between the house, those who dwell in it, and "their" city. That neighbors are often viewed as threats is only one of its consequences. Another is that the land is ravaged as single-family homes invade the outskirts; a phenomenon just as devastating as a natural disaster but for which human beings bear the

15 Eustaquio Tomás de Nicolás Gutiérrez, Chairman of the Board of Directors of Desarrolladora Homex (Homex Group), quoted by Álvaro Delgado, "Derroche al estilo García Luna", in *Proceso*, April 20, 2013; available at www.proceso.com.mx, accessed April 23, 2013.

16 Space Caviar (ed.), SQM: *The Quantified Home. Biennale Interieur*, Brussels: Lars Müller, 2014, p. 20.

sole responsibility. Another visible result of flawed housing policies is the depopulation of historic neighborhoods and the proliferation of residential complexes in outlying areas. On the one hand, cities spread uncontrollably to where open fields and waterways existed while, on the other hand, central areas are slowly emptying.[17] In Mexico, downtowns are becoming uninhabited and a large percentage of publicly funded housing is being built on environmental reserves or in hazard zones (ravines, mountainsides, volcanoes, etc.). These areas are also invaded by informal housing developments that, despite accounting for over 65% of all new construction in the country, it is still considered to be an "irregular" practice. The most significant building model in the country, however, cannot be written off as "irregular." When the temporary becomes permanent and the illegal becomes norm, we need to change concepts and laws.[18]

Current housing programs and regulations fail to acknowledge the real situation or the characteristics of the users. They do not take into account the variety of family structures –parents without children, singles, single-parent families, or people living together but not as couples– or the changes these experience over time. For example, the new reality of a growing number of dependent elderly people who live alone and whose life expectancy is increasing is not addressed. Meanwhile, the needs for temporary or emergency housing are considered anomalous when, in fact, they are as frequent as any other standard dwelling model. These realities challenge existing archetypes and call for different housing solutions as well as different relationships between housing, public services, and other ways of understanding collective living.

The quality of life in cities depends largely on its housing policies. Those policies determine whether houses are built as spaces to create a better society or as places with no regard for the opinions of users, architects, and city planners. The state's involvement is usually limited to granting mortgages; it does not demand a redefinition of minimum standards for the characteristics of the houses (natural light and privacy) and for the plots on which they are

17 See Paavo Monkkonen, "La segregación residencial en el México urbano: niveles y patrones", in *Revista de Estudios Urbano-Regionales, vol. 38, no. 114, Santiago de Chile, May 2012, p. 139.*

18 In 2010, urban dwellings represented 78.1% of Mexico's housing stock, and more than 65% of homes were informal constructions on illegally occupied land. Moreover, the majority of the population lives in hazard zones. See *Estado actual de la vivienda en México, 2014*, op. cit., pp. 14 and 22. See also Alejandro Suárez Pareyón, "La situacion habitacional", in Gustavo Garza (ed.), *La Ciudad de México en el fin del segundo milenio*, Mexico City: El Colegio de México, 2000, p. 393; and Mirtha Hernández, "Habitan 7.4 millones en zonas de riesgo", in *Reforma*, September 18, 2015, p. 2. This data refers only to Mexico City, where 2.2 million homes are registered in hazard zones.

built (whether they are isolated or built in hazardous areas). In other words: how noisy, ill-equipped and expensive can a house be?

The relation between housing, land, and social injustice is becoming increasingly apparent.[19] The term "housing classes" refers to residence-based social stratification.[20] For instance, the median size of homes in the southern outlying districts of Madrid is 40% smaller on average than houses in its northwest suburbs.[21] Yet beyond their physical dimensions, houses also express the levels of health, unemployment, and violence of a population.[22]

The recent social unrest in France has shown the rest of the world the consequences caused by the disparity in housing. Having begun in 2005 and lasting an entire decade, violent protests exploded in the massive housing projects (*grands ensembles*) and new cities (*villes nouvelles*) of the Parisian *banlieues* or suburbs. It is no coincidence that both models of urban growth lacked proper services, connective networks, and a sense of identity from the outset. This was called the "malaise of the periphery" or "sarcellitis," after Sarcelles, one of the most criticized modern residential complexes in Europe sardonically dubbed "The American City."[23]

This situation has spread across the planet: it includes examples from Pruitt-Igoe in the USA (the housing project whose demolition in 1972 signaled the death of the Modern Movement) to the walled city of Kowloon in China (the largest human anthill in the world, demolished in 1993). But it is not a disease; it is merely the result of models of social injustice perpetuated through housing arrangements. The ailment is nothing more than the problems created by the concept of ghettofication and short-term financial interests. Their consequences are much more costly than what building decent houses in the first place would cost. One of the most widespread forms of urban growth around the world is that of informal human settlements (IHS). They are currently home to about one billion people and that number is expected to double in just twenty years.[24] This suggests that improvised solutions have something positive

19 See P. Monkkonen, op. cit., *pp. 125-146.*

20 Term coined by John Rex and Robert Samuel Moore in *Race, Community and Conflict*, London: Institute of Race Relations, 1967.

21 The average size of dwellings on the northwest outskirts of Madrid is 1,350 square feet, but in the southern outskirts the average is 810 square feet. See Jesús Leal, "Segregación social y mercados de vivienda en las grandes ciudades", in *Revista Española de Sociología*, no. 2, Madrid, 2002, pp. 59-76.

22 Reinhold Martin, Jacob Moore and Susanne Schindler (eds.), *The Art of Inequality: Architecture, Housing, and Real Estate –A Provisional Report*, New York: The Trustees of Columbia University in the City of New York, 2015.

23 See Josep Maria Montaner, *La arquitectura de la vivienda colectiva: políticas y proyectos de la ciudad contemporánea*, Reverté, Estudios Universitarios de Arquitectura collection, no. 26, Barcelona, 2015, p. 42.

24 David Gouverneur, *Planning and Design for Future Informal Settlements: Shaping the Self-Constructed City*, New York: Routledge, 2015, p. XXIII.

that "state-sponsored" housing has been unable to address. The fact that large groups of people lack access to housing highlights the lethargic inefficiency of norms and procedures. In India alone, the government and private sector built half a million homes over a five-year period while eight million informal dwellings were raised in the same time and with less money.[25] When the government and developers are sixteen times less efficient than impoverished squatters, the incongruences of official housing policies become clear.

At the beginning of the 21st century, the financial crises triggered by market housing bubbles in different countries exposed the errors in housing policies. In Spain, the so-called "brick crisis" left over three million empty dwellings (which account for one in every three abandoned houses in Europe).[26] The problem with misguided housing policies is that the impact on the territory is immediate and the aftereffects can take decades to disappear and, in some cases, they never do. Yet housing policies also have the power to rebuild societies.

Recent real estate market crises have stimulated participatory models: new ideas such as "handmade" urbanism, cooperative housing, and concepts such as "co-living" and "open building" become viable alternatives for thousands of people without homes or jobs. This has renewed interest in techniques of appropriation inspired by informal architecture and in time-honored methods of community organization.[27] But this is not about returning to the 1960s when rural life and vernacular architecture was nostalgically vindicated. It is also not the product of a romantic vision of poverty. It is about people who live in prohibitively expensive cities and are trying to solve the problems that governments and architects have failed to address. Developing countries are viewed with interest given their adaptability, their ingenuity to make the most of limited resources, and how they handle the contingencies of accelerated growth. It is as if the term "developing country" implied a constant state of crisis that appears interesting to those eager to learn how to deal with dramatic living conditions. These places are no longer the laboratories where master planners could test their modern utopian ideas, as happened in the 20th century, but rather the site from which to learn about the users' own improvised dynamics.

25 Klaus Dömer, Hans Drexler and Joachim Schultz-Granberg (eds.), *Affordable Living: Housing for Everyone*, Berlin: Jovis Verlag GmbH, 2004, p. 42.

26 Cifras del Censo 2011 [2011 Census Figures], Instituto Nacional de Estadística (INE) at http://www.ine.es/censos2011_datos/cen11_datos_inicio.htm, accessed May 18, 2016. http://politica.elpais.com/politica/2015/06/23/actualidad/1435058233_803556.html, accessed May 2016.

27 See Marcos L. Rosa and Ute E. Weiland (eds.), *Handmade Urbanism: From Community Initiatives to Participatory Models*, Berlin: Jovis Verlag GmbH, 2013; and Richard Sennet, *Juntos: rituales, placeres y políticas de cooperación*, Barcelona: Anagrama, 2012.

Accustomed to large-scale problems and housing shortages that affect millions, the people who live there have many solutions at hand. At the very least, they are used to searching for more dynamic ways of producing, financing, and designing affordable houses.

In 2012, the Venice Architecture Biennale set a new precedent when it awarded the Golden Lion to an exhibition showing the transformation of the Torre David in Caracas. It presented a visual narrative of how a 45-story office building in the heart of the Venezuelan capital, left unfinished and abandoned, was occupied and turned into housing for hundreds of families. It was a skyscraper transformed into a vertical neighborhood of some three thousand people.[28] The fact that a collective, makeshift, illegal project was even considered in a competition traditionally reserved for *auteur architecture* revealed the power of solutions created by people willing to do anything but keep waiting on architects and governments for answers that never come.

Two years later, at the 2014 Venice Biennale, a group of architects and artists created an independent pavilion dedicated to Airbnb, the online platform established in 2008 that turns private homes into temporary rental spaces.[29] The pavilion was developed to analyze the domestic and urban effects of this improvised transnational hosting scheme in ordinary houses. It was a platform that explored the consequences of monetizing the home: taking a closed, private place and turning it into a publicly "advertised" space for commercial gain. The Airbnb model exemplifies the quest to harness the potential of domestic vacancies: it shows that we can overcome our habitual paralysis in order to envision houses differently and, even, make them profitable. This initiative aimed to bring cooperative consumption, the sharing economy, innovative concepts of ownership, and other ways of understanding resources, spaces, and services into the home. It has transformed the notions of temporary shelter and of exclusively residential neighborhoods and has even provoked the rejection, throughout several cities, of the improvised use of private homes for commercial rentals.

Airbnb is not an isolated case but rather part of a rejection of the unused dwelling. It is one of the better-known examples of spontaneous actions that rethink the house as a productive space. The idea of "homesharing," which

28 Justin McGuirk and Urban-Think Tank were the curators of the exhibition that won the Golden Lion at the 2012 Venice Architecture Biennale.

29 The name Airbnb is an abbreviated form of "air-bed & breakfast".

aims to legalize shared homeownership and remove zoning boundaries in cities, is based on the same systems used to share rides, bikes, or places to eat. These dynamics range from the SoHo (small office/home office) model to the pop-up restaurants that temporarily operate out of private homes. The latter is best illustrated the Restaurant Day (*Ravintolapäivä*), an initiative begun in Helsinki in 2011 and now active in forty-three different countries, where anyone can "open" their own restaurant for a day. Platforms like these, with a global reach are based on making use of what some people are not occupying and that others want but could not have until now. Although such initiatives are new to many countries, in others they are standard practices that have existed naturally for centuries, long before the advent of the Internet. Turning private residences into temporary hotel rooms, small daycares, laundry facilities, and workshops is a custom as old as the house itself. When children play "house," very soon they usually set up a shop, beauty salon, or restaurant inside in the same way any permissive or forward-looking neighborhood would allow.

The first workspace was the house and informal architecture has always included workshops and places of business in the domestic sphere. It has been an efficient model to reinstate public and commercial conditions suppressed in the preceding century by zoning policies that sought to compartmentalize cities by age, work or leisure hours, gender, and professions.[30] Yet to praise informal architecture is to forget the injustice it tacitly promotes within and outside its structure. On one hand, informal housing systems are well established and consolidated but, on the other, they are illegal despite the permissive attitude that exists in regards to them. They exist, therefore, in a juridical and statistical limbo that allows governments to shrink much of their responsibility while, at the same time, they serve to perpetuate inequality.[31] Venezuela's Torre David may have been applauded and praised at the Venice Biennale, but the story of this unfinished vertical slum has a darker side: the residents who died or were injured when they fell through unclosed openings or down staircases with no railings.

Some of the most visible signs of social inequality are found in houses. Cities in developing countries are increasingly based on two contradictory dwelling models: informal housing and gated communities. Both turn their backs

30 Dan Hill, "The Commodification of Everything: On Restaurant Day and Airbnb", in S. Caviar (ed.), op. cit., pp. 216-223.
31 This imbalance is illustrated by the fact that half of humanity lacks direct access to running water. See J. M. Montaner, op. cit., p. 124.

on each other and on the city, creating unbridgeable rifts between ghettos. Today's reality is far removed from the two predominant urban planning models of the 20th century: Ebenezer Howard's Garden City and Le Corbusier's Ville Radieuse.[32] Although these two archetypes were opposites –one sprawling and the other centralized– they both attempted to control the site of housing: they called for controlled islands clustered around a seamless green landscape, offering a vision of an ideal, predetermined way of life.

The exhibition *Foreclosed: Rehousing the American Dream*, held in 2012 at the Museum of Modern Art (MoMA) in New York, made patent the negative effects of an urban growth model based on detached, single-program homes, a model promoted as part of the "American dream" since the mid-20th century and made possible thanks to the supremacy of the automobile. This critique proposed a new premise: if we change the dream, we could change the city. In light of the countless individual dreams fueled by the polarized scenarios of today's cities, houses can no longer be designed for passive spectators, blind to the vital spaces of others, but for a society that builds shared dreams and also lives in them.

32 Aldo Rossi, *L'architettura della città*, Padua: Marsilio, 1966; English edition: *The Architecture of the City*, Diane Ghirardo & Joan Ockman (trans.), Cambridge, MA: MIT Press, 1982. (pp. 125-126 of the Spanish version).

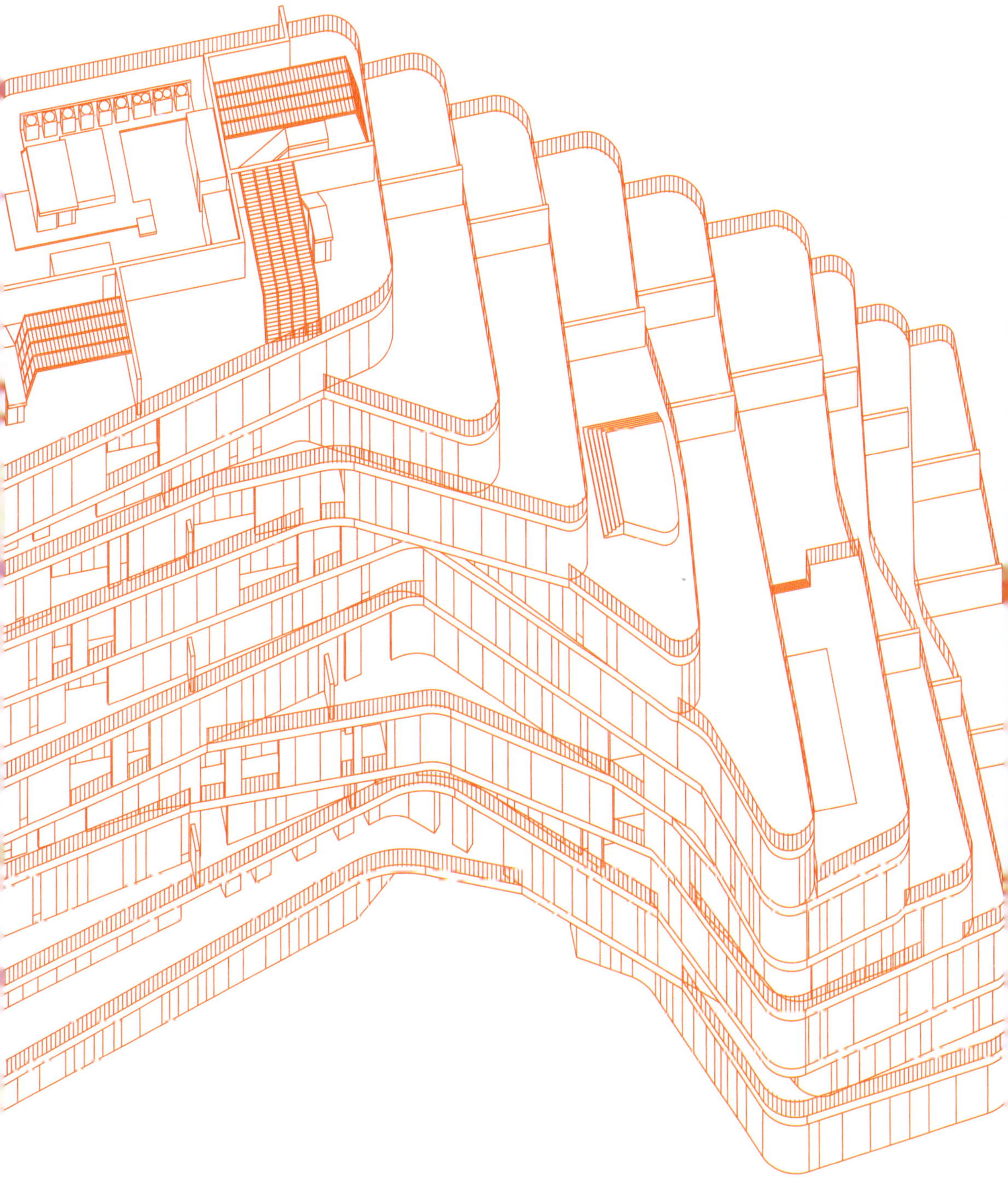

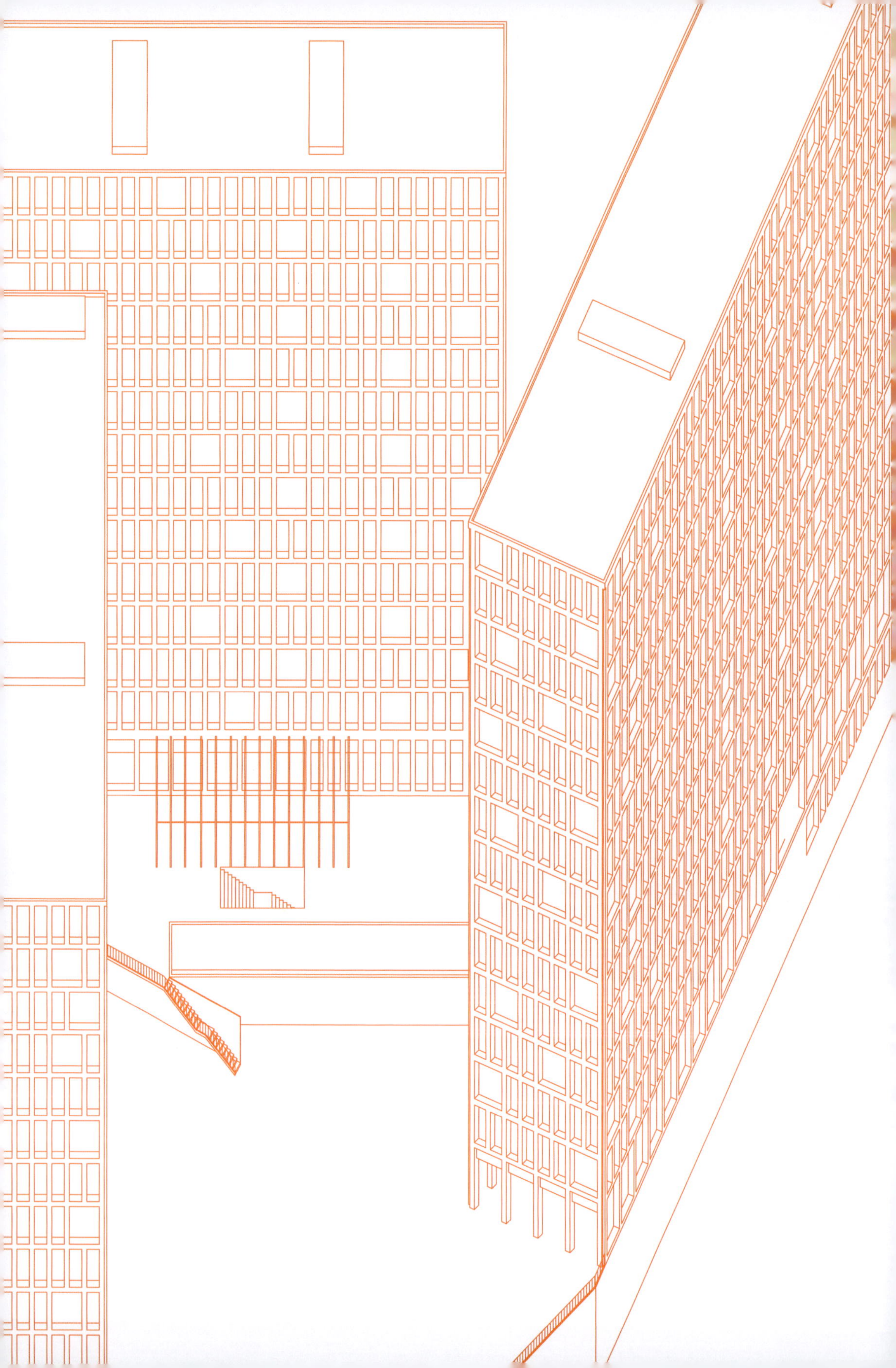

The Architecture of the House

Far from the functionalist model imposed by the totalizing programs of early modernity, we have created a fragmented, polluting habitat. We build cities characterized by the proliferation of houses without services, gated for the wealthy, and self-built in the case of that for the poor. Neither the well-planned cities proposed by Le Corbusier nor the balance between town and country that Ebenezer Howard dreamed of: our cities have grown unplanned and exacerbate environmental and social imbalances.

They are also far removed from the idea that cities are composed of familiar design archetypes as described by the Italian architect and critic Aldo Rossi in his 1966 publication, *The Architecture of the City*, one of the most influential books on architecture and urbanism of recent decades.[1] Rossi believed that there are two the basic ingredients of the city: its repetitive residential fabric, corresponding to the private sphere of the city and monuments, singular works with public character. While the former is forever transforming, the latter hardly changes at all and represents the continuity of cities. However, built environments are increasingly amorphous and the signs of collective will mentioned by Rossi are hardly perceptible. A simple aerial photograph of Mexico City, with its endless rows of houses lacking both services and monuments,

1 Aldo Rossi, *L'architettura della città*, Padua: Marsilio, 1966; English edition: *The Architecture of the City*, Diane Ghirardo & Joan Ockman (trans.), Cambridge, MA: MIT Press, 1982.

might represent any place on earth, challenging Rossi´s interpretation about the recognizable nature of the city. Within that same "city" there are territorial demarcations, like Ciudad Nezahualcóyotl or Iztapalapa, which are entirely devoid of public spaces and landmarks. These districts started out as informal settlements and today each houses more than two million people. They are anodyne areas with countless individual traits where nothing built there can be attributed to a collective will.

Although Rossi believed that the dwelling was the principal defining feature of a city and what set it apart from other cities, a topic in his book that attracted significant attention was the importance he gave to monuments. Legacies of this vision included the "re-monumentalization" of Paris promoted by President Mitterrand to mark the bicentennial of the French Revolution in 1989, the Guggenheim Museum Bilbao opened in 1997, and hundreds of projects that followed this phenomenon of spectacularization of cities. Many of the monuments built around the world following that logic are visually striking shells, mostly new museums or convention centers, often designed without considering the needs of the local population. Houses and monuments are based on opposing ideas –the logic of repetition in the case of residential typologies and the exceptional nature of the monument– and residential projects have tended to drift away from the ideas of architects. Yet these two constituent parts of the city could be seen today as a single entity. Why not develop a new concept of the monument associated with housing where the interdependence of private and public are clearly perceived? Why not see the home as a place of privacy while considering it also as a place of production and interaction? Today, over half a century after *The Architecture of the City* was published, we need to devise new models that permit other forms of association between the house (private) and the other (public); we need to design strategies based on their interrelationship.

According to Rossi, the modern city is the product of three major phases of change which, in turn, transformed modes of dwelling: the first one began with industrialization and severed the link between home and work that transformed the medieval city; the second originated with progressive industrialization which destroyed the sense of neighborhood by completely separating houses from production, administration, and consumption centers; and the third arose with the development of individual modes of transportation which, in turn, led to greater distances between the house and work and gave rise to the phenomenon of dispersion at a massive scale.[2] His analysis concludes with a description of this massive new urban scale –the city-region– whose effects could only be guessed at the time although today they are common anywhere in the world. Rossi believed that a city could change completely in just fifty years and he credited this transforming power to houses (dynamic elements) rather than monuments (fixed landmarks). His descriptions of Paris, Rome, London, and Berlin bear little resemblance to these cities as they are today. We must therefore take his interpretation one step further and redefine the house and its relationship with "the other" to create new territories which are no longer split along the lines of public and private, of residential and the rest.

Why can't we redefine the monument, so instead of being something static and motionless can be seen as a place where people dwell, where a true sense of belonging is built? Why not start working from a new urban model that reinstates the house as a cohesive element, bringing people and the environment closer together? Collective housing should be the new monument of the 21st century: a monument to the dynamic forces that redefine the relationship between public and private, between the habitable space and the territory. If we understand the planet as everyone's home then the old dichotomies –house vs. territory, individual vs. collective, center vs. periphery, work vs. leisure– will disappear.

Today we demand that cities not be designed for cars. Making non-polluting transportation part of a public policy to develop sustainable cities goes hand in hand with reinforcing the social function of public space. In informal settlements, which represent the most common construction method in the world, the proportion of public to private space is less than 1:10, far from a desirable 1:1 ratio (according to the Manhattan model). The wellbeing of cities depends on mobility and public spaces. An essential variable in this equation, however, is the configuration of the residential fabric. The defense of the "human dimension" of cities lies in the relationship between the house and everything else.

Continuing the transformations begun with the cave-dwelling of prehistoric times up to the machine-dwelling of the 20th century, we can now attain the dwelling as the ultimate collective monument, as an element for establishing new relationships between what belongs to one and what belongs to all.

2 Ibid., pp. 227-230.

Why not make the place where people live the symbol of a city? Collective housing, as the halfway point between the individual and the collective, between the neighborhood and the city, would be the basic element for reconciling walls that divide with spaces that connect.

The title of this chapter, "The Architecture of the House," deliberately echoes the title of Rossi's book, *The Architecture of the City*, in order to underscore the importance of considering that the architecture of the house *is* the architecture of the city.

The Loss of Neighborhood

From Tenements to Apartment Buildings

At the beginning of the 20th century, the housing situation in Mexico was similar to that in many other parts of the world: there were not enough homes and what existed was uncomfortable and unhygienic due to the effects of the Industrial Revolution that let to the overcrowding of cities and unleashed the subdivision of existing buildings into makeshift apartments with no natural light, bathrooms, or privacy. The houses, for the most part, were not owned by their occupants, so there was little interest in fitting them with new technologies, and only the negative consequences of industrialization impacted domestic life, chief among them was the shortage of housing for the working classes.

In those days, Mexican domestic architecture consisted of three basic types that had barely changed for decades: detached homes, communal patio houses or tenements (*vecindades*), and lodging houses (*mesones*).[1] In the first decade of the 20th century, the urban population grew by more than 60%.[2] As a result, the *vecindad*, the most common residential typology since colonial times, lost the spaciousness that had formerly characterized it. Its courtyards became

1 The *vecindad* (literally "neighborhood house") consists of various homes arranged around a central courtyard or shared corridor. [Translator's Note: in this text the term is often rendered as "communal patio house" or "tenement".]

2 According to the critic Ernesto Alva Martínez, the urban population went from 19 to 31% (ibid., p. 9). For data on demographic growth in Mexico City, see *Estadísticas sociales del Porfiriato, 1877-1910*, Secretaría de Economía/Dirección General de Estadística/Talleres Gráficos de la Unión, Mexico City, 1956, p. 9. In 1900, Mexico City has 344,000 inhabitants (51.4 people per acre), and by the mid-20th century the population had swelled to nearly 3 million, although the density was similar (51.8 people per acre). See Gustavo Garza (ed.), *La Ciudad de México en el fin del segundo milenio*, Mexico City: El Colegio de México, 2000, p. 242.

smaller, its sense of privacy was reduced and its hygienic standards were lowered. In Mexico City, one out of every six residents lived at a *mesón* which provided temporary accommodations for people with no permanent home; here they shared poorly ventilated rooms packed with rows of beds placed on, often, unpaved floors.[3] Few people owned the houses where they lived: over 80% of all residential structures were rented.[4] This explains why one of the most important demands of the 1910 Revolution was the worker's right to decent housing.

After the Revolution, technological development became more accessible and prompted innovations such as electricity, new energy sources, indoor plumbing and sanitation services, modern equipment in kitchens, bathrooms, and programmatic differentiation between spaces destined for specific activities. Industrialization had introduced new typologies –such as factories and schools–, and better transport systems –trains, trams and cars– that distanced home and workplace and eliminated from the houses the activities that had once made them self-sufficient production spaces. Houses ceased to be places for farming, producing, and doing business to become exclusively devoted to domestic purposes. This led to the reduction of people who worked and lived in them and a concept of hygiene developed that not only meant cleanliness and providing modern services within the houses but also getting rid of everything unrelated to family life or the very idea of the nuclear family. As a result, the distance between the private sanctum of the home and the street's public character increased.

In the second decade of the 20th century, population growth in the capital city and technical progress led to the creation of a new housing typology: blocks between three and five stories tall, built specifically for residential purposes. With the desire to bring order to the city, the concept of the apartment building that ushered a new era of modernization was forged. The first apartment buildings were to be rented to middle and upper class employees. The buildings maintained the traditional central courtyard or corridor as well as common laundry areas and *tendederos* (patios with clotheslines). Over time, they incorporated modern conveniences and international customs with the intention of simplifying housework. Three projects illustrate the modernization of the concept of *vecindad* and the birth of apartment buildings: the

3 Jonathan Kandell, *La Capital: The Biography of Mexico City*, New York: Holt and Company, 1988, p. 387.

4 Ernesto Alva Martínez, *Vivienda en edificios de apartamentos y conjuntos horizontales de arquitectos en México*, Mexico City: Comex, 1999, p. 10.

Buen Tono (1913), the Condesa (1917) and Vizcaya (1922) blocks. The first proclaimed a new logic of domestic productivity linked to the factory and to industrialized building systems while maintaining the traditional character of the communal patios; the second adapted a mixture of both programs when it incorporated the neighborhood (*vecindad*) model in the interior and, on the outside, a four story high block and independent street accesses to the houses; the third combined the design of the neighborhood (*vecindad*) within a layout of taller buildings and the addition of new technologies (it was one of the first buildings to use elevators and a hydraulic foundation system). However, these innovations were only available to the middle and upper classes and a legal system to provide the means by which anyone could become a homeowner and different people could own the same shared building or property still did not exist.

The Year of the Mexican House

In the post-revolutionary period, a new domestic culture was created, rooted in the civic values promoted by Mexico's first Minister of Public Education, José Vasconcelos. An educational reform led to combat the illiteracy that affected over 80% of the population and the redefinition of affordable housing "considered the nation's greatest shame". The redistribution of land after the social revolution implied also the democratization of knowledge.

The newspaper *Excélsior* announced that 1925 would be "the year of the people's house" to promote a movement intended to dignify domestic architecture and, as such, educate the masses.[5] As a result, architecture was marked by the desire to reassert Mexico's national sovereignty and by the establishment of new rights of society. In a text entitled "How do the Mexican people dwell and how should they dwell?" Alfonso Pallares, president of the newly-established Sociedad de Arquitectos Mexicanos (The Society of Mexican Architects [SAM]), spoke of the need to provide decent housing for millions of people but, above all, he emphasized the need to teach them how to dwell.[6] It was not just an architectural problem or one of hygiene but of creating a domestic

5 "1925 será el año de la casa popular", in *Excélsior*, December 28, 1924, quoted in Ramón Vargas Salguero and J. Víctor Arias Montes (eds.), *Ideario de los arquitectos mexicanos*, vol. II: *Los olvidados*, Mexico City: Instituto Nacional de Bellas Artes, 2010, p. 94.
6 Alfonso Pallares, "¿Cómo habita el pueblo mexicano y cómo debía habitar?", in *Excélsior*, November 23, 1924, quoted in *op.cit.*, p. 111.

culture. Knowing how to dwell in a house meant knowing how to conserve, a vital lesson at a time defined by the changes that industrialization was enacting on cities. It also meant knowing how to improve: how to introduce the latest technology and the concept of comfort in homes but most importantly it meant knowing how to appreciate those conveniences and that appreciation could only be taught by raising the educational level of occupants. The new culture of inhabitation was, therefore, based on a synthesis of human and cultural values. The shaping of an educated society had to begin at home. As Pallares explained, "Mexico will be a learned nation when its people learn to house themselves."[7]

The desire to create a modern, uniquely Mexican housing model was part of the need to organize and control urban growth. In 1925, the country celebrated the 600th anniversary of the founding of Mexico-Tenochtitlán. As such, the call to reinvent the Mexican house was bound up with reinventing the city itself. That year, Carlos Contreras, a pioneer of urbanism in Mexico, attended the conference of the International Federation for Housing and Planning (IFHP) in New York where he presented a visionary planning project for the country and a rough draft of the first master plan for the Mexican capital.[8] In it, Contreras defined future residential areas to the southwest, as well as worker's housing areas linked to the factories, on the northwest side, and to public transportation. Contreras defined the creation of new housing linked to a system of parks, recreational areas, circulation, services, natural reserves, and farmland. He also promoted the creation of laws to regulate home construction, encouraged the inclusion of indoor plumbing, water systems, and electricity, and suggested that residential building projects should consider waste collection and fire safety measures. Contreras' involvement ranged widely from regulations on home rentals to restrictions on raising animals in houses. The first step toward putting the city in order was to organize life within the home.

Contreras contributions focused on finding the best way to organize the nation's territory. Apart from funding the National Association of Planners of the Mexican Republic, he promoted the use of vernacular building techniques, promoted the Affordable Housing Act, and advocated for the construction of

7 *Ibid.*, p. 114.

8 At the conference, Contreras presented the rough draft of the First Regional Plan and of the Master Plan for Mexico City. This was the basis of the 1933 Regional Plan for the Federal District, which largely defined the city's layout. See Enrique Ayala Alonso, "Tres décadas de modernización de la Ciudad de México", in Carlos Sambricio (ed.), *Ciudad y vivienda en América Latina, 1930-1960*, Madrid: Lampreave, 2012, p. 347.

apartment buildings up to six stories high surrounded by open spaces. The state acted slowly on these ideas and, as a result, the plans to improve housing and control urban growth failed to materialize. Despite this, the efforts of Contreras and Vasconcelos' followers to create *educated* housing managed, in those early years, to link the idea of modern dwelling to a sense of culture and urban planning.

The Renovation of the House

In the first quarter of the 20th century, new technological developments propelled the redefinition of the domestic space and altered both the historical model of cities as well as the very concept of local identity. In homes, carriage houses were replaced by garages, storage cellars by pantries, spaces for ice-boxes by kitchens with refrigerators, and cesspools by sewage pipes. New materials – reinforced concrete and steel– and new construction systems made it possible to rethink dwelling models. The experimentations materialized in the early 1920s and 1930s in new residential areas like Condesa, Cuauhtémoc, and Polanco, and in the first housing developments for state employees, such as the Postal (1921) and Federal (1924) neighborhoods, whose vast empty spaces led to the question: what types of houses should be built on those lands that would ultimately define the city?

At the time, the will to build was promoted principally by developers and owed much to the work of engineers like Modesto C. Rolland, Miguel Rebolledo, and Roberto Gayol, as well as to the innovations introduced by construction companies and materials manufacturers. The new models of affordable housing were widely publicized via the free magazines *Tolteca* and *Cemento*, published by Cementos Portland Company, which month after month, popularized the new architectural forms to their readers.[9]

Housing was, not only, a critical factor in modernizing the country's architecture, but also essential to the definition of a national post-revolutionary identity that emerged in opposition to foreign influences. The ideal of the *Mexican house* epitomized the search for uniquely Mexican values. The first issue of the journal *El Arquitecto* (1923), published by the Sociedad de Arquitectos Mexicanos, launched the following challenge: "Thousands of houses have cropped

9 This campaign was spearheaded by the publicist Federico Sánchez Fogarty.

up but where is the Mexican house, the house of and for Mexicans? We have imported every style, killed the courtyard and replaced it with the *hall*, shrunk the bedrooms down to the smallest possible size, eliminated potted plants and put caricatures of gardens in their place. In short, we have made a concerted effort to relinquish what is ours."[10] The insistence on local housing was part of a larger trend closely linked to the muralist movement spearheaded by artists Diego Rivera, José Clemente Orozco, and David Alfaro Siqueiros that sought to revive native traditions and urged people to take pride in ones own culture and on what was Mexican. This happened at a time when the "typical American home," later dubbed the "California-style house," was being introduced; altering forms, building processes, and the value of local history.

At first the term "modern house" was used quite skeptically, fearing that the sense of efficiency meant the reduction of size and budget. The creation of the first mortgages for low-income homes in 1901 jump-started an emerging residential construction that was based on economizing measures, which in most cases, only made space cheaper but not more productive or efficient. Some of the principal features of traditional architecture were eliminated in the name of an economy of means. The first attempts to rationalize affordable housing, therefore, drew harsh criticism from the defenders of Mexico's historic cultural heritage. Since 1905, the architect Nicolás Mariscal had lashed out against those who made copies of "Anglo-Saxon houses" which, by reducing space and quality, adversely affected the courtyards, balconies, and the very sense of the home. According to Mariscal, "The desire for profit has become so acute that, in order to avoid waste, they have managed to make walls whose surface area is an exact multiple of the wallpaper area and the windows are sized to match the dimensions of commercial lumber. Here, the order of things has been inverted: now it is the needs that adapt to the materials."[11] This "inverted order" signaled the emergence of a concept based on principles of standardization promoted primarily after World War I in Central European countries with the ideas of *Existenzminimum* (minimum subsistence space) and adopted in Mexico after the Revolution.

10 Israel Katzman, *Arquitectura contemporánea Mexicana*, Mexico City: Instituto Nacional de Antropología e Historia/Secretaría de Educación Pública, 1963, p. 81.
11 Ibid., p. 60.

New Functions of Housing

Houses in post-revolutionary Mexico reflected social changes and the new values of efficiency and class justice. Technological advances made housework easier and lightened the workload of domestic staff. But all of that was not enough. Modernity was not just about building houses with new ideas and new methods but also about making them affordable to everyone. Modernity had to be synonymous with utility and efficacy but also with social justice: it needed to yield more and to more people.

In the late 1920s and early 1930s, as the urban population increased more than ever and technology evolved rapidly, old houses became replaced by taller, better equipped, and more affordable buildings. This unleashed the creation of housing for rent that could be affordable to different social classes and led to greater freedom developing programs, forms, and layouts that would express the new modes of inhabitation of a diversified society. But in order to make room for the new, it was necessary to do away with the formulas of the past, eschewing the styles during the Díaz dictatorship and of buildings marked by the incongruence of their function, appearance, and context. Form had to be the result of a constructive logic and programmatic needs. It had to be in tune with metropolitan contexts characterized by speed, new modes of transportation, luminous signage, and new typologies like movie theaters, restaurants, parking lots, gas stations, office buildings, and skyscrapers. The most important thing was to consider the new functions for new types of users.

Architects born at the turn of the century, such as Francisco J. Serrano and Juan Segura, began the search for solutions attuned to technological advances and changing lifestyles. Three buildings serve to illustrate the kind of projects conceived to house a new urban society, eager to enjoy modern services and be identified with a sense of innovation: the Isabel housing complex (1929) and the Ermita building (1931), both designed by Juan Segura, and the Jardín housing complex (1931), by Francisco J. Serrano. Following the democratic spirit of the times, those three housing projects incorporated community services and sought to extend the benefits of new living standards to everyone.

The Isabel complex and the Ermita building are paradigms of a new urban proposal that transformed into a collective space what was once a family-owned *finca* (ranch) on an old country estate in the Tacubaya district. On a larger scale, the project called for additional housing structures, shops, offices, recreational areas, and a hospital. Although the master plan was never fully executed, it did redefine the way of understanding housing and its relationship to services in a new urban environment. The Isabel complex was a new interpretation of the traditional *vecindad* –with two private communal patios– that combined two typologies: the single-family row house and the apartment building block. For its part, the Ermita building was a symbol of the transition to a plural, avant-garde, democratic city. This eight-story building was the first vertical housing structure in the country and the first to incorporate a variety of uses such as stores, offices, different types of residences, and a large movie theater.[12] The Ermita building was designed around a central covered courtyard, a social space that served as a vestibule for the apartments, and pioneered the notion of offering tenants entertainment in their own building. Located at the intersection of two major avenues, the building expressed an unmistakably metropolitan character as far removed from the crowded, insalubrious old houses in the downtown area as it was from the new detached homes being built in recently created neighborhoods. While the houses in the new estates were surrounded by green areas and formally influenced by the ideal of the Garden City, as formulated in England by Ebenezer Howard in the late 19th-century, the Ermita glorified the collective sense of cooperative housing which Howard himself, influenced by the utopian socialism of French thinker Charles Fourier, had proposed in his early days. In the Ermita, Juan Segura crystallized the idea of the building as a social condenser and for the first time housing was designed with different types of users in mind: single people, childless couples, and short-term tenants (many of which were Republican exiles of the Spanish Civil War). The building was influenced by apartment houses that were proliferating at the time in cities like New York and Chicago, and, with the idea of simplifying housework, advocated by European and American defenders of socialism and gender equality, Segura designed apartments for working-class citizens that had begun to incorporate "free time" into their lives and, as a result, recreational activities needed to be available to everyone. Consequently, domestic chores and entertainment acquired a collective, urban dimension. The Ermita echoed the Corbusian metaphor of the apartment building as a great ocean liner but made it more inclusive by emphasizing its vertical, diverse, and permeable nature. It was not a stranded ship but an element open to the city and an active part of it, tearing down the boundaries between the isolated residential building and the urban system.

12 *La vivienda comunitaria en México*, Mexico City: Instituto del Fondo Nacional de la Vivienda para los Trabajadores, 1988, p. 270.

The Jardín building complex, consisting of apartments arranged around a central garden, was a synthesis of the collective urban block and the green rural landscape. Like the Ermita building, Francisco J. Serrano's project was closer to Fourier's notion of the phalanstery (a cooperative residential building with common services) than to the rows of suburban single-dwellings of the new neighborhoods. The buildings of the Jardín complex, raised on pilotis, extended the houses into the garden and the garden, in turn, into the street. By combining different housing typologies and different terraces, an inclusive notion of dwelling was provided that was designed specifically for the local climate. As a result, the reduced size of the dwelling space was not so noticeable because of the link created between the advantages that urban life provided as well as the freedom of the open landscape.

Prototypes of Equality

In the mid-1920s, architects who had completed their studies after the Mexican Revolution changed the ways of living, driven by a desire to create more equitable societies. Juan O'Gorman, Juan Legarreta, Álvaro Aburto, Carlos Tarditi, Enrique Yáñez, Alberto T. Arai, and Raúl Cacho proposed to leave behind the injustices and styles of the past. This generation was the first to consider houses for the working class, who would finally own their own homes. The search for equality produced an architecture of simple forms capable of meeting any person's basic needs with a minimum of resources. In this way, lifestyles, urban models, and the relationship between work and home were reinvented. While the references had once been palaces and monumental works and later haciendas and convents, now the rural home, hut, and factory would become the emblems of that desire for change. As O'Gorman said: "(it was about) what was useful, the useful house, the machine, the workshop, and the factory, as opposed to the flower vase, to crested closets and to closet-crested houses."[13] In this age of renewed values, spaces, and forms, the house acquired importance as the space that most defines people's lives and became the laboratory for testing the architectural revolution proposed by figures such as Frank Lloyd Wright and Le Corbusier. It was the perfect place to combine modern influences with

13 Juan O'Gorman described the "Elorduy Minimal House" (1930), designed by Legarreta, as "the first experiment in housing for workers and of technology at the service of the majority". See Juan O'Gorman, in *El Arquitecto. Órgano de la Sociedad de Arquitectos Mexicanos*, special memorial issue dedicated to the architect Juan Legarreta, October 1934, p. 18.

the patriotic values elicited by the fervor of the revolution. The new emphasis on home economy and optimization required a redefinition of traditional habits, the sense of privacy, and even the concept of individual property. The advantages of collective housing had to be reconsidered and the prejudices that had annihilated the traditional model of the *vecindad* had to be overcome.

New ways of life were materialized in several prototypes of affordable housing. The first emerged as university assignments thanks to professors José Villagrán, Guillermo Zárraga, Juan Segura, Francisco Serrano, and José Luis Cuevas who encouraged their students to find a coherent balance between needs, building processes, culture, and context. Two thesis projects, submitted by Carlos Tarditi and Juan Legarreta, illustrate the incursion of architects into the realm of minimal housing. Carlos Tarditi's professional thesis from 1924 offered an analysis of the traditional *vecindad* that led to a regulation for the construction of functional *vecindades* and three prototypes for different income levels. Juan Legarreta's 1930 thesis became, on the other hand, the first constructed prototype of a functionalist home for the Mexican working class: "Elorduy Minimal House" (1932), built in the Peralvillo neighborhood.[14] This project represents the social and political transformation of his day. Like the Ermita building, the location itself was a bold statement. The Peralvillo neighborhood is a faithful reflection of the history of social and urban changes in Mexico: under Díaz's dictatorship, what was once a farm during the colony became a recreational area for the upper classes and the site of the country's first racetrack and an exclusive private club. After the Mexican Revolution, the racetrack was torn down and the land was divided into plots for affordable housing payable in installments. Under the administration of Plutarco Elías Calles, known as the "Supreme Chief of the Revolution," the land was handed to a working-class cooperative of settlers.

"Elorduy Minimal House" initiated the logic of mass produced collective housing. It looked like a single-family home, but in fact it contained two separate apartments. The layout followed the strictest economy of means with the service areas arranged in a row and the living room and bedrooms in the same space. The bedrooms were actually a series of beds separated by curtains, offering greater spatial flexibility and providing different uses during the day and night. The floor plans of both apartments were identical except for their separate entrances and the size of the *azotehuelas* (small backyards or areas

14 Enrique X. de Anda, *Vivienda colectiva de la modernidad en México: los multifamiliares durante el periodo presidencial de Miguel Alemán (1946-1952)*, Mexico City: Instituto de Investigaciones Estéticas-Universidad Nacional Autónoma de México, 2008, p. 100.

for washing and hanging laundry); it was much larger in the ground-floor house and also served as an outer vestibule. This first domestic manifesto of constructive rationality had several important implications for the concept of standardized efficiency. On the one hand, its modernity was not incompatible with traditional aspects like the *azotehuelas*; on the other, the strict repetition of elements was flexible enough to allow differences between the ground-floor apartment, with its front courtyard, and the residence upstairs, which was fitted with larger windows to let more light in and to make the most of its corner location. This modification of the corner window does not appear on the original plans, which showed identical facades on both levels. This makes evident Legarreta's need to go beyond the requirements of the strict economy of means. By making these alterations during the building process, Legarreta downplayed the project's repetitive nature, establishing a discourse of unity rather than just reproducing identical pieces.

Another example of how the rigorous principles of the modern movement were modified to integrate local conditions is the project of the twin homes for the Behn and Zöllinger families in the Del Valle district (1929) designed in Switzerland by Hans Schmidt and Paul Artaria, two of the leading exponents of European radical rationalist avant-garde. The houses were an exercise in simplifying both the structure and the layout; managing to design two homes that looked like one and to allow the families to share the garden and terraces. There is a major discrepancy between the 1929 plans on file at the Federal Institute of Technology in Zurich (ETH) and the built version: the servant's room was removed to create a shared terrace in the middle of the top floor. This break in the continuity of the two symmetrical facades indicates that the space, light, sun, and views were more important than strict repetition of the different parts of the program. Like Legarreta's "Elorduy Minimal House", the regulated plans and modular logic were disregarded in order to open up the dwellings to the exterior and improve the communication between the two homes in accordance with the lifestyles of their occupants. Another exemplary prototype of mass produced housing adapted to local conditions was the "Experimental Peasant House" designed by Álvaro Aburto and his teacher Carlos Obregón Santacilia and built in the countryside of Michoacán in 1928. In it, basic rationalist principles were combined with the use of local materials and with a consideration for traditional ways of life. It incorporated the *zaguán* (hallway) as a multipurpose transitional space between exterior and interior; the kitchen was separated from the house; and the *tapanco* (in Mexico, a mezzanine/

loft multipurpose space) was used in a reinterpretation of the colonial "cup-and-saucer" design where the lower and upper floors were intertwined, allowing a more flexible use of space. These designs increased spatial possibilities even within the strict limitations and scant square footage available to affordable housing. The geographical and cultural reality was the starting point for devising solutions not found in architectural treatises.

Subsequent housing projects designed in Mexico by Swiss architect Hannes Meyer and by the German architect Max Cetto followed a similar course. This is evident in the clear comprehension of local materials and site conditions expressed by their projects, but also in their advocacy of traditional ways of life. Looking to the *vecindad* for inspiration, Meyer introduced in 1942 the concept of multi-family residential complexes in Mexico with his Lomas de Becerra project. Although it was never built, it paved the way for later designs based on the premise of generating diverse typologies with a minimum occupancy of the site, high-density housing, and a strong connection between the residence, the public space, services, and work.

Lives in Competition

In the early 1930s, the working class still awaited for the government to fulfill its promise of providing them their own homes. The Sociedad de Arquitectos Mexicanos insisted on the importance of studying the problem of workers' lodgings and of holding employers responsible for providing their workers with hygienic housing.[15] Hoping to spur the government to action with specific projects, the architect Carlos Obregón Santacilia, as director of the SAM, organized a "Minimal Worker's House" competition in 1932 which was envisioned to generate ideas for the first publicly-funded houses for the working class.[16] The purpose of the competition, arranged in collaboration with the government of the Federal District, was to revitalize the marginal areas that had been settled along the northeast edge of the city and which were known as the "slum horseshoe." The competition initiated a debate about what affordable housing should be like. The winners were all architects under the age of

15 This duty was set out in Part XII of Article 123 of the Mexican Constitution, and in Clause III of the Labor Act article which stipulated that "employers have the obligation to provide comfortable, hygienic housing for their workers".

16 Obregón Santacilia incorporated the private company Muestrario de la Construcción Moderna, and enlisted the assistance of Aarón Sáenz, the Federal District Department Chief, to organize the competition and have the government build the first workers' homes.

thirty: Juan Legarreta was awarded first place, Enrique Yáñez second, and Carlos Tarditi and Augusto Pérez Palacios tied for third. The winning project by Legarreta was constructed in the Balbuena neighborhood and became the first low-income housing complex built by the government. Legarreta´s Balbuena project incorporated ideas from Yáñez's second-prize proposal: a reinterpretation of the "cup-and-saucer"design with the living/sleeping area on the *tapanco*, or mezzanine, and a workshop on the ground floor. The project was designed around common service areas, and led to two more residential areas for workers in San Jacinto and La Vaquita built the following two years, also designed by Legarreta. These three neighborhoods included spacious public areas that would also benefit adjacent neighborhoods, parks and gardens, athletic fields, markets, and schools placed at the central part of the project. However, these services were only partly completed and the model that was tirelessly repeated for decades across the country was that of the detached home lacking services, workspaces, and the sense of productivity that had characterized the home for thousands of years.

The Communal House

A series of housing projects designed by Juan O'Gorman between late 1929 and the early 1930s illustrate the growing commitment of architects to society, to the economic situation, and to the desire to create flexible spaces. These works were conceived to transform society through new types of houses that offered a wider range of possibilities to interpret life, the landscape, local history, and international tendencies.

O'Gorman's submission to the 1932 "Minimal Worker's House" competition was called "Transition"; it received an honorable mention and it was the first attempt to create multi-family building complex in Mexico.[17] O'Gorman designed different versions of units: from the minimum cell to three-story longitudinal housing blocks arranged around common service areas, raised on pilotis, and having rooftop terraces. The complex also included spaces to plant crops as well as workspaces on the ground level of the houses.[18] In the descriptive summary of his project, the author headed off potential criticism by noting: "There is absolutely no need to get rid of flower pots, birds, climbing

17 E. X. de Anda, op. cit., p. 102
18 Ibid., p. 102.

vines, etc.; on the contrary, there would be even more possibilities in this respect and the street would preserve the same popular, picturesque quality it has today."[19] O'Gorman's "scientific" homes were full of color, plants, and reflected an interest in local traditions.

Two houses built later by O'Gorman in the Altavista neighborhood represent the constructed manifesto of the Revolution's ideals: the studio-houses he designed for his father, and the house for Diego Rivera, and Frida Kahlo were single-family homes for the intellectual elite. They were, however, part of the discourse on affordable housing and the idea of a standard prototype. O'Gorman believed that cost per square foot should be the same for a working-class and a wealthy person's home. In the Altavista houses, he took the quest for economy to new extremes by simplifying the forms, spaces, and building systems. Yet the economy of means did not lead him to sacrifice spatial or visual qualities or to overlook the importance of the landscape. The houses' connection to the outside gave them an uncommon richness: not only did they achieve, for the first time in Mexico, a radical transparency between the domestic interior and exterior but they also made explicit a domestic lifestyle that extended beyond the four walls to incorporate work and a new concept of family. Both homes were designed as places of work, as part of the landscape, and as tools that would define new ways of living.

O'Gorman combined modern methods and materials (concrete, steel, large glass surfaces) with traditional elements (fired clay, artisanal details, colors inspired by popular architecture and local vegetation) and reconsidered the programmatic use of space: eliminating the service rooms forced him to come up with solutions for simplifying housework. By questioning what was essential to a house and thinking of its daily maintenance, his design proposed a reinterpretation of the individual's basic needs. Spaces like the vestibule or entry hall, the breakfast room, basements, cellars, service corridors and service stairs were no longer required. The spatial simplification reconfigured the traditional domestic layout that divided spaces into separate sectors and brought about uses that did not correspond to those of the traditional family. Materials and forms changed because the individual had changed; the house was, finally, the "individual's own home," capable of projecting the identity of its occupant outward. The different areas of Diego and Frida's residence illustrate this idea based on the unique needs of each occupant: Diego's house was separate from Frida's but connected to it by a bridge and it is close to the adjacent structure

19 Ibid., p. 103.

intended to serve as the workshop for Frida's father. Each house expressed the differences between each user. This acknowledgment of individual needs and circumstances did not mean giving up on the all-important principles of mass production and economy of means.

In the Altavista houses, O'Gorman made tangible the exploration begun in three of projects that never materialized but nevertheless changed the way architecture is understood: the "houses for workers", the "houses for journalists", and the "Communal House". These projects were based in what the author termed "technical architecture," exclusively functionalist, and particularly evident in the "Communal House", the architect no longer saw the house as an isolated object or serial element but as a collective compound. He gave up the idea of the reproducible single-family house scattered across the land and, instead, focused on the densely-populated building with collective services following Le Corbusier's *Immeubles-villas* project. O'Gorman incorporated aspects that were quite innovative, even in comparison with Corbusian postulates, such as the collective workspaces for residents, the random arrangement of terraces and protruding balconies on the upper floors, the incorporation of local vegetation on the rooftop, the use of native materials, and the introduction of a curved form which was unusual for the time. The three existing drawings of the "Communal House" reveal a singular exploration: one shows a facade detail that breaks the regularity of the linear block with cactus-filled terraces, exterior staircases, crenelated rooftop, and a hanging garden. Another drawing shows the facade in perspective, with a note by the author that emphasizes the importance of collective services and the use of pilotis to elevate the building in order to leave the ground floor free for studios and workspaces. The slightly curving wall in the central part of the building reveal the architect's formal, organic experimentation, which is more pronounced in the final perspective drawing. In that third drawing, the entire facade curves and the "functionality" of the regular standardized block acquires a different connotation. These three drawings foreshadowed the struggle against the rigidity that would ultimately mark the death of the modern movement. O'Gorman's project for the "Communal House" emphasized the idea that when affordable houses finally became the property of their tenants, this change needed to be expressed on the exterior. The individuality of each occupant should be manifest in the configuration of the building while also maintaining the advantages of standardized elements. His design addressed both aspects –individuality and standardization– and the facade was a visionary reflection of how the architect's design should accommodate different forms of dwelling. The individualized nature of the house had to be made apparent in the use of varied solutions to suit different types of users.

The Immensity of the House

In the mid-20th century, macroeconomic growth and the disproportionate population increase in the country were accompanied by a desire to formulate a new social structure within a new urban order. This triggered the simultaneous launch of plans for regional development and national programs for social housing, schools, and hospitals. As a result, residential projects increased in scale and apartment complexes became portions of the metropolis. House and city formed an inseparable bond: the former was more and more dependent on the latter, with homes relying on urban community infrastructures; and the city with the increasingly visible consequences that the proliferation of single-family units had for the territory.

The first projects intended to satisfy these mass housing needs were created in the late 1940s: multi-family complexes designed to organize society's ways of living and of building cities. These complexes were promoted by the state in an attempt to control urban sprawl and link housing to public services. In this way, the construction of new homes went hand-in-hand with the appearance of social centers, recreational and leisure facilities, transportation networks, and public spaces. The first multi-family complexes –among them the Unidad Esperanza by Carlos Lazo and Antonio Serrato; the Unidad Modelo by Mario Pani, Félix Sánchez Baylón, Carlos B. Zetina, José Luis Cuevas, Domingo García Ramos and Homero Martínez; and the Centro Urbano Presidente Alemán (CUPA), primarily designed by Pani and Salvador Ortega– redefined the dynamics of land occupancy and the state's role in society: affordable housing for workers had to be guaranteed, but those homes also needed to have access to all the basic services of electricity, water, sanitation, education, and healthcare. The Unidad Independencia project, led by Alejandro Prieto and José María Gutiérrez in 1960, exemplifies the best of this integral vision: a complex that dissolves into gardens, pathways, theaters and common areas.

Housing complexes quickly went from occupying urban land to forming superblocks that colonized the peripheries and transformed slum areas and obsolete industrial zones into new residential neighborhoods. In just fifteen years –between the late 1940s and the early 1960s– the size of these complexes multiplied by 100: they went from having 200 homes to about 20,000. This dramatic change of scale required large teams of architects, urban planners, and engineers, as well as new types of construction companies with the capacity to work on an unprecedented scale. This facilitated new processes for building, manufacturing, and distributing materials and, above all, a new understanding of the territory.

Mario Pani was the foremost advocate of these multi-family developments: in the Unidad Modelo complex (1947), he introduced the superblock scheme for the first time in Mexico; in the CUPA (Conjunto Urbano Presidente Alemán, 1949), he quintupled the number of homes planned for that site but with a built surface area of just 20% and the remaining surface destined as garden areas; and with the Nonoalco-Tlatelolco complex (1964) he proposed the regeneration of 238 acres north of the capital –an area of wasteland and plots occupied by workshops, small warehouses, and informal dwelling– to house nearly 100,000 residents. Each of these multi-family projects, intended to guide the transformation of marginalized territories into new urban territories, illustrated a clear understanding of one of the principles of the modern movement: high-density occupancy as the solution to the city's housing needs. The projects attempted to leave unbuilt as much land as possible, promoting greater typological variety, more public services, better connections with the urban fabric, and less segregation among different social classes.

In the second half of the 20th century, the idea of using housing projects as the basis of urban planning was juxtaposed by the realities that resulted from the unbridled growth of cities. Two situations highlighted the new scale of the problem: on the one hand, the inability of providing housing for the most disadvantaged members of the population grew and, on the other, the large-scale housing complexes created new issues around the problem of social integration. The social crises that emerged following the 1968 student movements highlighted the state's inability to organize the life of the inhabitants through large projects conceived to maintain social order. As a result, a series of works emerged –removed from the idea of the architect-planner and totalizing urban designs– that were closely related to the changing needs of the inhabitants. During the 1960s and 1970s, a number of diverse and adaptable strategies centered on self-construction were developed. Among the most important ones are Pedro Ramírez Vázquez's "The House that Grows," Christopher Alexander's housing complex in Mexicali, and a series of projects in Guadalajara by

Alejandro Zohn. In these three cases, there was an attempt at pushing for a high housing density, a greater typological variety for different economic levels, and the integration of the work of the community.

Two works by Zohn, the Ricardo Flores Magón housing complex and the CTM Atejamac complex (both from 1977), exemplify a territorial development model based on an understanding of local dynamics. These works managed to make diversity and chance coexist with a sense of order in which the architect's expertise was complemented by the building skills of the future occupants themselves and their changing needs. These projects were able to reconcile aspects long regarded as opposites: mass construction and individualized spaces, and privacy in structures for shared use. Both complexes represent the last time that politicians, architects, and urban planners worked together on large-scale projects for the benefit of society. Self-building was an integral part of Zohn's plans for these complexes. This required skills training programs and projects that allowed for variations on a master typology: houses made to grow and accommodate businesses, workshops, or offices. Behind homogeneous facades, the homes could vary in size, layout, height, and design. He also devised transitional areas between the most private and the most public spaces: small porches at the entrance to each home, balconies in the bedrooms, and front yards that allowed the houses to be integrated with the street while also creating a sense of identity. Rather than having clearly visible boundaries, the homes extended into public spaces like the main square, the community building, the shops, the daycare center, or the health clinic. The Flores Magón complex was also one of the most successful planned self-built programs in Mexico: the collective participation of the future residents in the construction work reduced costs by 40%.[20]

In the final decades of the 20th century, population growth and the lack of political organization led to the end of the urban planning that produced an unprecedented destruction of the territory. After the catastrophic aftermath of the earthquakes that hit Mexico City in 1985 and the neoliberal policies implemented at the beginning of the 1990s, the government left its duty to provide citizens with decent homes in the hands of privately-owned companies. As a result, residential projects were no longer concerned with normalizing the urban fabric or improving the living conditions of its inhabitants. As a result, the stated desire of linking the houses with services and public space was lost.

20 Rábago Anaya, Jesús, *Alejandro Zohn: ingeniería, arquitectura, planeación*, Guadalajara: Secretaría de Cultura de Jalisco, 2011, pp. 71-81.

Present-day urban growth is based on three housing models that favor segregation: residential ghettos distant from communal services, self-built homes on the peripheries, and high-density residential blocks without services or public space which saturate the existing services of the urban centers. Although they seem quite different, the three are products of a lack of connection with the city. This is especially visible in the gated communities and in the informal settlements, that operate on the physical and legal fringes of the city: generally speaking, both are fairly inaccessible, governed by internal laws, and often manage their own services, such as the water supply, electrical power, roads, and drainage systems. Both models deny their connection to the rest of the city, even though they depend on it for subsistence. This physical and social removal often occurs in communities located on adjacent lots that turn their backs on each other. Both privatization and self-management –one formal and the other informal– are attempts to remedy the ineptitude of the state. They are isolated responses that reinforce the rupture of the social fabric and create "dual cities" with polarized housing developments.[21]

Urban growth based on the creation of the unplanned single-family house is one of the main causes of the devastation of natural reserves. The Catalan photographer Jordi Colomer described the situation accurately in a 2009 documentary film entitled *Avenida Ixtapaluca (Houses for México)*. His footage exemplifies the repetitiveness of devastating patterns resulting from hundreds of cardboard cookie-cutter houses spreading like an unstoppable tide and that are juxtaposed to the natural landscape, thus exaggerating their decontextualized character and its sense of almost artificial life. In his video, the first aerial views highlight the geometric order of the Cartesian disposition of the houses and it is almost impossible to tell the difference between them and, even, if what we are looking at is a photomontage. Only the sound of the video that is made up by the sounds of the street –children playing, dogs barking, music, street peddlers, and some laughs– humanize the scene. Colomer's visual narrative shows the effects of residential construction on the natural and urban landscape, as do the photographs of Livia Corona, Pablo López Luz, Melanie Smith, and Jorge Taboada. The large swaths of repetitive housing appear to be realities that can only be captured through the distance allowed by aerial photography. It might seem that such realities can only be captured from

21 In just forty years, from 1960 to 2000, the population of marginal residential areas in Latin America multiplied by five. See J. M. Montaner and Z. Muxí, op. cit., p. 192. Marginal settlements occupy at least 50% of the total surface area of Lima, 38% of Rio de Janeiro, 40% of Caracas, and 35% of Bogotá. See Eduardo Neira, *El desarrollo sustentable y las metrópolis latinoamericanas*, Mexico City: Red Latinoamericana de Estudios Ambientales Urbanos/El Colegio de México, 1996.

the distance afforded by aerial photography. From that vantage point, details become uniform, repercussions are flattened, and everything looks like part of a tapestry woven in a repetitive pattern that goes on indefinitely and that makes us forget about the lives within. Colomer explained this reality well with a phrase he used to present his photographic project of the peripheries: "Ixtapaluca is one of several cities in the metropolitan area of Mexico City. A city suddenly popped up there for eighty thousand people, all living in identical houses [...] the residents compete with each other to turn that imposing geometric grid into a genuine city. They set up temporary markets, build new stories on the roofs, occupy the gardens, paint the houses a different color... But perhaps they are swallowed up by that Kafkian planning."[22]

To make the contradictions between urban development and the nature of the very territory visible to a broader population, in 2012, I, along with an interdisciplinary group, made an intervention in Mexico City's Zócalo (the second largest plaza in the world and through which nearly one million people pass through every day) that consisted in mapping at a large scale the fundamental aspects that define the city. The intervention consisted of drawing a map of the capital on the concrete plaza and adjoining streets at a 1:500 scale. During the following four days, different levels of information about the elements that make up the territory were added: bodies of water, political boundaries, natural reserves... Every day, over this gray surface, a new layer of a different color was added and, on the third day, hundreds of small trees in flowerpots were placed so that anyone could modify the configuration of the territory. The idea was to emphasize the changing and manifold character of the city and to make visible the inane policies that are foreign to the nature of the site such as the rivers that are placed in tubes underground, the drainage that sends rainwater down the sewer, and the still-existing lakes that are depleted of water to make room for more building. Understanding the outcome of arbitrary processes is the first step in changing them. That project, along with this book, emerged from a desire to stimulate the imagination into thinking of new forms of inhabitation and of collectively building the city. The goal is to make clear that cities are not the sum of private sanctuaries, but spaces for constructing public life based on new patterns of coexistence between the individual and the civic and on a broader comprehension of the public dimension of the domestic sphere. We need houses and cities that we can understand and in which we feel understood.

22 Jordi Colomer, *Avenida Ixtapaluca (Houses for México)*; available at http://www.archdaily.mx/271308/video-avenida-ixtapaluca-houses-for-mexico-jordi-colomer/, accessed July 2017.

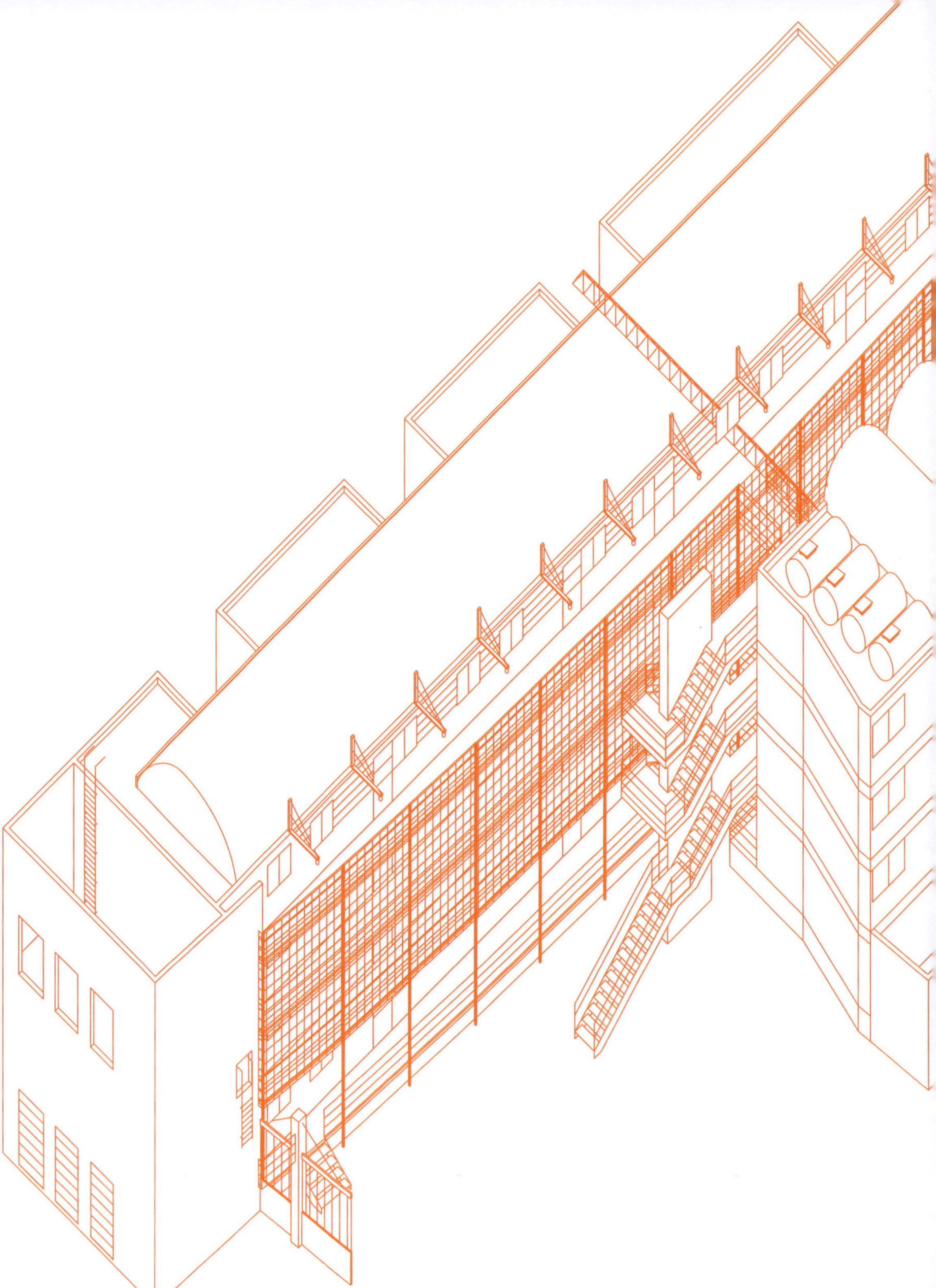

Building Houses with Words

Houses are built with ideas, sometimes expressed in drawings and spaces and, at other times, in words. In many cases, however, ideas that are written or merely verbalized in interviews or notes in scattered texts have been omitted from the most important architectural records. Yet the sum of these fragmentary statements and ideas is a vital analytical tool for pursuing more profound lines of debate and understanding the priorities that have characterized each era and the personal preoccupations of their authors. For instance, what have architects who worked in Mexico, a country whose population shot from 14 million inhabitants in 1917 to 120 million in 2017, said about housing? And, more importantly, what remains to be said?

Doubts and concerns are a substantial part of the process of designing and of communicating architectural projects. In other words, we must broaden our analytical perspective and understand what it means to an architect to design houses that lack public services or to build a house where the size of a closet is large enough to accommodate the entire home for a low-income family. These topics are part of the everyday work of the architecture profession but are barely addressed. For example, talking about the house should imply that we address issues of transportation, the use of resources, rainwater harvesting, and the future life of buildings; the impact and consequences of architectural projects. Here I am alluding not only to extreme cases such as earthquakes and mudslides where millions have been entombed by their houses, but to small errors and cases of neglect, and also to the everyday problems that people experience everywhere in the world as a result of their houses or, simply, of their attempts to have a house. This is something that architectural publications, schools, and governments generally disregard. Acquiring, maintaining or even just living in a house are issues that are much more complex than what the facades of buildings suggest.

The interest to compile testimonies of architects who have addressed the theme of housing over the last one hundred years was motivated by the fact that their words provide a parallel perspective to the works, creating a portrait of each era and its priorities. These selected quotations reveal which aspects of housing and dwelling were being debated across time, or what circumstances led to a revision of the foundations and parameters of residential architecture. Through different voices that are essential in order to understand contemporary Mexico, it is possible to understand that to speak about the house implies to speak about dignity, principles of hygiene and functionality; tradition and modernism; the advantages and drawbacks of different typological models; the relationship between popular housing and the city; the idea of productive dwellings; the connection between domestic and urban architecture; and housing policies and land policies. These are essential discussions in order to blaze new trails in the relationships between people, buildings and the world.

Rather than seeing these statements as unrelated ideas, we can visualize them as a constellation that shows the different perspectives throughout time, and form new dialogues in order to debate ideas and political, economic and urban matters. For example, Juan O´Gorman considered the house as an element to force the modesty in the lives of the rich and establish a balance between different social classes, while Luis Barragán proclaimed houses should be a luxury available to everyone, personal shelters where anyone could have a piece of sky and a small garden, and for Pedro Ramírez Vázquez the house should be a system capable of growing alongside the possibilities of the families. Some authors discuss historical matters, while others allude to the desires of occupants or cost-related issues; sometimes their words are couched in tones of grievance or protest, and in other cases they are enthusiastic about the possibility of improving people's lives. Together, they offer us a glimpse not only of each author's personal takes on the past, but also of the engines driving the machinery that will define the houses of our future.

70 Projects

The 70 projects that follow pertain to different authors and conditions, but as a whole they illustrate the priorities that have defined private life within a common territory. To gather contrasting projects –from a housing prototype of 24 square meters to a housing development with hundreds of buildings on a site of almost one million square meters– is a way of envisioning the topic. This is not an inventory of domestic models or built forms, but a magnifying lens for visualizing the broad range of possible living patterns and for understanding buildings in their context.

The group of drawings gives shape to a mapping of the domestic realm where the abstract character of the drawings is highlighted with the goal of representing the home in a closer and more complete way. For this, the essence of the projects is compressed into the small drawings and is accentuated when each project is represented with two layers, each on a different type of paper: the first is a line drawing of the project on a transparent sheet and the second is a color drawing on a white surface. This emphasizes the different layers and the depth that exists between the limits of a wall, a hole that becomes a window, an entrance, or a patio. The axonometric drawings of the projects codify the houses in a way not much different than that of an aerial perspective that flattens and homogenizes its particularities. Thus, lifting the first translucent page and discovering another layer underneath reflects an interest in opening the houses and discovering what lies beyond those residential bulwarks in our cities. If inside we find nothing more than a uniform colored surface, then this indicates there are still many more layers to uncover.

Ciudad de México / Escala 1:500, 2013
Installation of Derek Dellekamp, Fernanda Canales, Rozana Montiel and Gustavo Lipkau, among others. Photography: Surya Son

70 Projects

168	1994	Tláloc complex	Alberto Kalach, Daniel Álvarez, Axel Arañó, Felipe Buendía, Rebeca Cotera Salvador Ferreiro, Julio González and Moisés Miserachi	
172	1996	Veracruz complex	Javier Sánchez, Ernesto Sánchez and Lorenzo Farfán	
174	1998	Portal Bretaña	Gonzalo Gómez-Palacio and Gustavo Eichelmann	
178	1999	Stacked housing	Reinaldo Pérez Rayón	
180	2000	Ámsterdam Building	Isaac Broid, Fernando Donis, Benjamín Campos and Alfredo Hernández	
182	2001	Housing for artists	Fernando Romero, Juan Pablo Maza, Gerardo Asali, Pablo Quiroga, Víctor Jaime and Adriana Lara	
186	2003	AR58	Derek Dellekamp	
188	2004	13 de Septiembre	Javier Sánchez, Juan Reyes, Iris Sosa, Mariana Mas and María Elena Reyes	
192	2008	FR43	Juan Carral and Juan Pablo Valdés	
194	2009	Atrio de San Francisco Apartment	Mauricio Rocha and Gabriela Carrillo	
196	2010	Tlacolula 11H	Derek Dellekamp	
200	2010	Elemental Monterrey	Alejandro Aravena, Gonzalo Arteaga and Fernando García-Huidobro	
202	2010	Lisboa 7	Francisco Pardo and Julio Amezcua	
206	2012	Alfonso Reyes 200	Jorge Ambrosi and Gabriela Etchegaray	
208	2012	Liverpool 61	Jorge Arvizu, Ignacio del Río, Emmanuel Ramírez, Diego Ricalde and Olga Romano	
210	2012	Reforma 27	Alberto Kalach	
214	2014	Casa Caja	César Guerrero, Ana Cecilia Garza, Carlos Flores and María Sevilla	

216	2014	Modular house	Óscar Hagerman and Xuxcab inhabitants	
220	2014	Regional single housing	Alberto Kalach + TAX	
222	2014	Bosco Housing	Alberto Kalach + TAX	
224	2014	Antonio Sola	Jorge Ambrosi, Gabriela Etchegaray	
228	2014	Bucareli hybrid complex	Juan Herreros	
230	2015	High Park	Michel Rojkind	
234	2015	Rinconada Margaritas	Luis Aldrete	
236	2015	Sustainable Housing	Tatiana Bilbao	
238	2015	CH-ReUrbano	Cadaval & Solà-Morales	
242	2016	Central Park Interlomas	Migdal Arquitectos	
244	2016	Un Cuarto Más	Rozana Montiel	
248	2016	Del Territorio al Habitante	Alberto Kalach + TAX	
250	2017	Productive House	Fernanda Canales	
252	2017	Donceles Studios	Juan Carral	
256	2017	Mar Tirreno	Frida Escobedo	
258	2017	Ermita Iztapalapa Building	Manuel Cervantes	
260	2017	Red Tower	Zeller & Moye	
262	2017	Monte Albán Building	Fernanda Canales	
264	2017	MAJI Building	Salvador Macías and Magui Peredo	

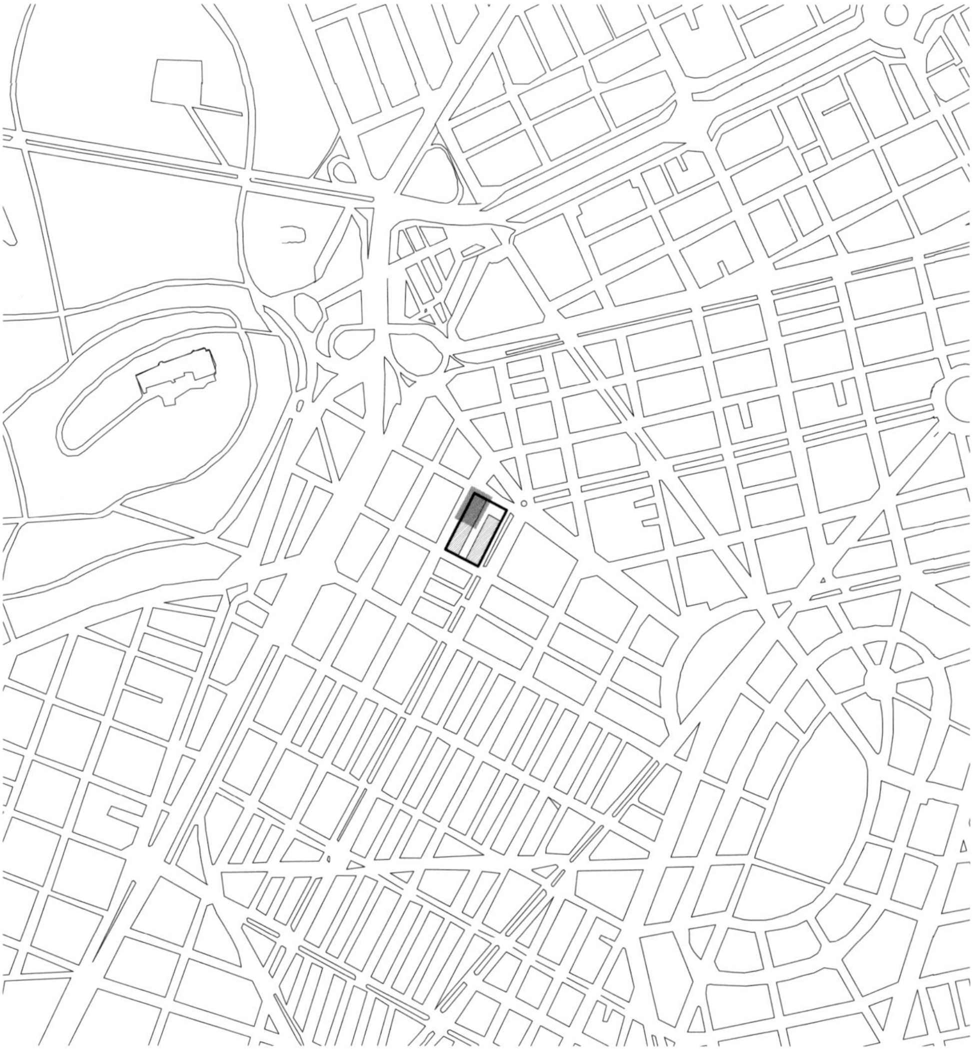

1917, Conjunto Condesa, Thomas S. Gore

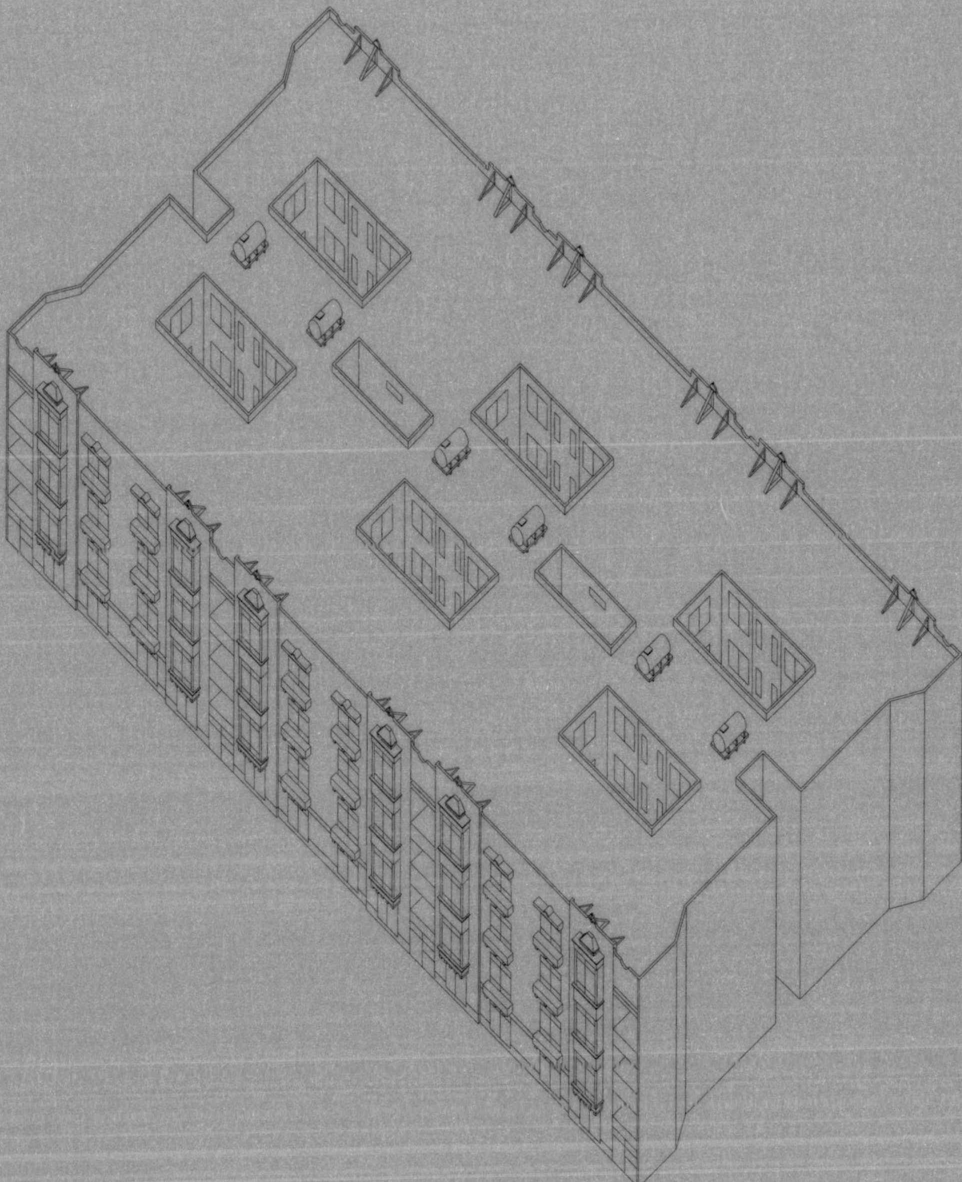

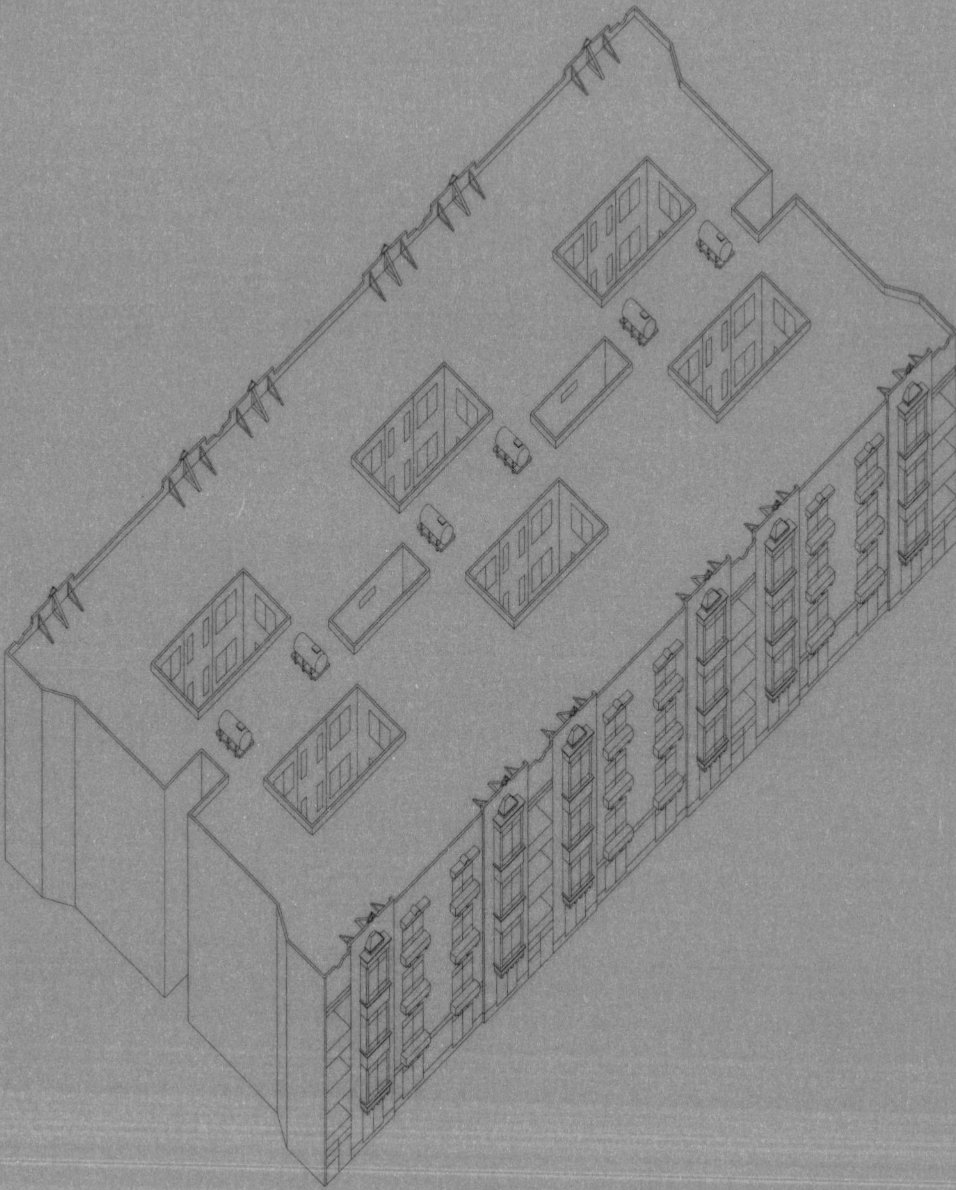

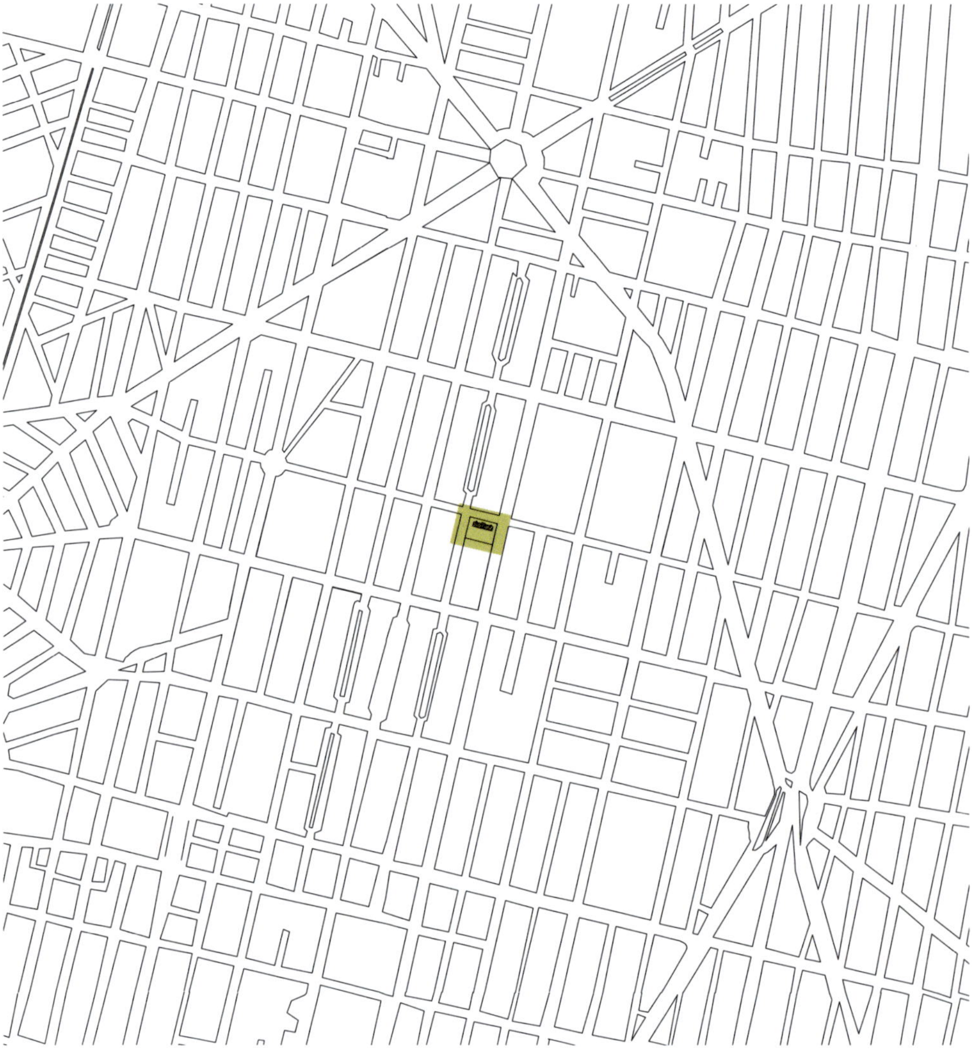

1929, Behn-Zöllinger Houses, Hans Schmidt and Paul Artaria

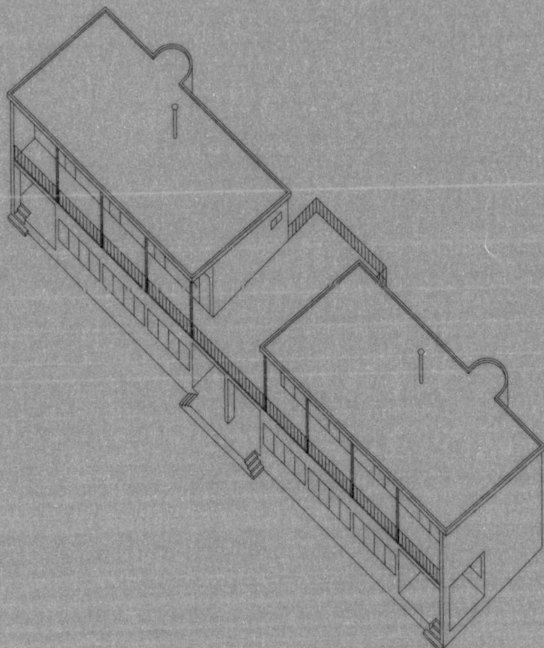

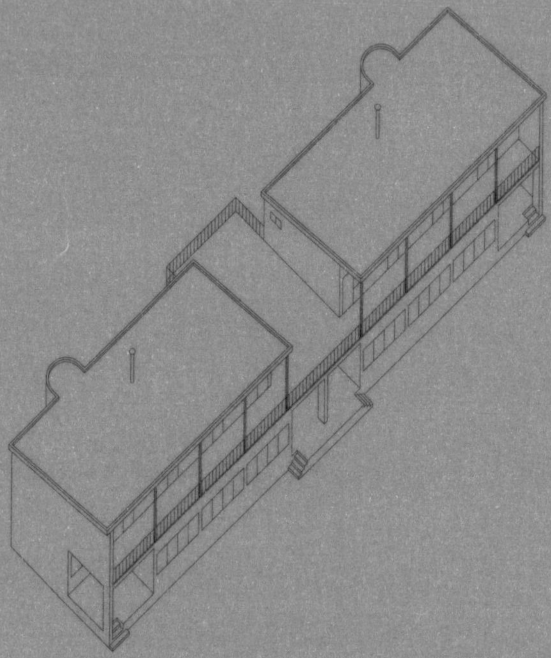

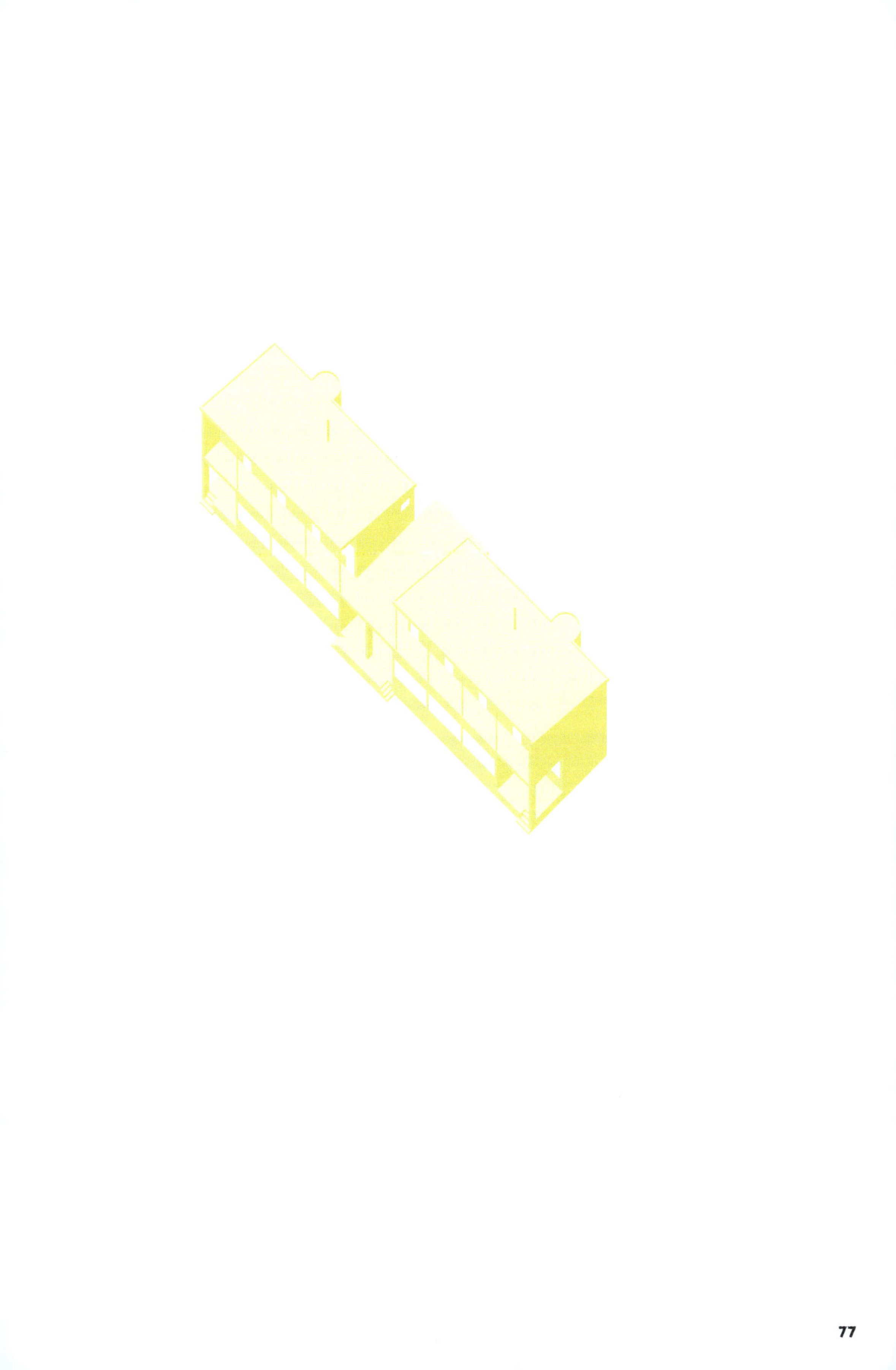

"The tenement, that humblest of housing stock, is much the same today as it was back then [...] but back then those homes had something expressive about them."[1]

Federico Mariscal, 1913

"Thousands of houses have cropped up, but where is the Mexican house, the house of and for Mexicans? [...] we have made a concerted effort to relinquish what is ours, [and this] constitutes a betrayal of our sky, our flowers, our social possibilities."[2]

Alfonso Pallares, 1923

"It is well known that 80% of the Republic's population is illiterate; what proportion of said residents lives in dwellings suitable for civilized men?"[3]

Alfonso Pallares, 1924

"If only tenements, without losing their intense vernacular flavor based on tradition and custom, could acquire a measure of civilization and culture befitting the modern concept of life and cleanliness."[4]

Bernardo Calderón and Juan Galindo, 1924

"The typical houses of Puebla, Oaxaca, Veracruz, and our capital present very significant differences which tell us how Puebla differs from Oaxaca, and Oaxaca from Veracruz and Mexico City."[5]

Federico Mariscal, 1924

1 Federico Mariscal, "La casa", lecture, Casa de la Universidad Popular Mexicana, October 21, 1913, in Federico Mariscal, *La patria y la arquitectura nacional,* Mexico City: Imprenta Stephan y Torres, 1915.
2 Alfonso Pallares, quoted in Israel Katzman, *Arquitectura contemporánea Mexicana,* Mexico City: Instituto Nacional de Antropología e Historia/Secretaría de Educación Pública, 1963, 01.
3 Afonso Pallares, "¿Cómo habita el pueblo mexicano y cómo debía habitar?", in *Excélsior,* November 23, 1924, published in Ramón Vargas Salguero and J. Víctor Arias Montes (eds.), *Ideario de los arquitectos mexicanos*, vol. II: *Los olvidados,* Mexico City: Instituto Nacional de Bellas Artes, 2010, 110.
4 Bernardo Calderón and Juan Galindo, "1925 será el año de la casa popular", in *Excélsior.* December 28, 1924, published in Ramón Vargas Salguero and J. Víctor Arias Montes (eds.), Mexico City: Instituto Nacional de Bellas Artes, 2010, op. cit., p.94.
5 Federico Mariscal, "El estilo de la casa mexicana debe ser el que mejor cuadre", in *Excélsior,* March 16, 1924, published in Ramón Vargas Salguero and J. Víctor Arias Montes (eds.), Mexico City, op. cit., p. 49.

c. 1929, Houses for workers, Juan O'Gorman

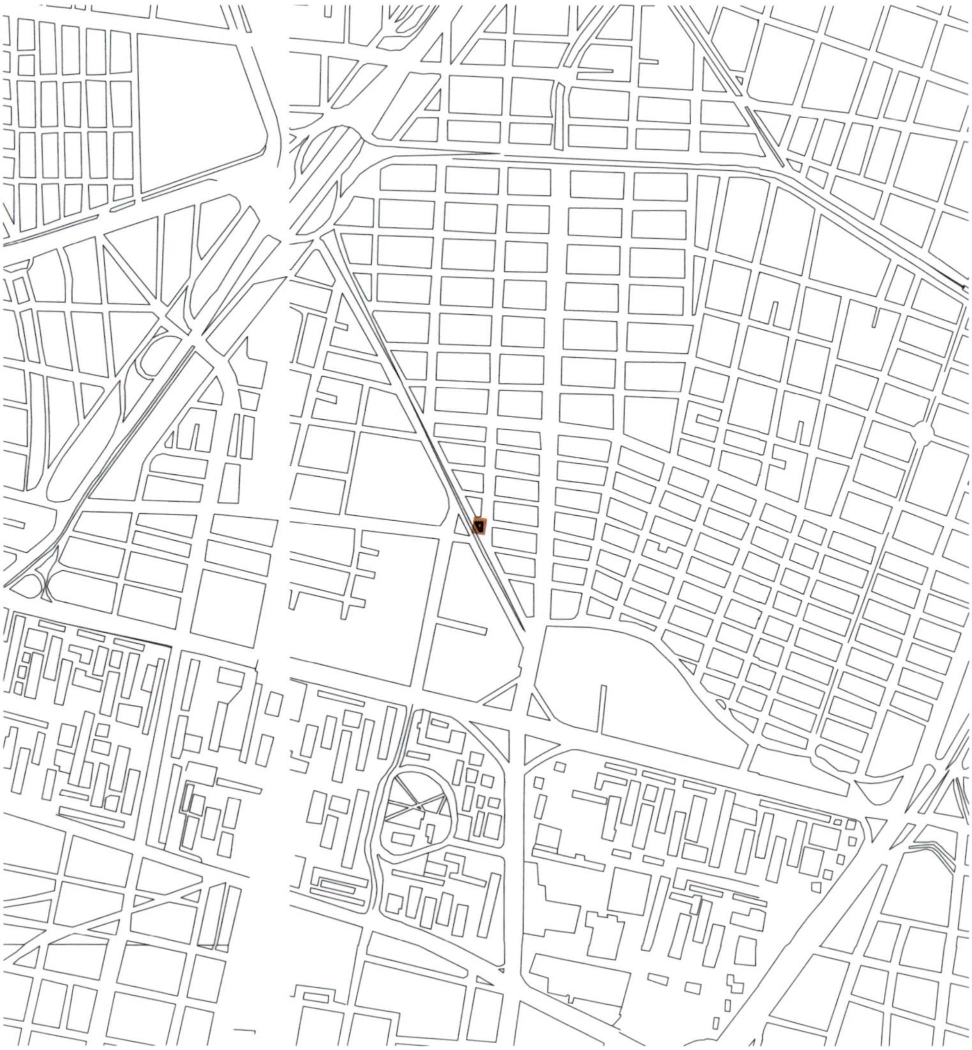

1930, Elorduy Minimal House, Juan Legarreta

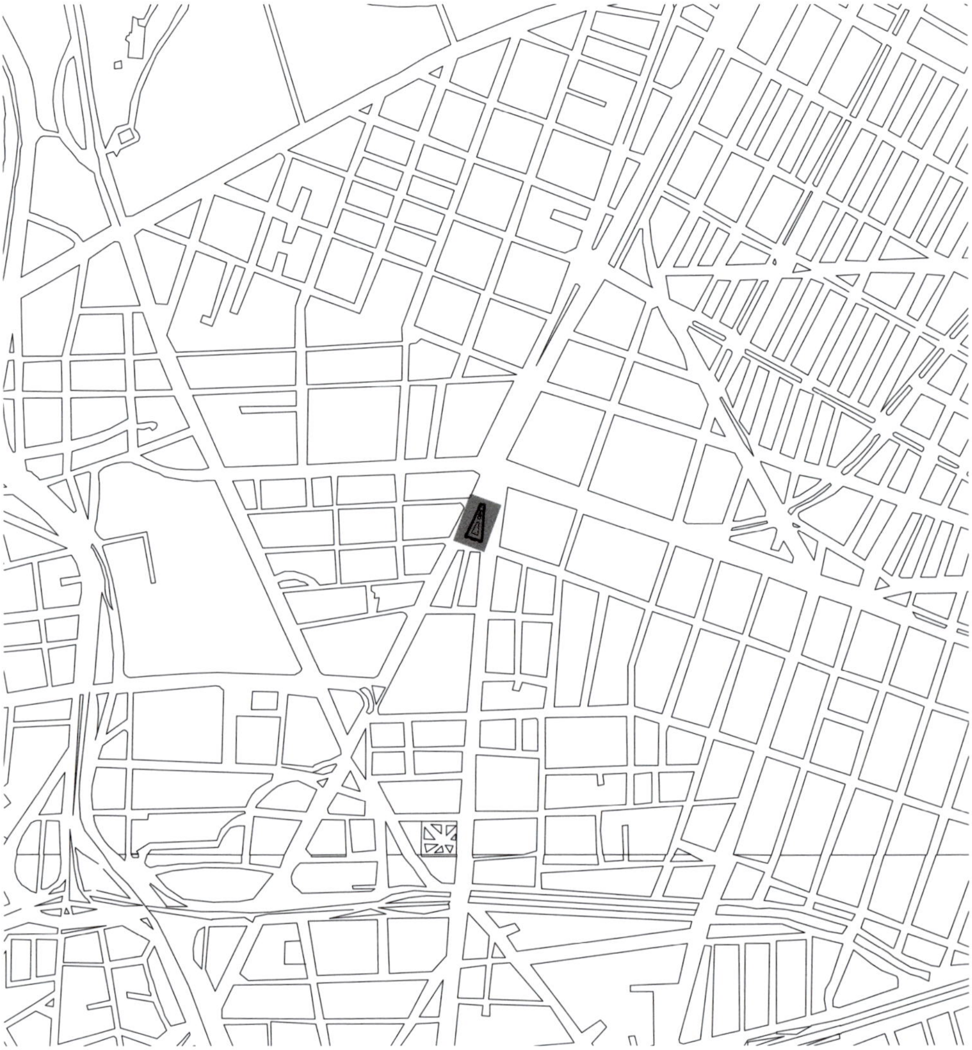

1931, Ermita Building, Juan Segura

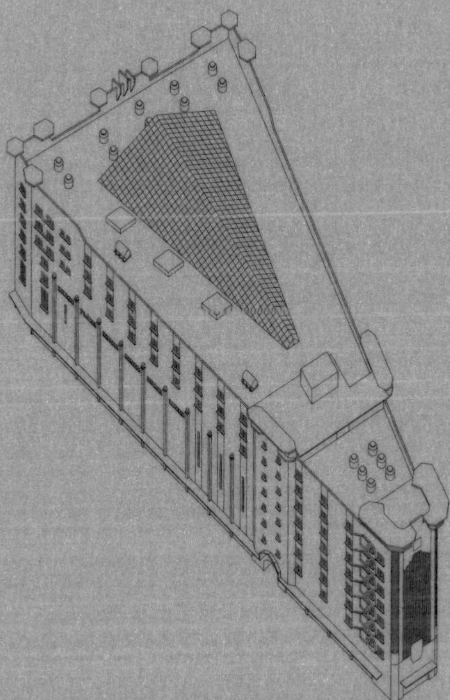

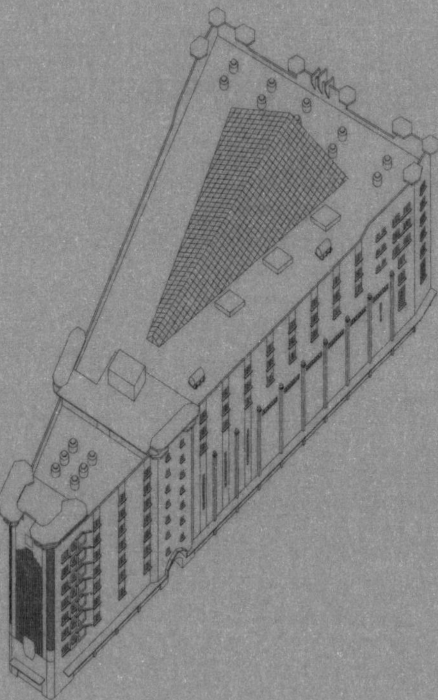

"The blame lies with the state, with the great institutions, with the intellectuals, professionals, and capitalists. Each shares its portion of blame if material and economic –and consequently moral– improvement has not occurred in a stable, disciplined, systematic way for the social classes that huddle on the outskirts. Their miserable housing conditions constitute one of the nearly invariable premises of those denouements of illness or bloodshed that end in hospitals or prisons."[6]

Luis Prieto y Souza, 1926

"Every house should have air, light, sun, water, and a garden."[7]

Carlos Contreras, 1927

"At least 60% of our population is poisoning themselves, both morally and physically, by living in infested shacks and miserable rooms inside tenements."[8]

Silvano Palafox, 1930

"We must seek to make our houses gardens, and our gardens houses."[9]

Luis Barragán, 1931

"The concept of a *private home* should be discarded. The future lies in collective living; its embryonic forms are already developing."[10]

Hannes Meyer, 1932

6 Luis Prieto y Souza, "Problemas del momento material y económico de las clases sociales", in *El Universal*, September 26, 1926, published in Ramón Vargas Salguero and J. Víctor Arias Montes (eds.), Mexico City, op. cit., p. 138.

7 Carlos Contreras, "¿Qué cosa es la planificación de ciudades y regiones?", in *Planificación*, no. 1 (September 1927), published in Vargas Salguero and J. Víctor Arias Montes, eds., Mexico City, op. cit., p. 170.

8 Carlos González Lobo, *Arquitectura en México durante la cuarta década: el Maximato, el cardenismo. Apuntes para la historia y crítica de la arquitectura mexicana del siglo xx, 1900-1980*, vol. II, Cuadernos de Arquitectura y Conservación del Patrimonio Artístico, nos. 22 and 23, Mexico City: Secretaría de Educación Pública/Instituto Nacional de Bellas Artes, 1982, 89.

9 Luis Barragán, "Apuntes de Nueva York. Ideas sobre jardines" [1931], in Antonio Riggen, *Luis Barragán: escritos y conversaciones*, Madrid: El Croquis Editorial, 2000, 15.

10 Hannes Meyer, "Der Architekt im Klassenkampf", in *Der Rote Aufbau*, no. 13, Hamburg, 1932; Spanish version: *El arquitecto en la lucha de clases*, Havana: Arte y Literatura, 1981, 86.

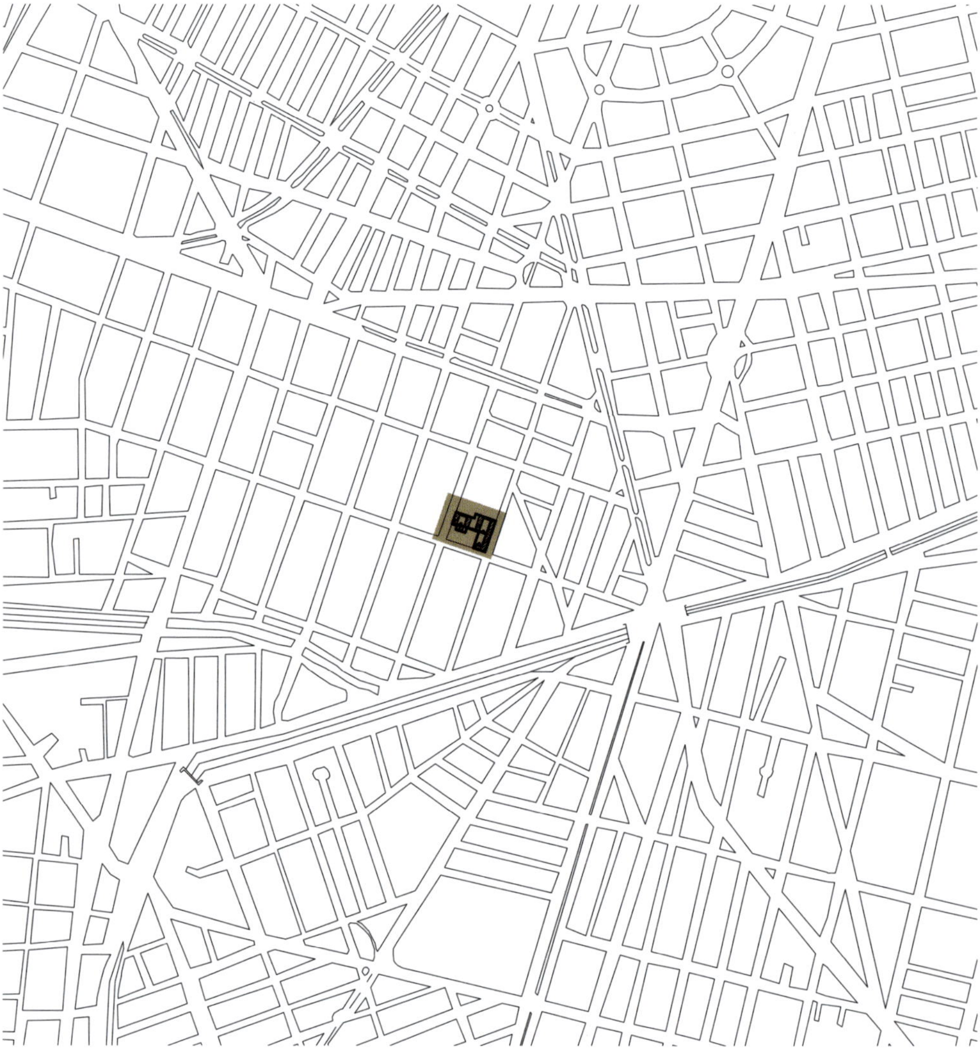

1931, Jardín complex, Francisco J. Serrano

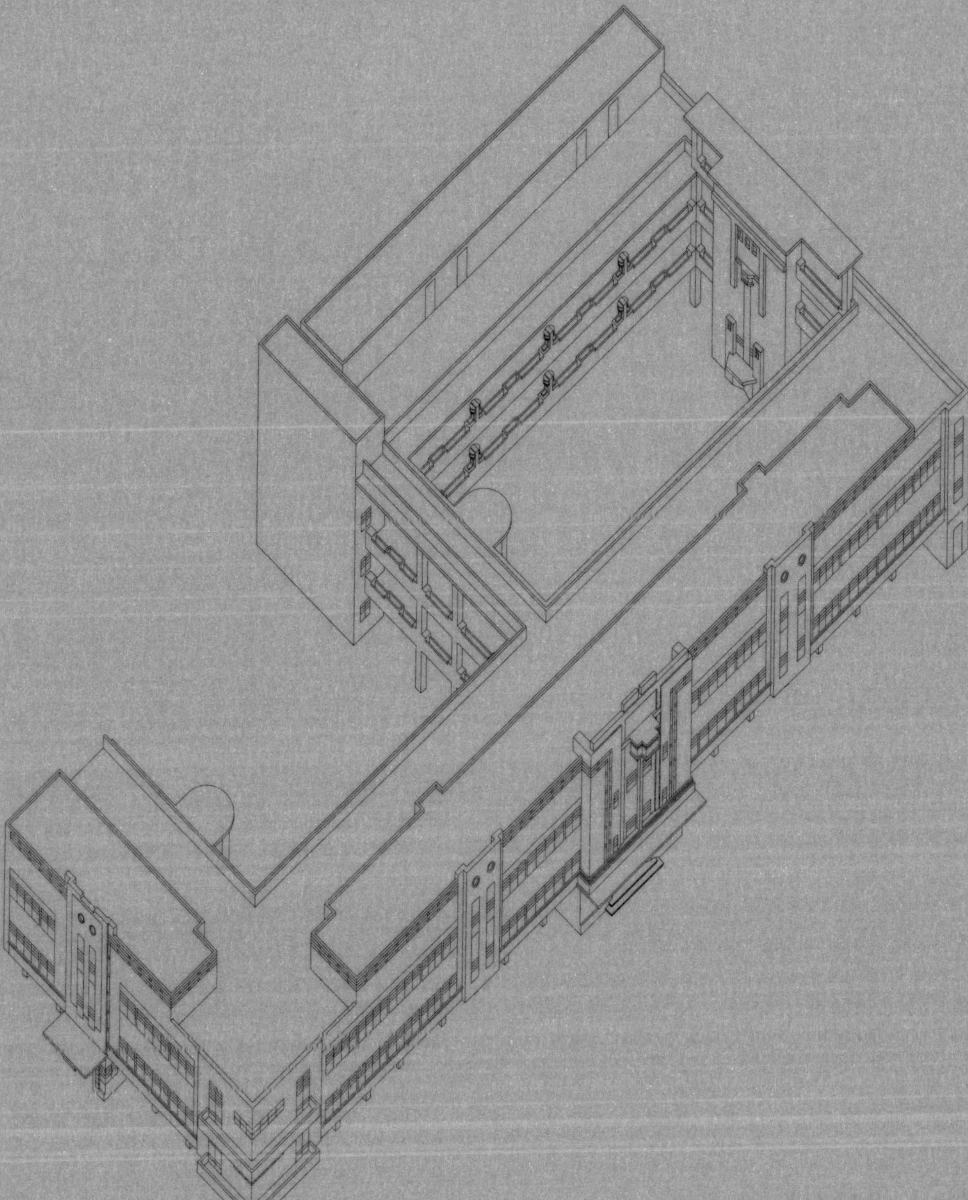

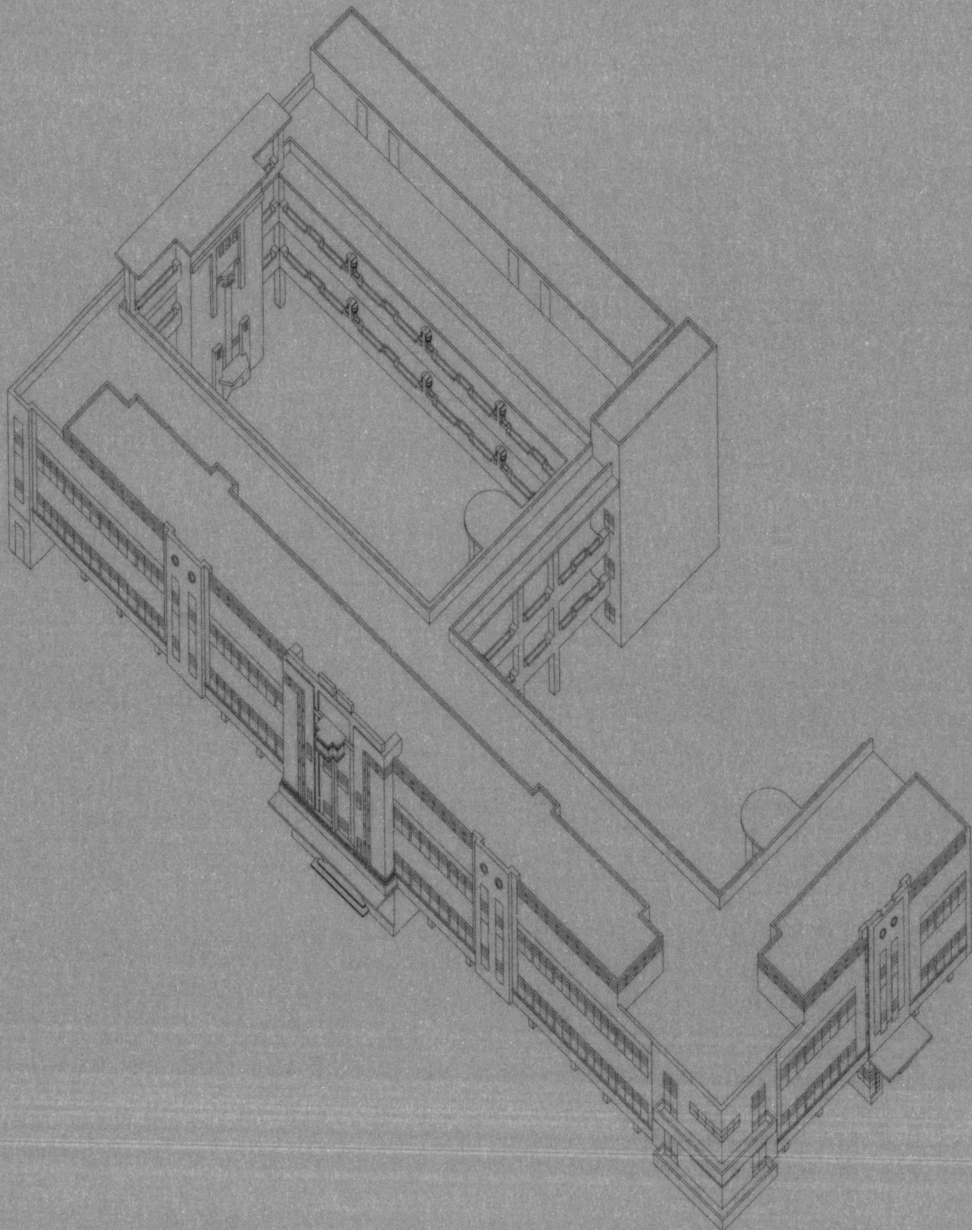

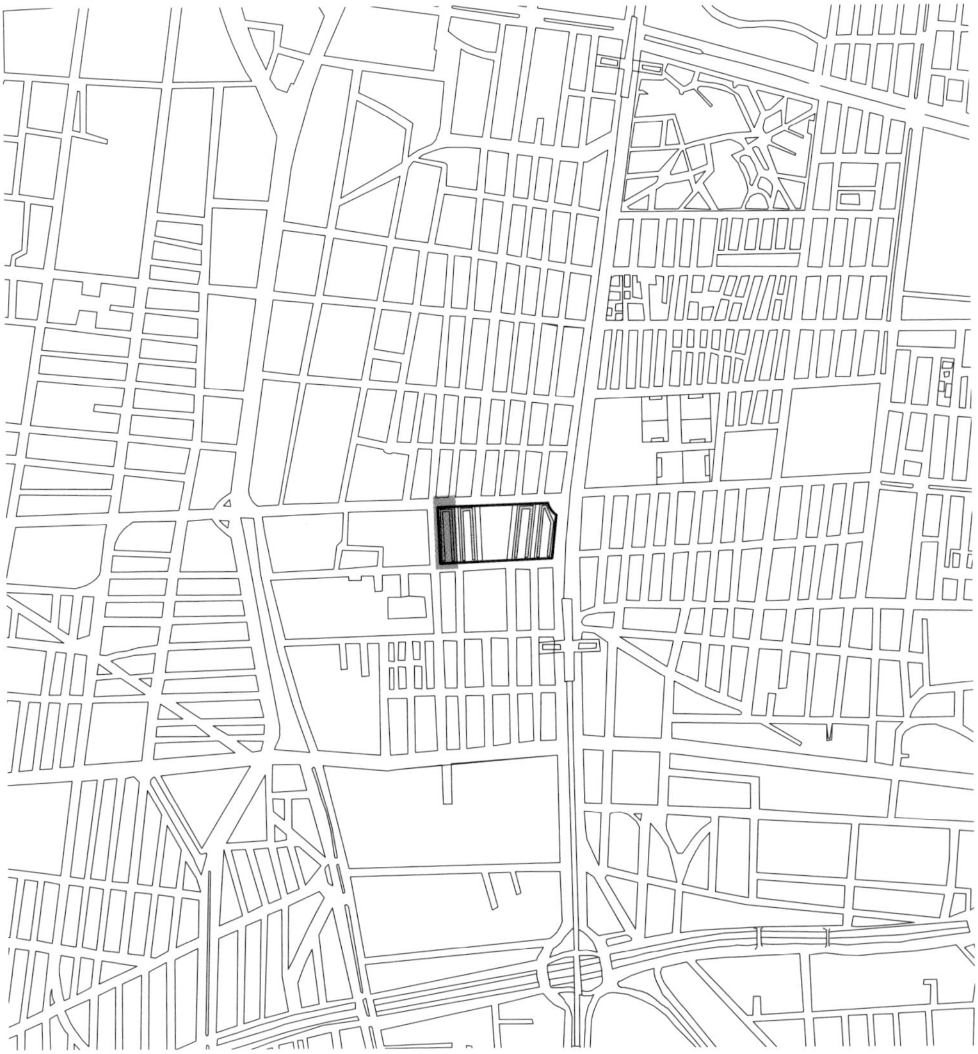

1932, Minimal Worker's House, Juan Legarreta

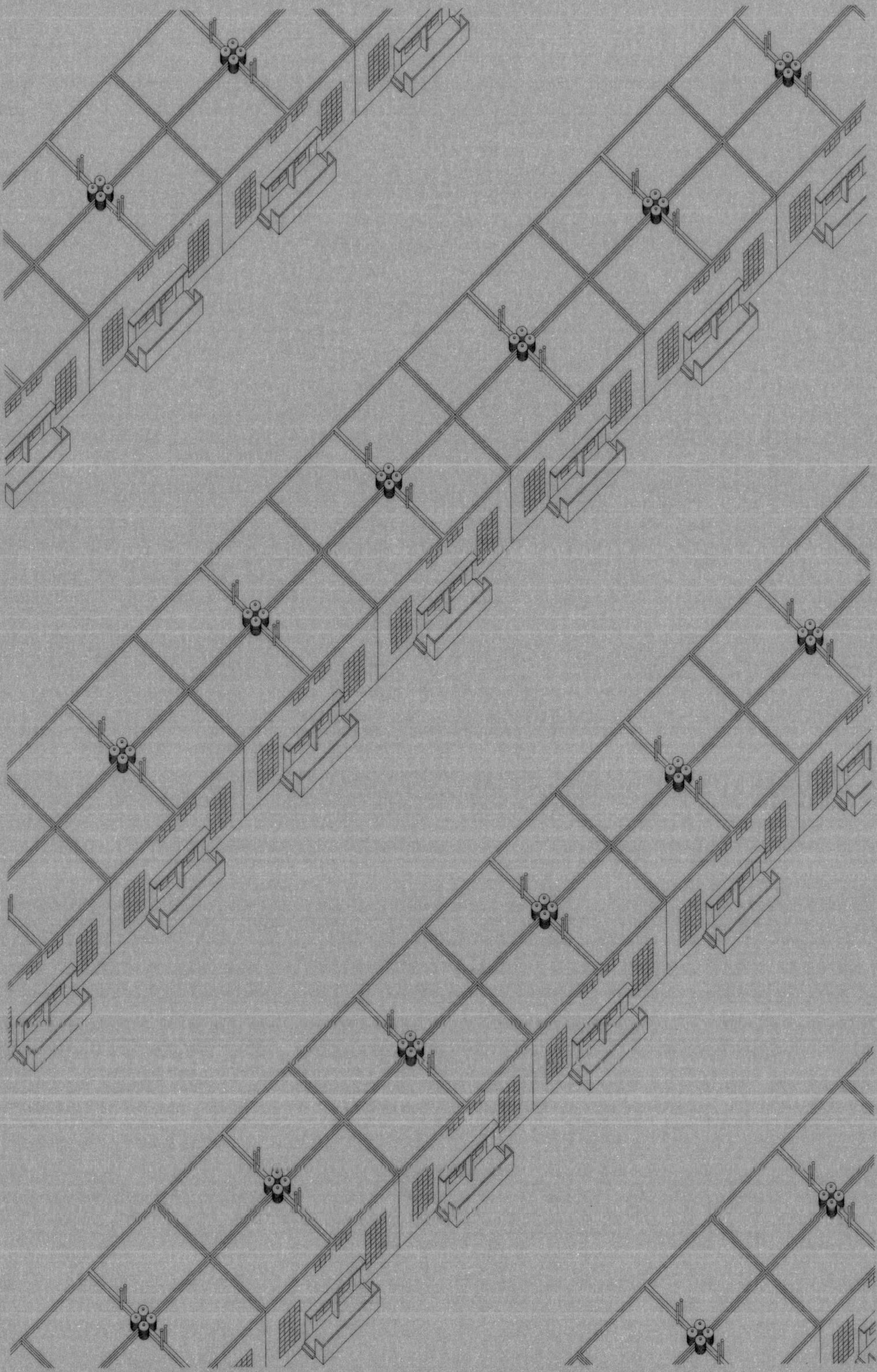

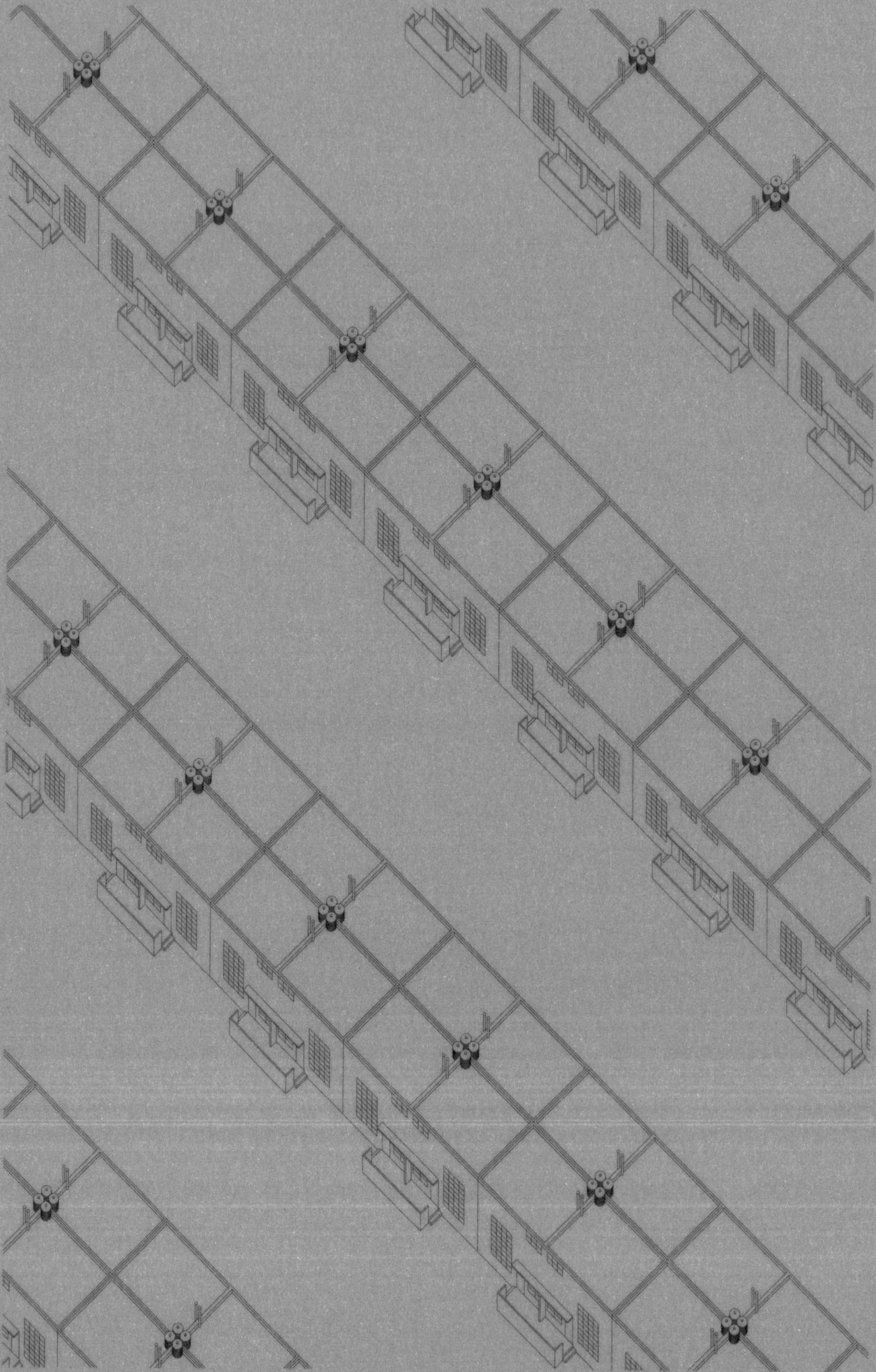

"The prime directive is 'My house must not be like other houses', and this superfluous, vain reasoning makes us overlook the true rational principles of efficiency to meet the spiritual needs of a fool."[11]

Juan O'Gorman, 1933

"A nation that lives in huts and single rooms cannot speak architecture. We must build the house of the people. The esthetes and rhetoricians –devil take them all!– can debate about it afterwards."[12]

Juan Legarreta, 1933

"The door in a worker's home will be the same size as one in a philosopher's home."[13]

Juan O'Gorman, 1933

"One day, the sharecropper and worker will rise up in a new revolution if the former continues to live in an African hut and in the latter in a crowded tenement."[14]

Álvaro Aburto, 1933

"We can guarantee a smiling population, in a city with gardens enough for all [...] a city where, having abolished the differences of a class-conscious society, human life recovers its truly human dimension."[15]

Juan Legarreta, 1933

11 Juan O'Gorman, "Pláticas sobre arquitectura", lecture given in Mexico City in 1933, printed in *Cuadernos de Arquitectura*, Mexico City: Direccion de Arquitectura y Conservación del Patrimonio Artístico Inmueble/Consejo Nacional para la Cultura y las Artes/Instituto Nacional de Bellas Artes, 2001, 20. First edition, Mexico City: Sociedad de Arquitectos Mexicanos, 1934.

12 Juan Legarreta, "Pláticas sobre arquitectura", op. cit., p. 39. First edition, Mexico City: Sociedad de Arquitectos Mexicanos, 1934.

13 Juan O'Gorman, "Pláticas sobre arquitectura", op. cit., p. 54. First edition, Mexico City: Sociedad de Arquitectos Mexicanos, 1934.

14 Álvaro Aburto, quoted in Israel Katzman, Mexico City: Instituto Nacional de Antropología e Historia/Secretaría de Educación Pública, 1963, op., cit., p. 154.

15 Luz María Granados Roldan, *¿Un funcionalista radical? Juan Legarreta*, Architecture BA thesis, Mexico City: Universidad Iberoamericana, 1987, 146.

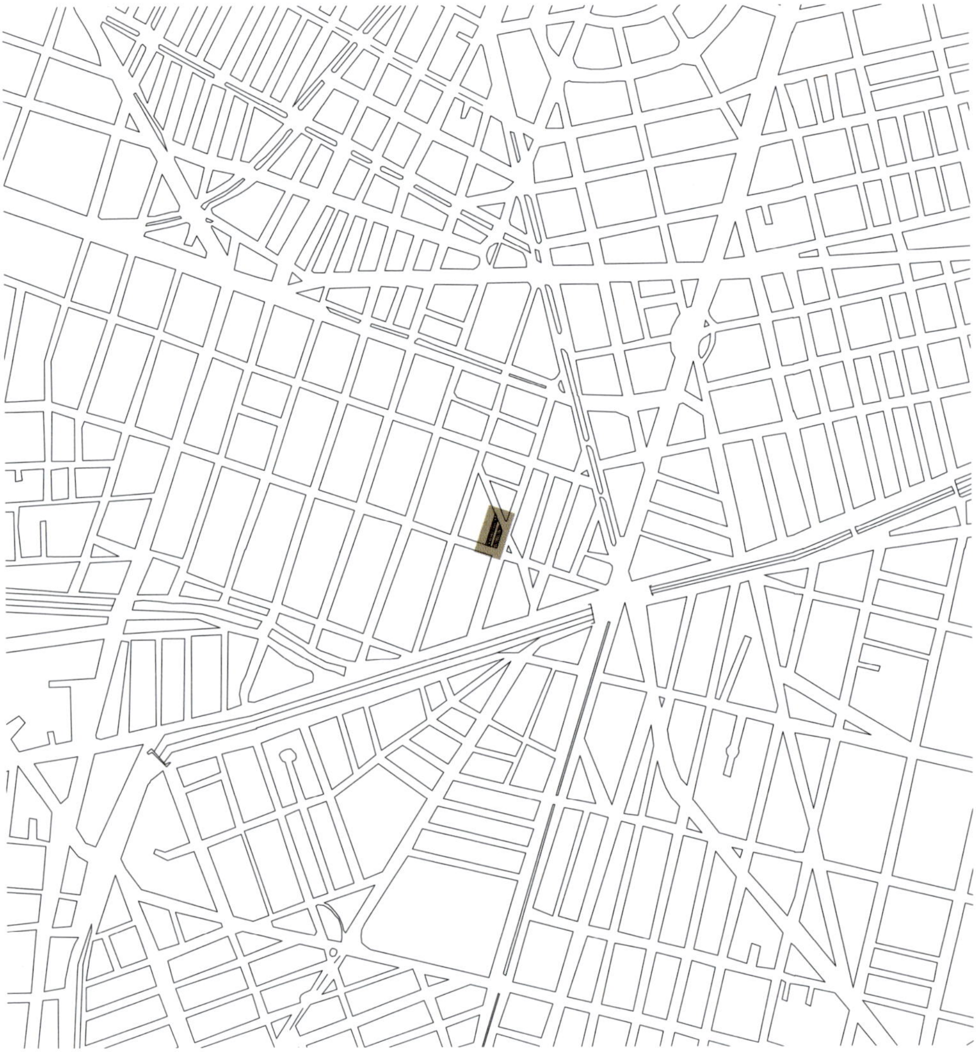

1934, Martí Building, Enrique Yáñez

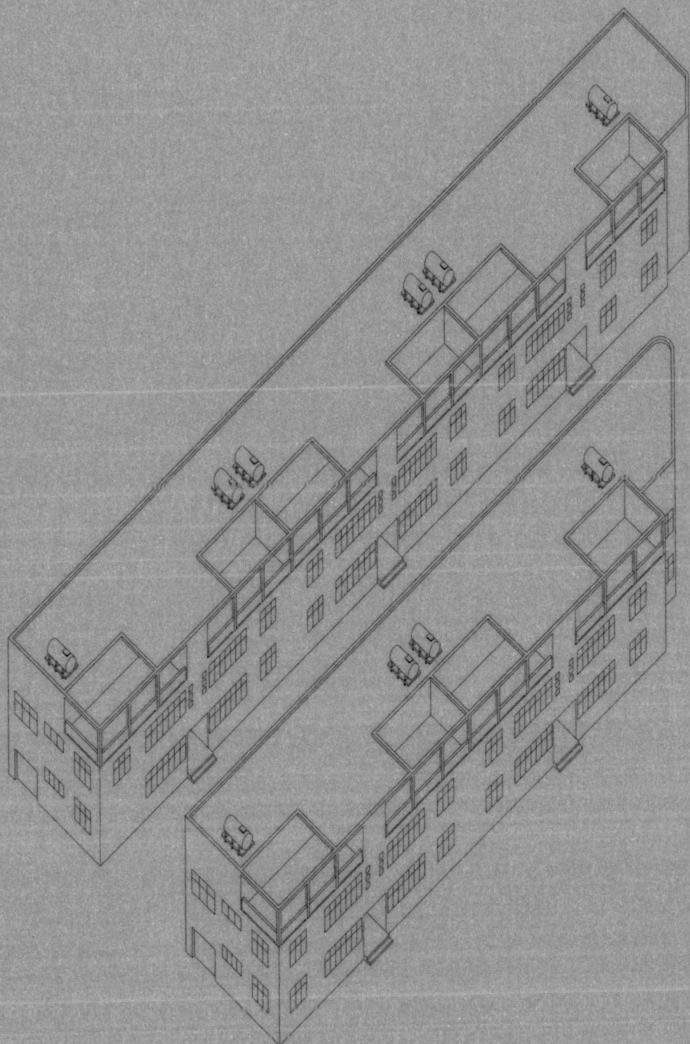

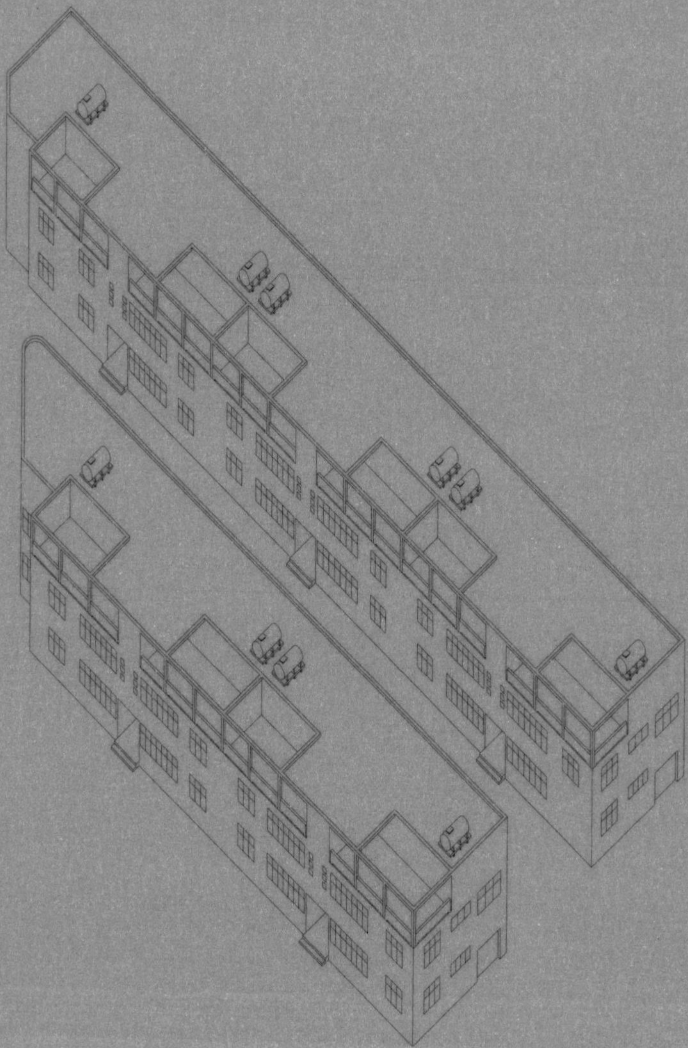

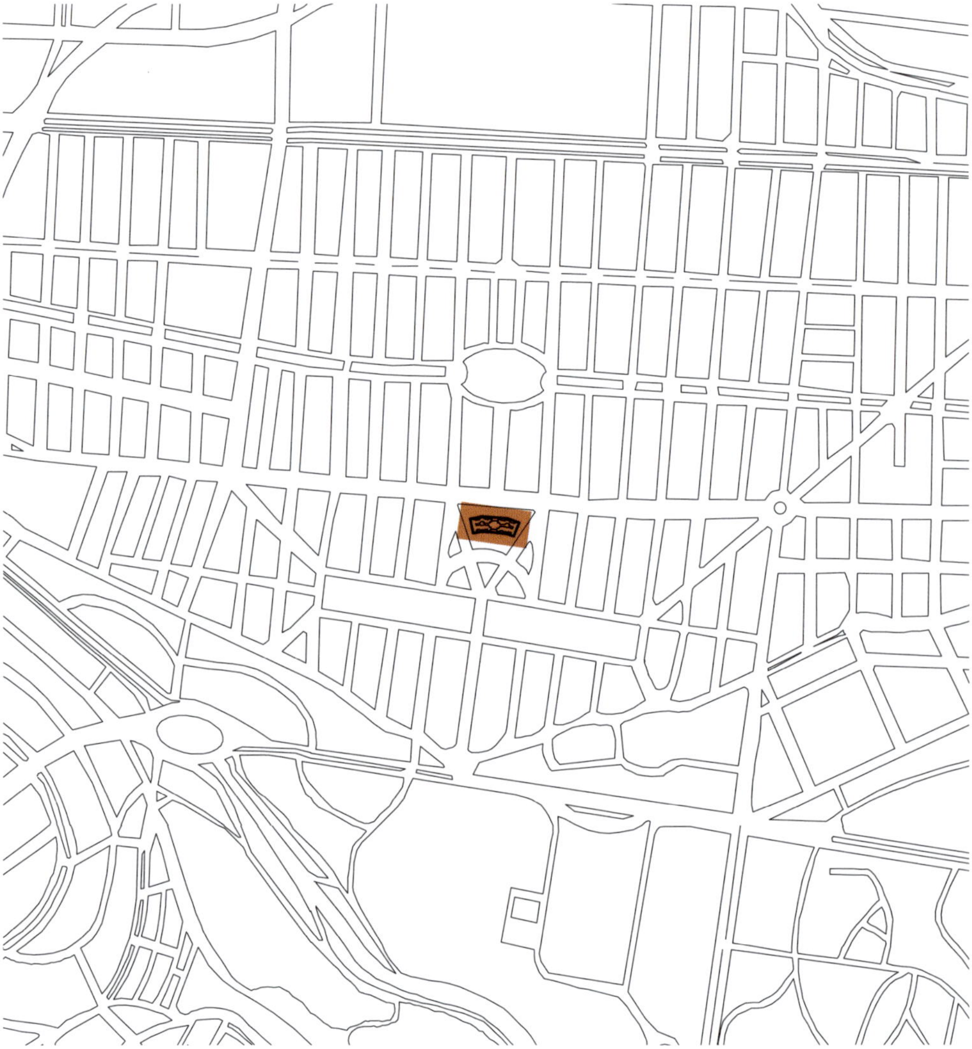

1939, Polanco Passway, Francisco J. Serrano

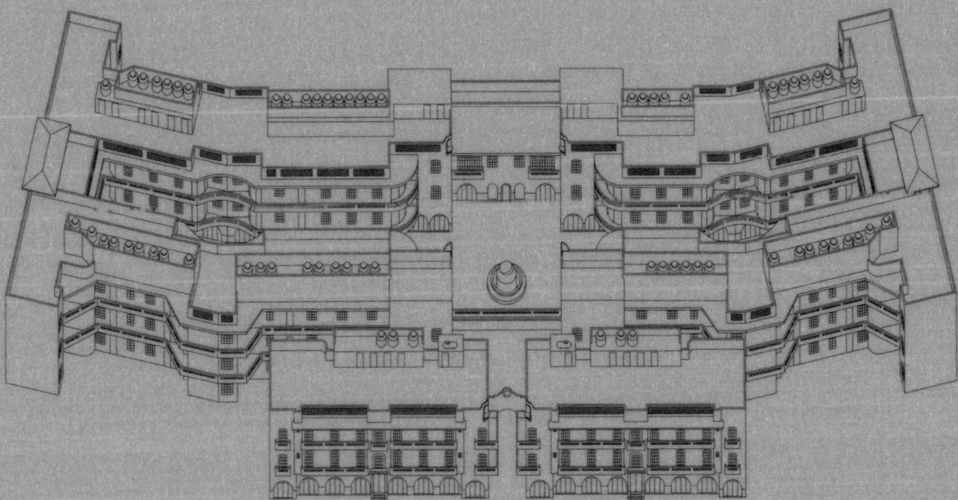

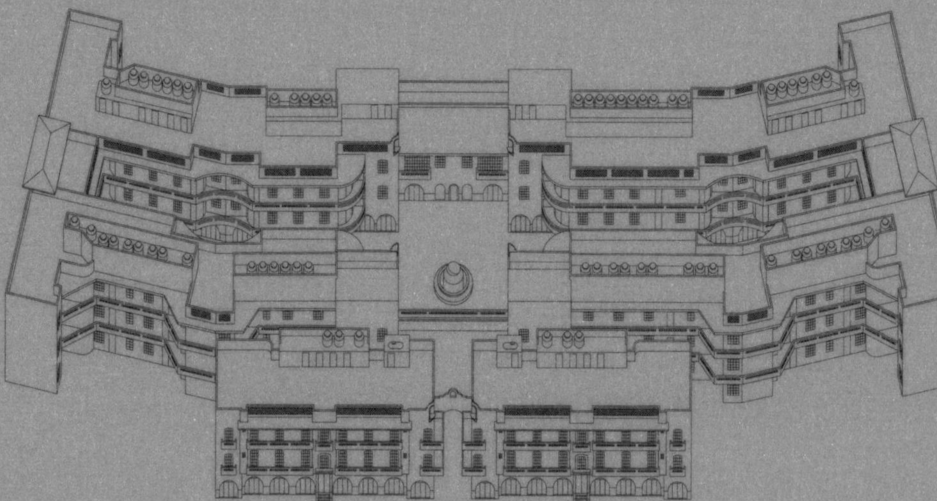

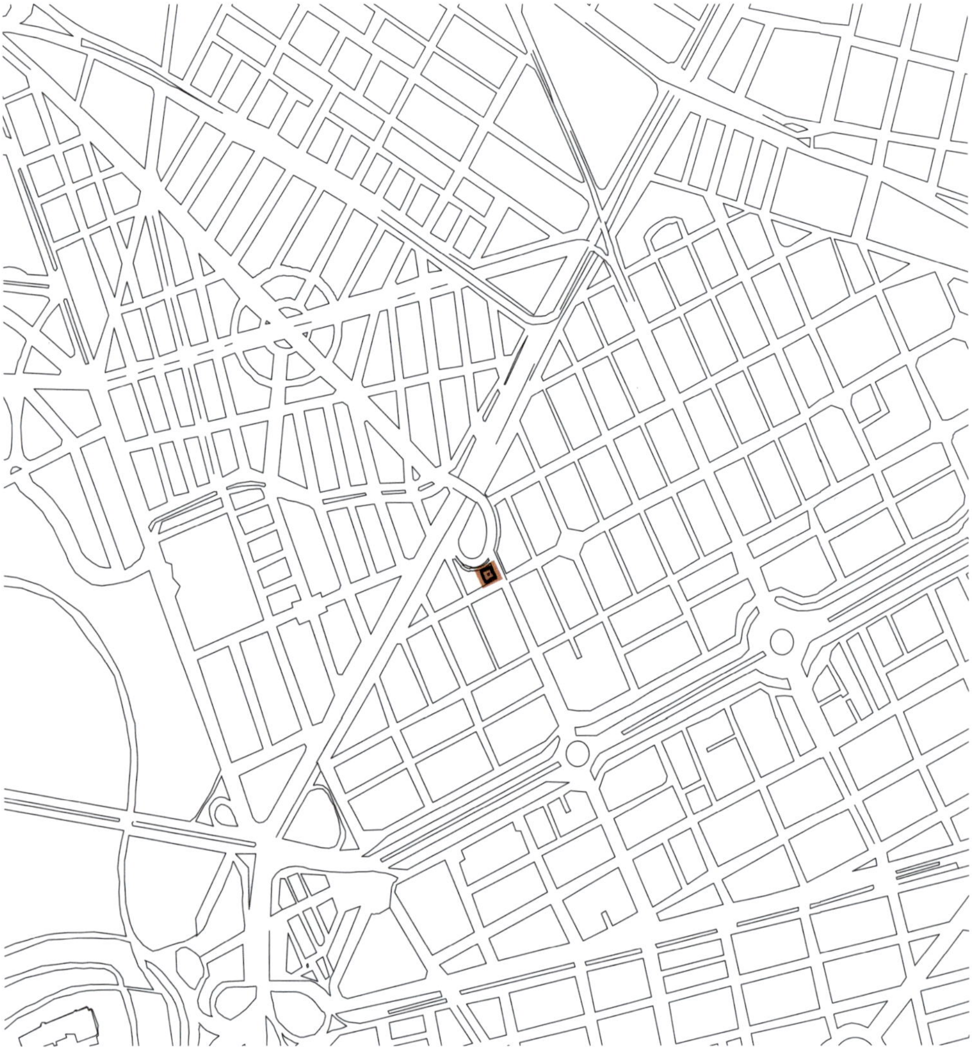

1939, Garza Building, Luis Barragán and José Creixell

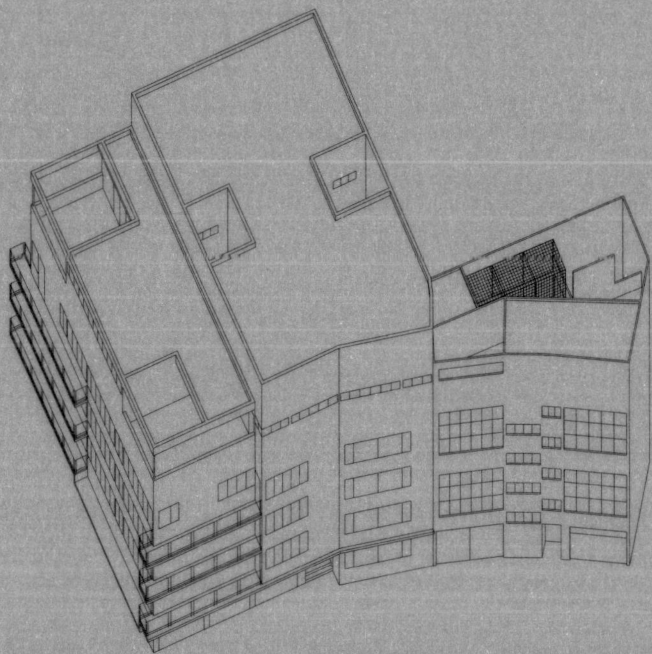

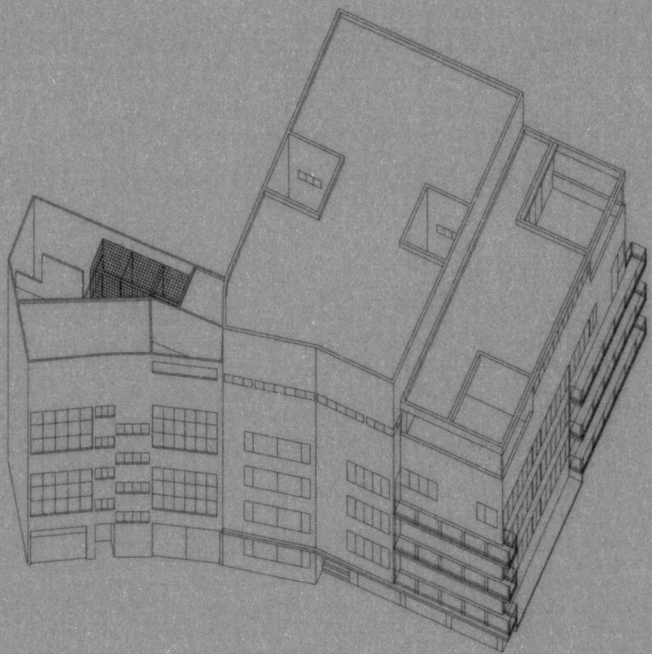

"Air and sunlight for workers currently living in pigsties and tenements."[16]

Juan O'Gorman, 1934

"No architectural proposal explains the tension of class struggle in bourgeois society more immediately or effectively than the residential construction."[17]

Hannes Meyer, 1935

"Given that the majority of Mexicans live in huts, single rooms, and insalubrious tenements, we insist that not a single cent of public funds be spent on architectural monuments, ornamental avenues, etc."[18]

Álvaro Aburto, Raúl Cacho, Ricardo Rivas
y Luis Cuevas, 1937

"Architecture may yet become revolutionary if it can fully satisfy the collective need to dwell."[19]

Unión de Arquitectos Socialistas
(Alberto T. Arai, Raúl Cacho, Enrique Guerrero
and Balbino Hernández), 1938

"Out there [in the countryside] is where we must learn how to build rural homes for Mexico, not in our offices."[20]

Carlos Contreras, 1938

16 *El Arquitecto. Órgano de la Sociedad de Arquitectos Mexicanos*, special memorial issue devoted to the architect Juan Legarreta, October 1934, 18.
17 Hannes Meyer, quoted in Alexander Klein, *Vivienda mínima, 1906-1957,* Barcelona: Gustavo Gili, 1980, 13.
18 Álvaro Aburto, Raúl Cacho, Ricardo Rivas and Luis Cuevas, "El problema de la arquitectura y el urbanismo en México", *Edificación*, no. 1, January February 1937.
19 Alberto T. Arai, Raúl Cacho, Enrique Guerrero and Balbino Hernández, "Memoria del proyecto de la Ciudad Obrera de México", in *Arquitectura y Decoración*, no. 11, September 1938, 202-214.
20 Carlos Contreras, lecture "Sobre el problema de la habitación rural urbana y semiurbana", August 17, 1938, quoted in Enrique X. de Anda, op., cit., p. 105.

1940, Tropical Rural House, Alberto T. Arai

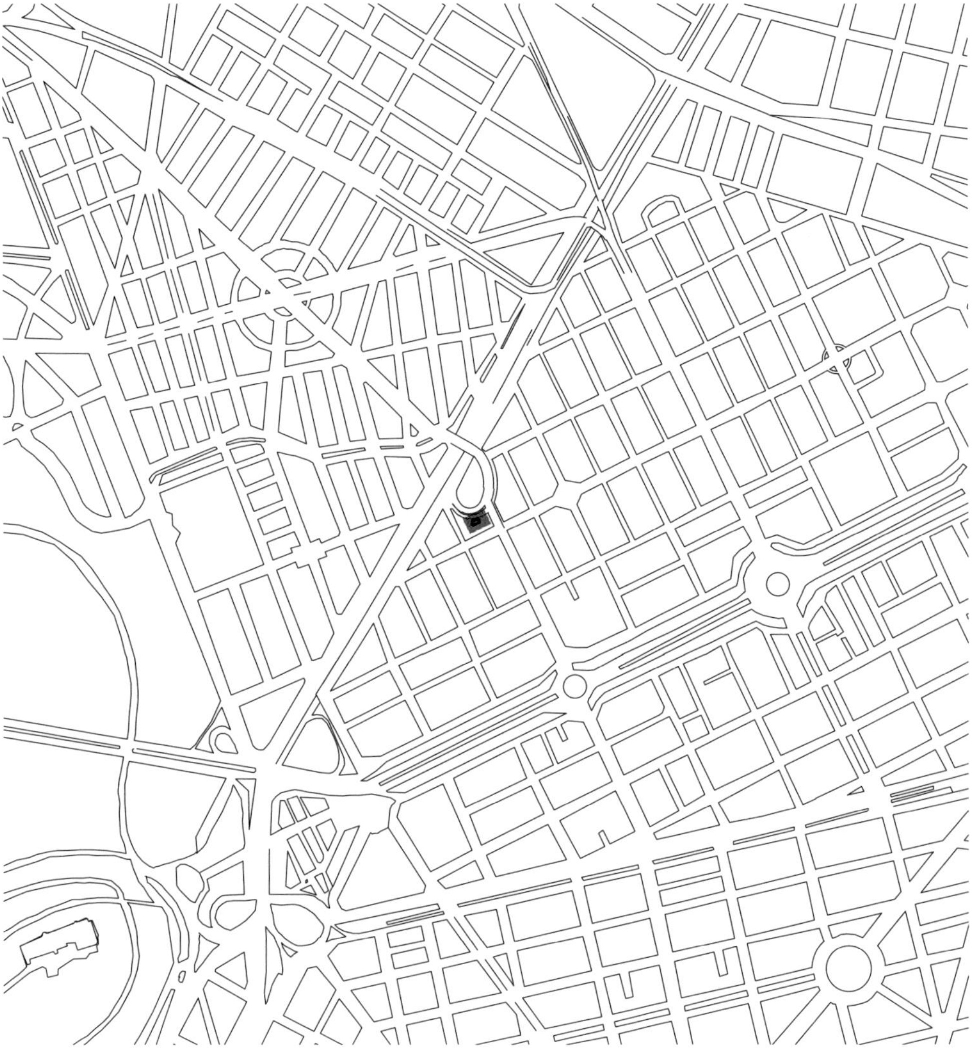

1941, Building for artists, Luis Barragán and Max Cetto

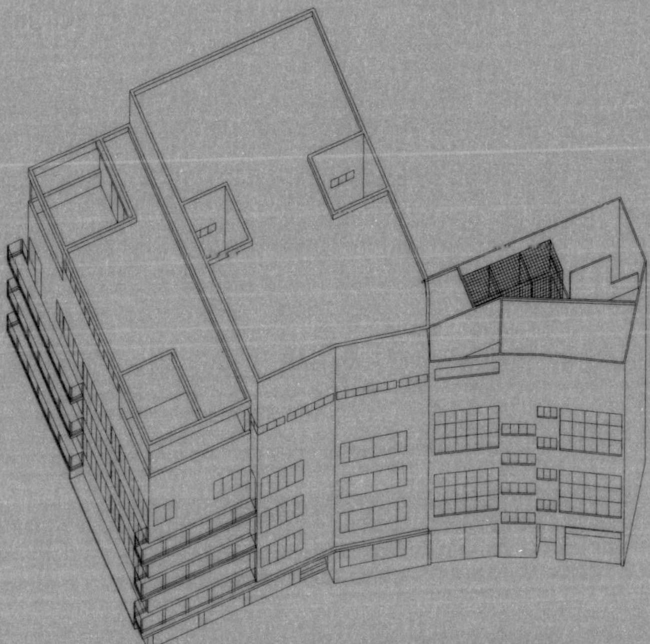

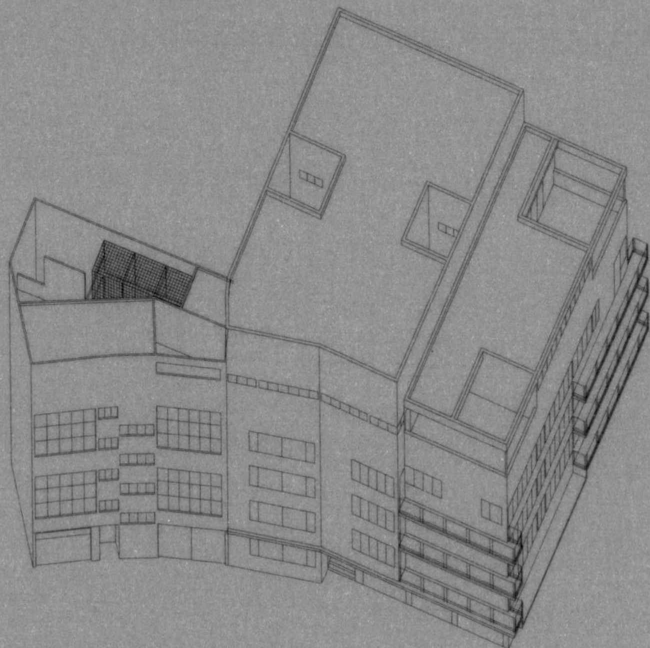

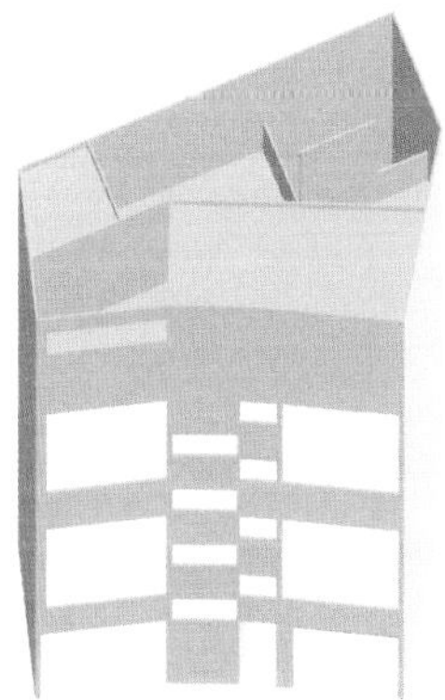

"The housing development of the property speculator uses all sorts of folksy elements to appeal to the patriotic instincts of potential buyers, hoping that this architectural flattery will distract them from the robbery."[21]

Hannes Meyer, 1938

"Building vertically is a very good way of concentrating (families), but unfortunately it has the disadvantage of creating structures that cast shadows, depriving each other of sunlight, air, and gardens; and even if we aim to create numerous detached edifices that take up a small portion of the lot and leave ample room for gardens, it is still a dangerous undertaking."[22]

Francisco Serrano, 1938

"My clients know and care nothing about these matters; what they want is architecture that sells and gives them big returns on their investment. The high demand for housing guarantees that profit, and the rest doesn't matter: what people want is a roof to live under."[23]

Luis Barragán, 1938

"The glaring contradiction between the great spaciousness of urban Mexico and its terrible traffic congestion is due to a lack of coordination between the city's residential and work areas, a product of unrestrained property speculation and the frenzied pursuit of private interests."[24]

Hannes Meyer, 1943

21 Hannes Meyer, lecture "La formación del arquitecto", Escuela Nacional de Arquitectura de la Academia de San Carlos, September 29, 1938, published in *Hannes Meyer, pensamiento*, Cuadernos de Arquitectura, no. 5, Mexico City: Dirección de Arquitectura y Conservación del Patrimonio Artístico Inmueble/Consejo Nacional para la Cultura y las Artes/Instituto Nacional de Bellas Artes, 2002, 22

22 Francisco Serrano [August 17, 1938], in Enrique X. de Anda, op., cit., pp. 103 y 104.

23 Luis Barragán, "Reflexiones sobre la arquitectura moderna en México, DF, y EEUU" [1938], in Antonio Riggen, Madrid: El Croquis Editorial, 2000, op., cit., p. 21.

24 Hannes Meyer, "La Ciudad de México: fragmentos de un estudio urbanístico", *Arquitectura México*, no. 12, April 1943, 96.

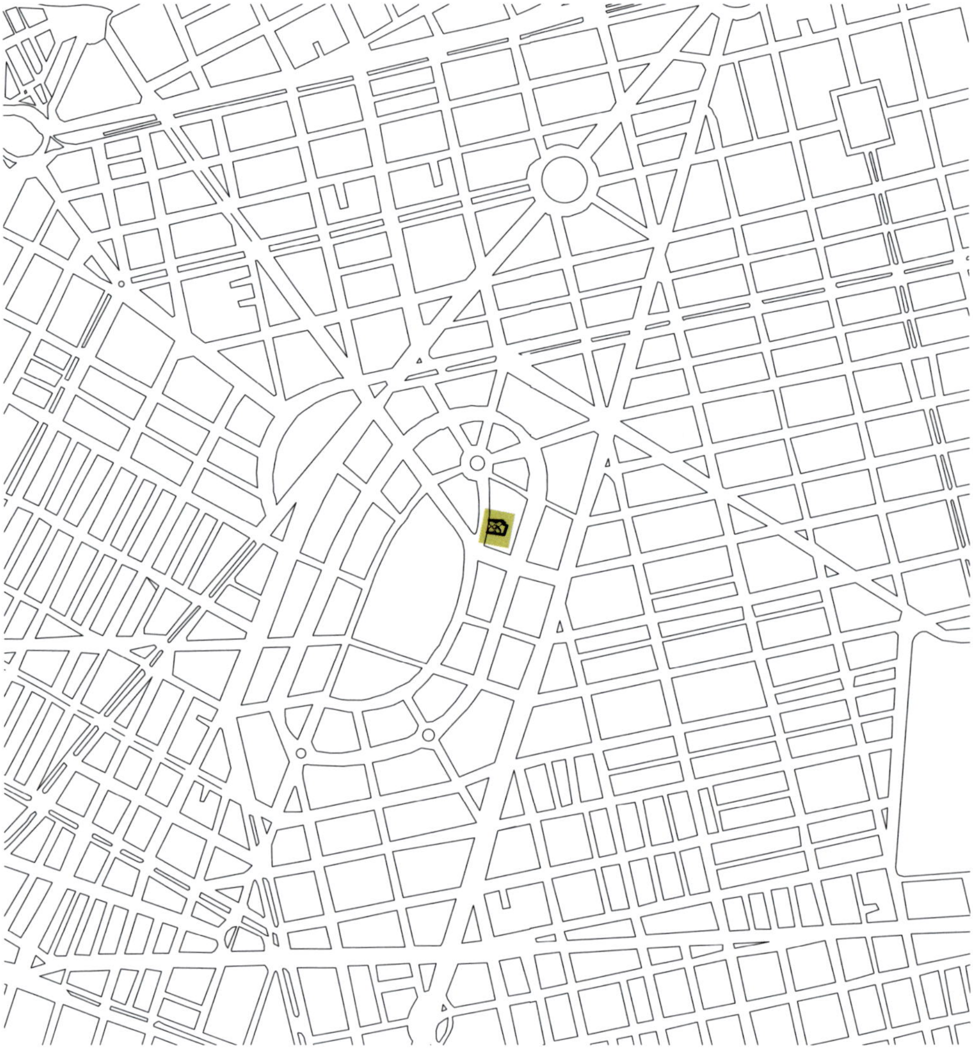

1942 Basurto Building, Francisco J. Serrano

c. 1947, Unidad Modelo complex, Félix Sánchez Baylón, Carlos B. Zetina, Mario Pani, José Luis Cuevas, Domingo García Ramos and Homero Martínez

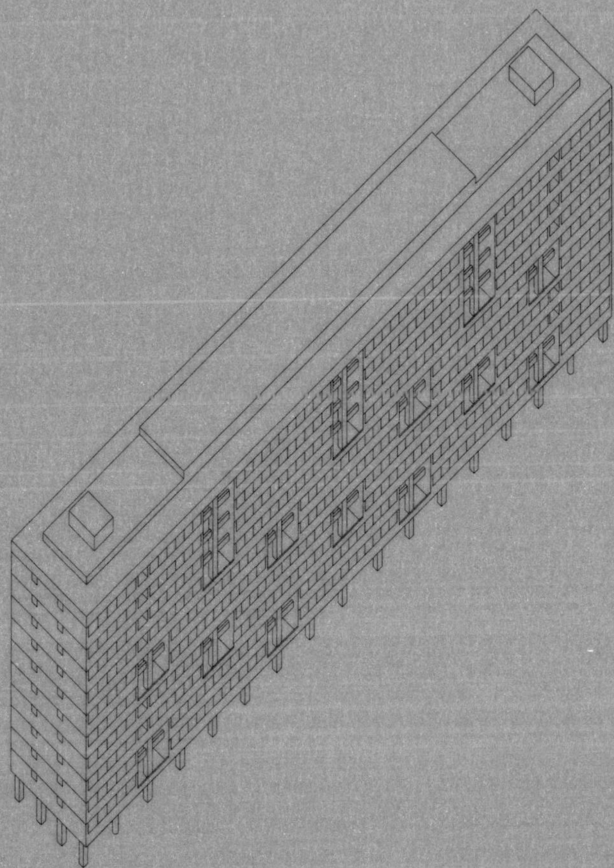

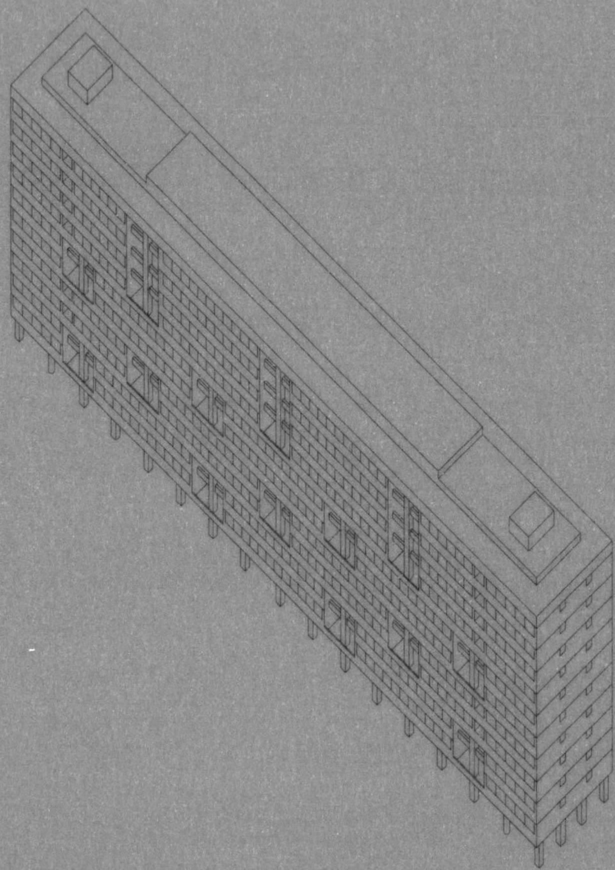

1949, Centro Urbano Presidente Alemán (CUPA), Mario Pani, Salvador Ortega, J. de Jesús Gutiérrez and Jenaro de Rosenzweig

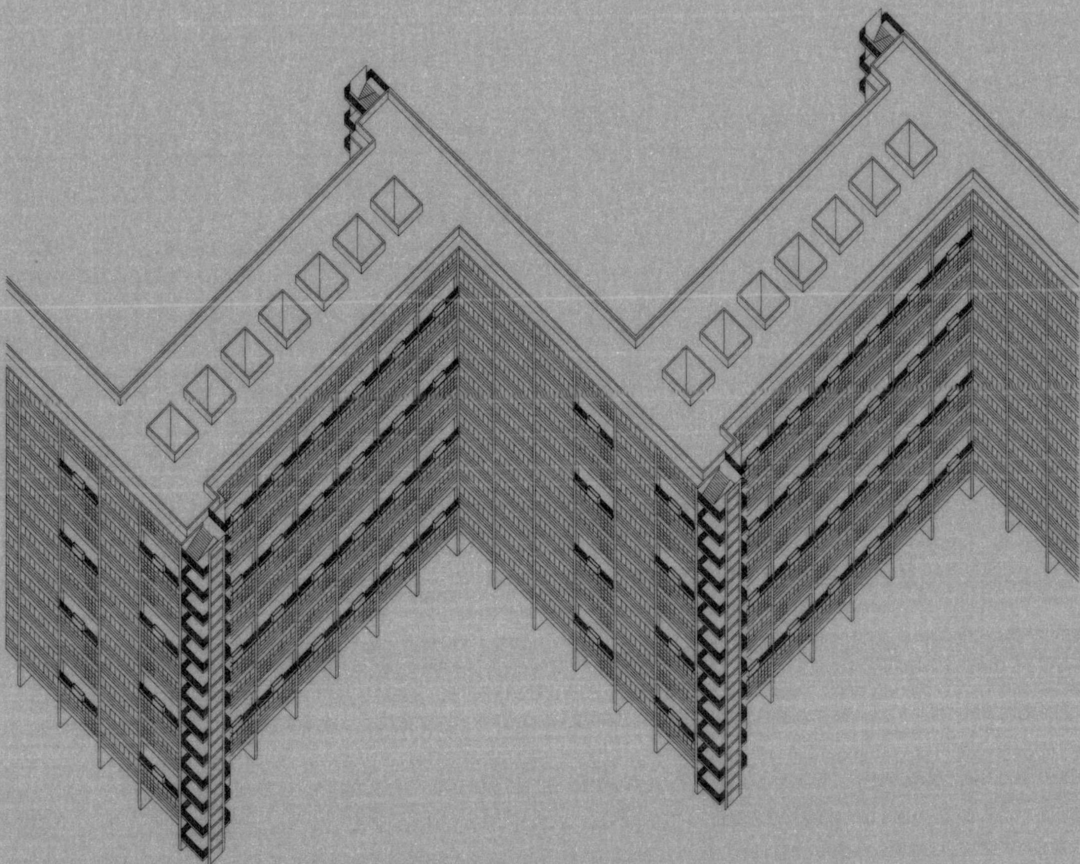

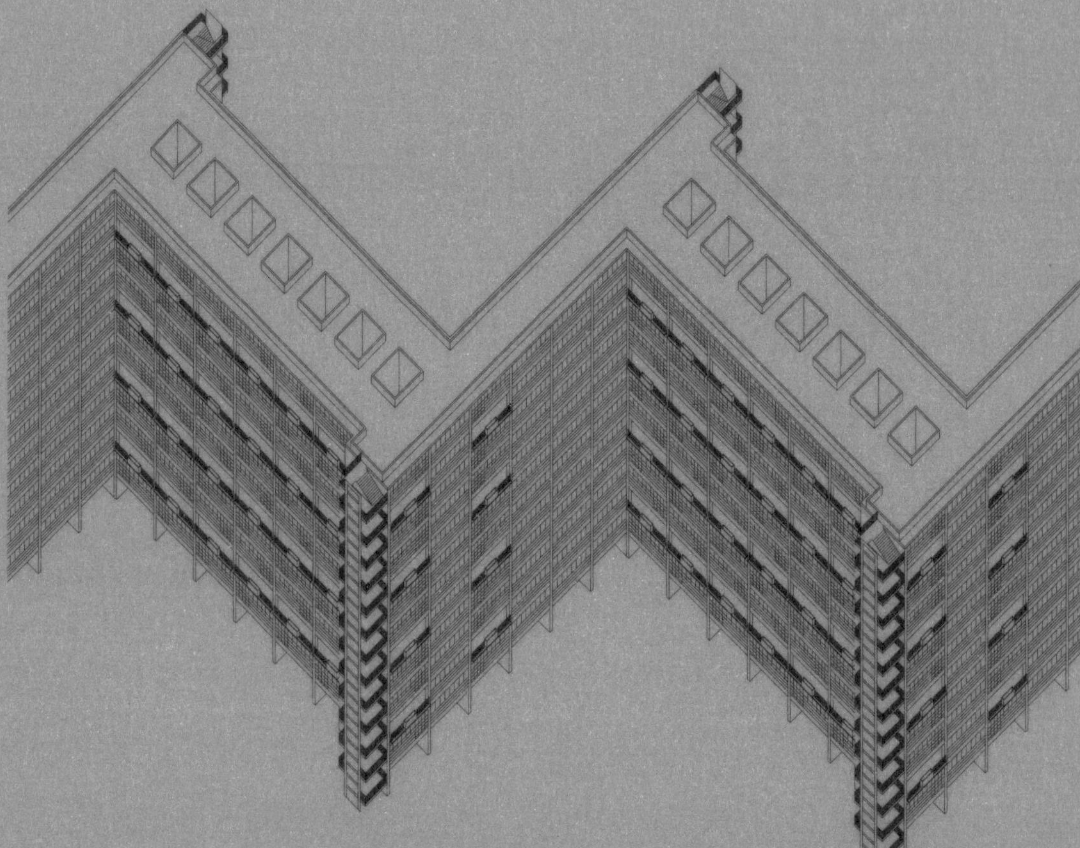

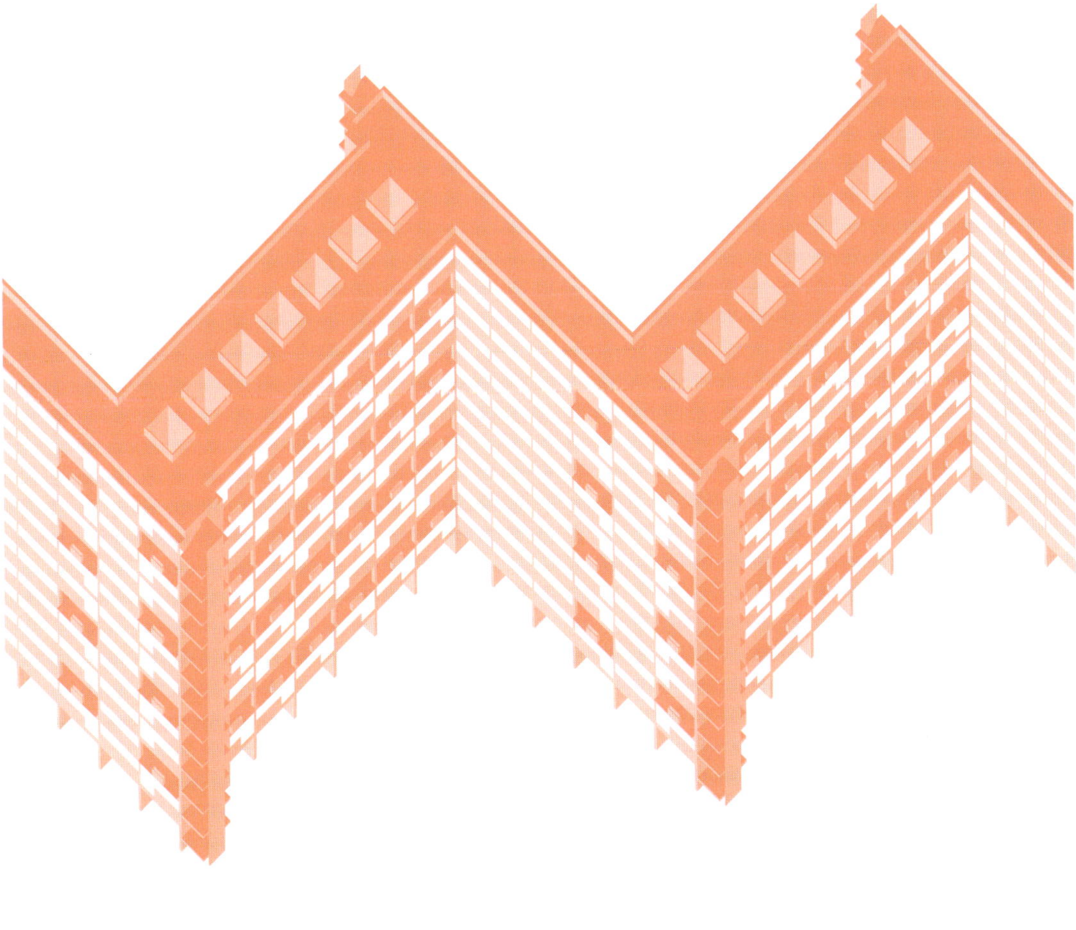

"[We propose] equality of orientation and maximum sunlight in homes, an arrangement that will foster a sense of neighborly community."[25]

Hannes Meyer, 1943

"When economics is no longer the determining factor in architectural projects, these, more noble and just from a social perspective, will begin to satisfy one of the most vital human longings: a better dwelling for a better man."[26]

Jorge L. Medellín, 1945

"The house continues to be built as an individual thing, with arbitrary characteristics spawned by our whims."[27]

Guillermo Zárraga, 1945

> "The house must be a machine whose mass-produced elements are assembled or mounted. It will consist of parts, like an engine. And each will be identified by a letter or number in the spare parts catalog: for example, a section of wall with a built-in light switch, a socket and a doorbell outlet might be called AZXN-14."[28]
>
> Guillermo Zárraga, 1945

> "It remains to be seen if the members of our humblest class, and those most in need of homes, who today made do in a shack [...] or a single room, with a brightly painted entrance featuring at least one worn stone step, a flowerpot of medicinal herbs or blossoms, and a reed cage with a bird inside; it remains to be seen if they will give up all this to live in an impersonal igloo, a concrete version of the Eskimo ice house."[29]
>
> Carlos Obregón Santacilia, 1947

25 Hannes Meyer, "La Ciudad de México: fragmentos de un estudio urbanístico", *Arquitectura México*, no. 12, April 1943, 183.

26 Jorge L. Medellín, "La habitación frente a la psicología del trabajador", in *Arquitectura y lo Demás*, vol. I, no. 6, October/November 1945, 23-32. In Ramón Vargas Salguero and J. Víctor Arias Montes (eds.), *Ideario de los arquitectos mexicanos*, vol. III: *Las nuevas propuestas*, Mexico City: Instituto Nacional de Bellas Artes, 2011, 343.

27 Guillermo Zárraga, vol. I, no. 6, October/November 1945, op. cit., pp. 33-36.

28 Guillermo Zárraga, ibid., pp. 33-36.

29 Carlos Obregón Santacilia, *50 años de arquitectura mexicana, 1900-1950*, Mexico City: Patria, 1952, 67.

1949, Ala Minimal House, Félix Candela

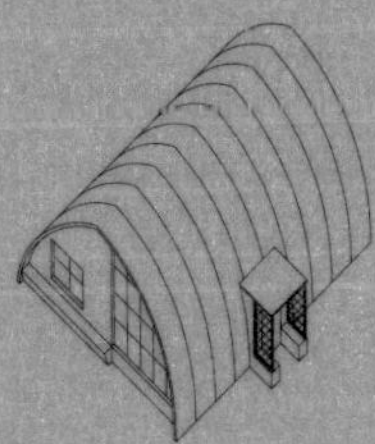

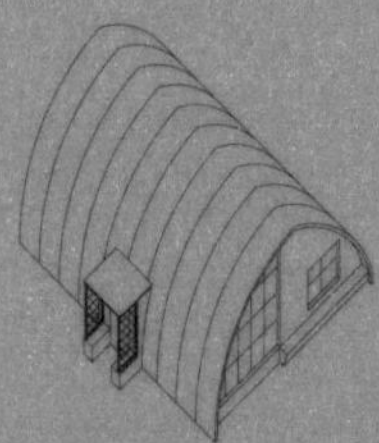

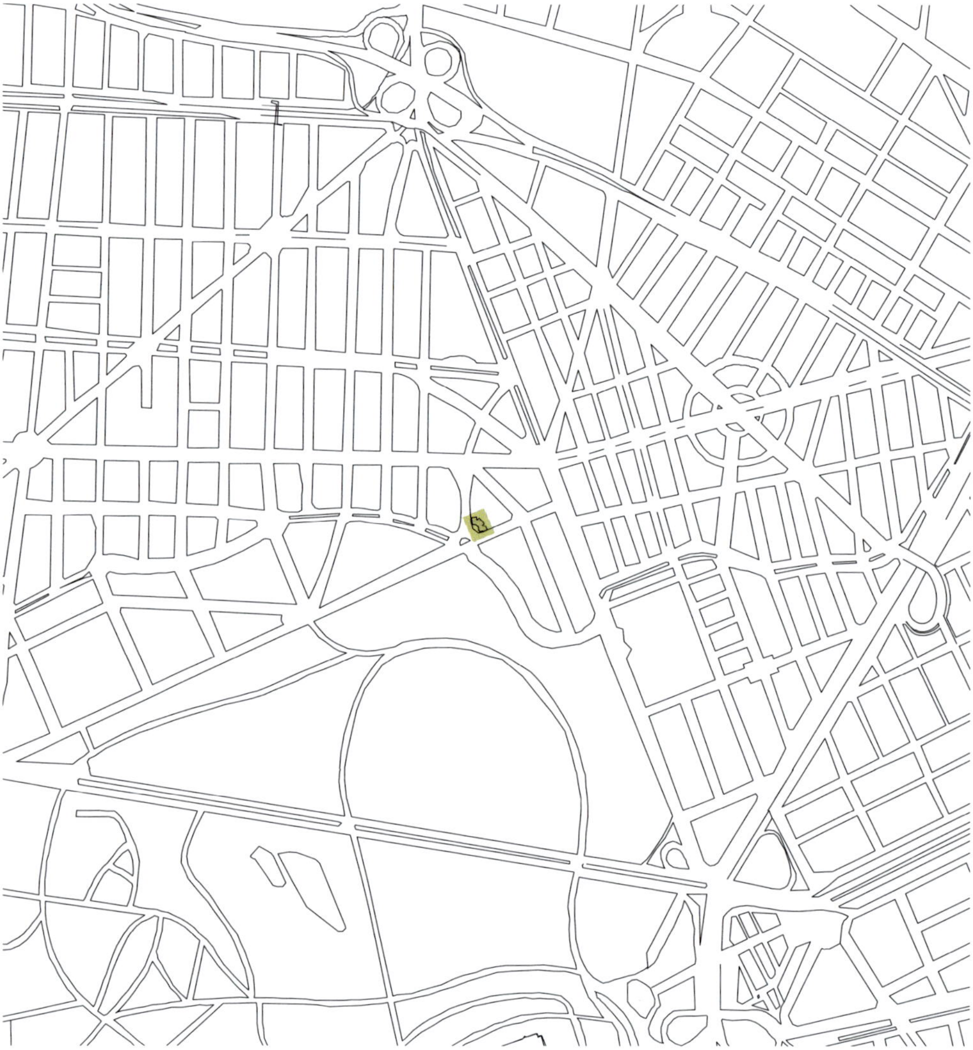

1953, Fundición Building, Abraham Zabludovsky

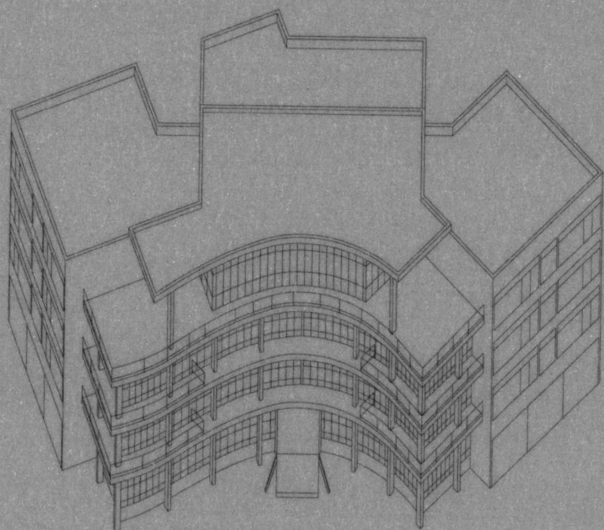

"Shoddy, barely habitable constructions of incredibly poor quality [...] that kind of rubbish is the only thing people can really afford with what they are able to save."[30]

Mario Pani, 1949

"The CUPA [Centro Urbano Presidente Alemán] was the first apartment block built in Mexico. Curiously, it was made while Le Corbusier was building the Unité d´habitation in Marseille. [While they] are constructing a building of three hundred and fifty apartments over three years, here in Mexico we're finishing a building with one thousand apartments!"[31]

Mario Pani, 1949

"Architects have started to do what tailors have not yet been able to achieve: create made-to-measure rental homes."[32]

Alberto T. Arai, 1950

"I wonder if, aside from private gardens for homes, we are capable of building gardens that feel private for residential developments."[33]

Luis Barragán, 1951

"Until 1930, nothing had been done to improve affordable living conditions in Mexico. However, it was a matter of concern for several architects."[34]

Carlos Obregón Santacilia, 1952

30 Mauricio Gómez Mayorga, "El problema de la habitación en México: realidad de su solución, una conversación con Mario Pani", in *Arquitectura México*, no. 27, April 1949, 67-74.

31 Pablo Quintero (ed.), *Modernidad en la arquitectura mexicana: 18 protagonistas*, Mexico City: Universidad Autónoma Metropolitana-Xochimilco, 1990, 461.

32 Alberto T. Arai, *La raíz humana de la distribución arquitectónica*, Mexico City: Ediciones Mexicanas, 1950, 26.

33 Luis Barragán, lecture "Gardens For Enviorment: Jardines de El Pedregal", California, October 6, 1951, in Antonio Riggen, op. cit., p. 38

34 Carlos Obregón Santacilia, op. cit., p. 65.

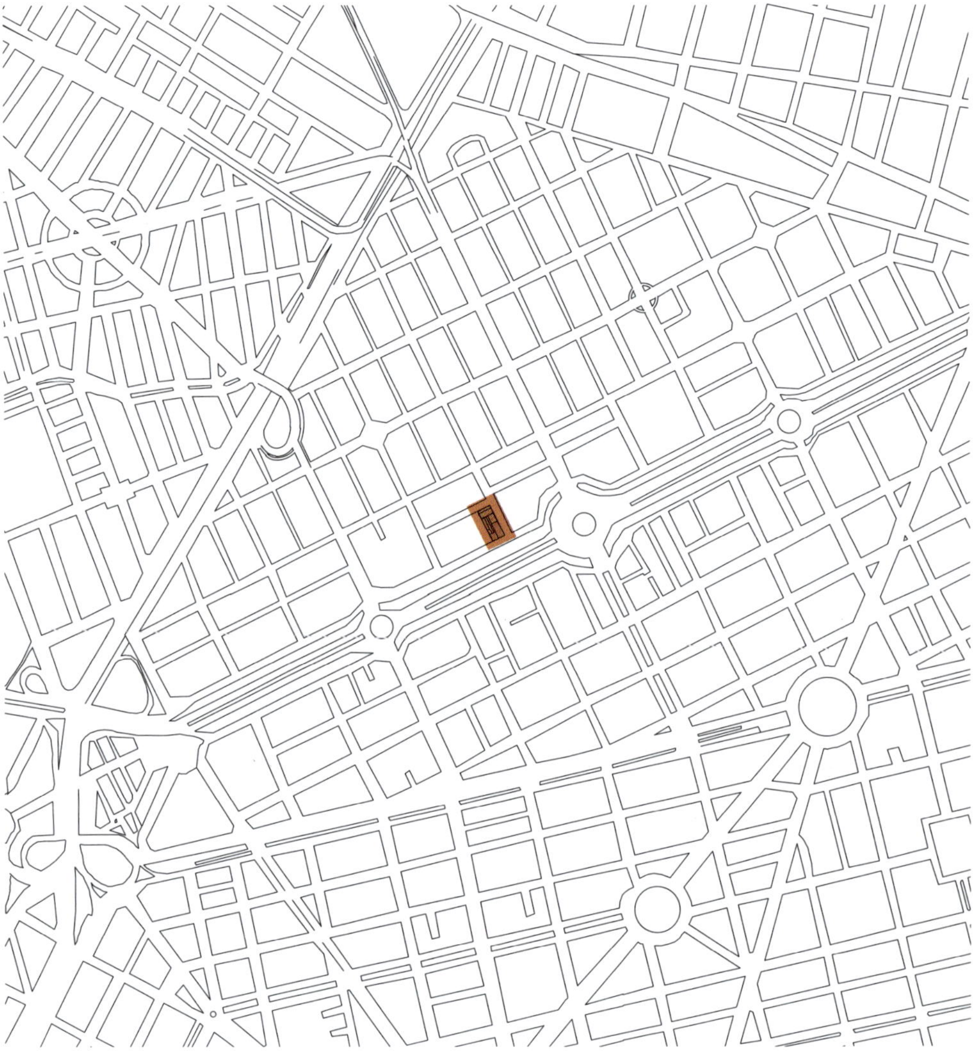

1956, Reforma Condominium, Mario Pani and Salvador Ortega

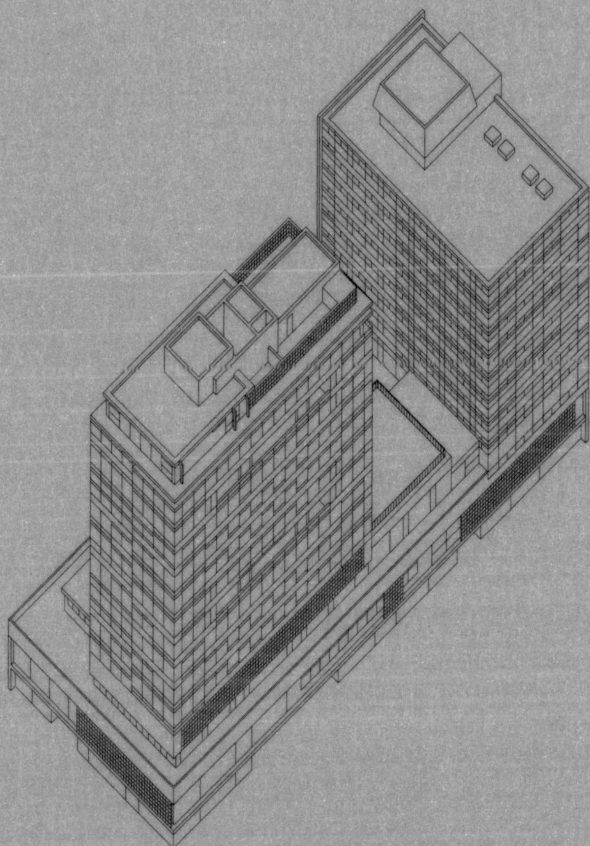

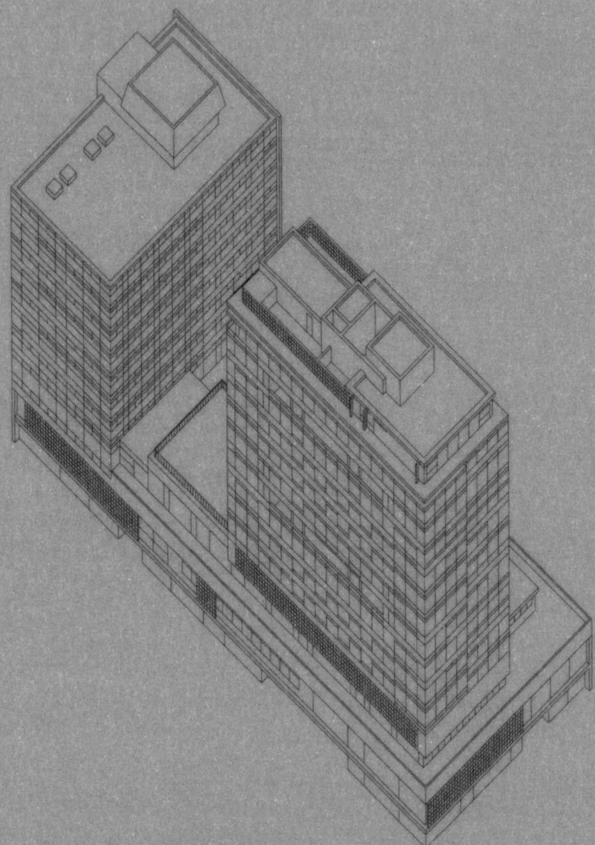

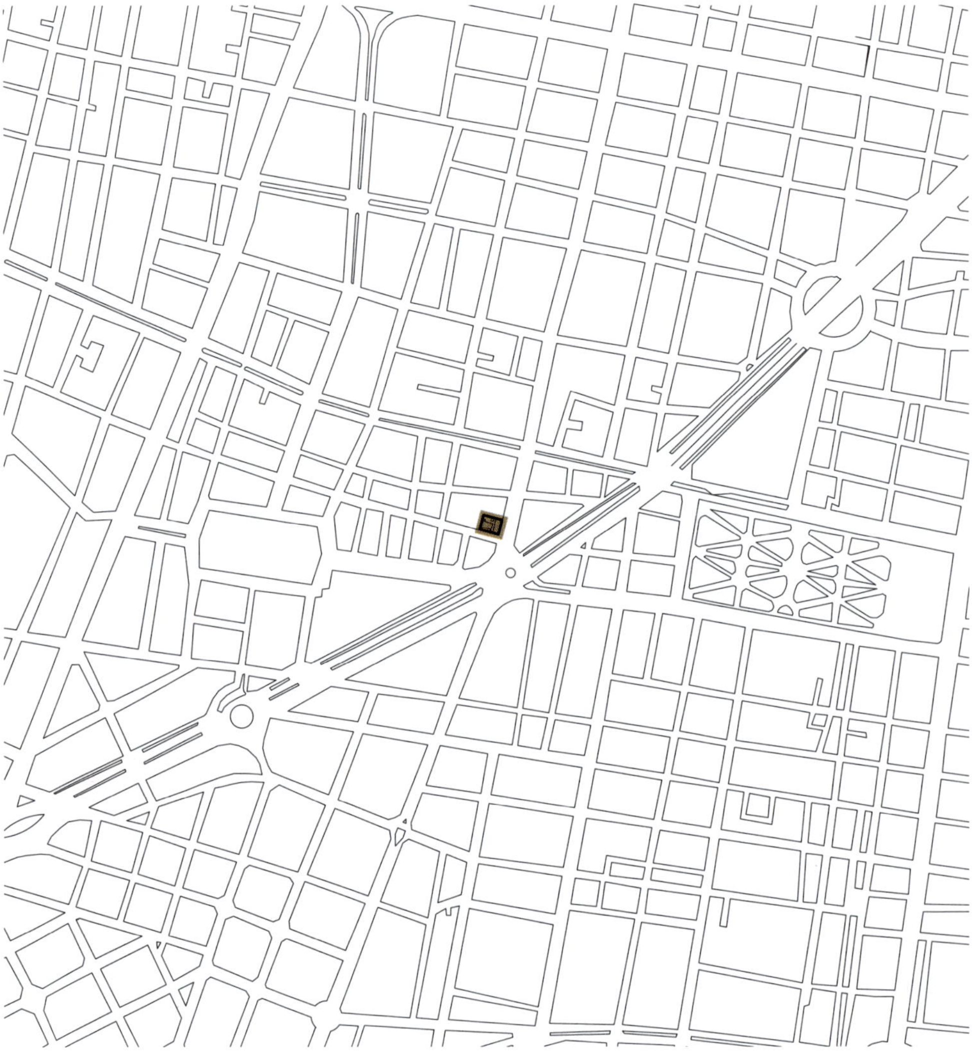

1958, La Nacional Insurance Building, Augusto Álvarez and Enrique Carral

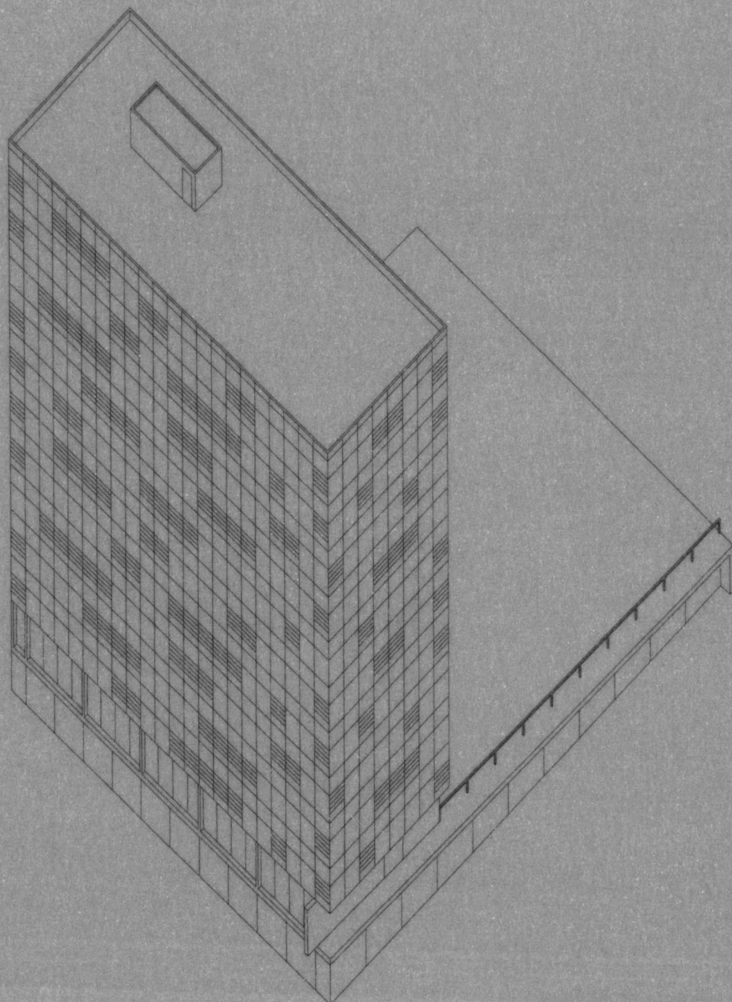

1958, Barra de Navidad, Teodoro González de León

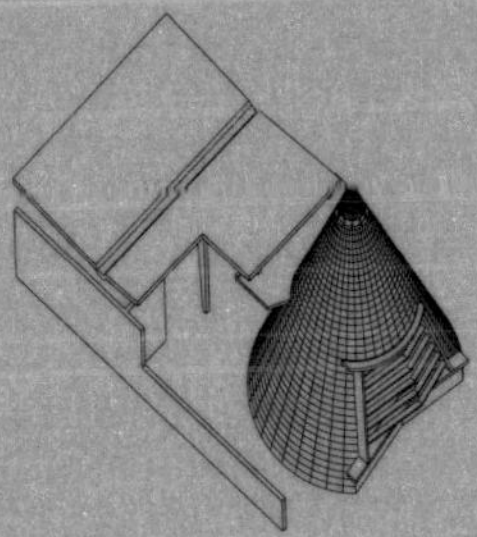

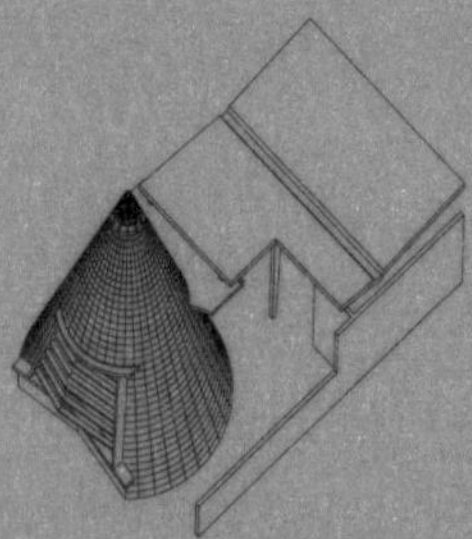

"The inhabitants of these houses [designed by Juan Legarreta in Balbuena] have made minor additions –tile roofs, parapets shaped like decorative crests, brightly painted exteriors, etc.– that clearly express their nonconformity with dull, mechanical, cookie-cutter forms."[35]

Juan O'Gorman, 1952

"Before 1947, no serious efforts were made to solve the problem of affordable housing [...] up until today, that is, in five years [...] some 12,000 units will have been built, a figure which at most meets 20% of our growing population's need."[36]

Félix Sánchez Baylón, 1952

"Functionalism was reduced to an effective means of slashing construction costs [...] maximum profit on minimum investment."[37]

Juan O'Gorman, 1953

"In our view, the answer to where and how we can provide affordable housing lies in the superblock."[38]

Domingo García Ramos, 1956

"The more urban a collective housing scheme is, the greater the difference between the customs and habits of its occupants."[39]

Alberto T. Arai, 1956

35 Juan O'Gorman, "Crítica a la arquitectura mexicana contemporánea", Academia de Artes, Mexico City, December 9, 1952, in *La palabra de Juan O'Gorman,* Mexico City: Universidad Nacional Autónoma de México, 1983, 167.
36 Félix Sánchez, "La realidad mexicana y las nuevas concepciones arquitectónicas urbanísticas en materia de habitación popular", in *Estudios*, no. 1, January 1952, 43-50.
37 Juan O'Gorman, "En torno a la integración plástica", in *Espacios*, Mexico City, July 16, 1953, n. p.
38 Domingo García Ramos, "La planificación de la habitación popular", lecture given to the Society of Mexican Architects, July 24, 1956, printed in *Ciclo de conferencias sobre vivienda popular,* Mexico City: Sociedad de Arquitectos Mexicanos/El Colegio Nacional de Arquitectos Mexicanos, n. d.
39 Alberto T. Arai, "La casa mexicana", Sociedad de Arquitectos Mexicanos, June 5, 1956, op. cit., p. 25.

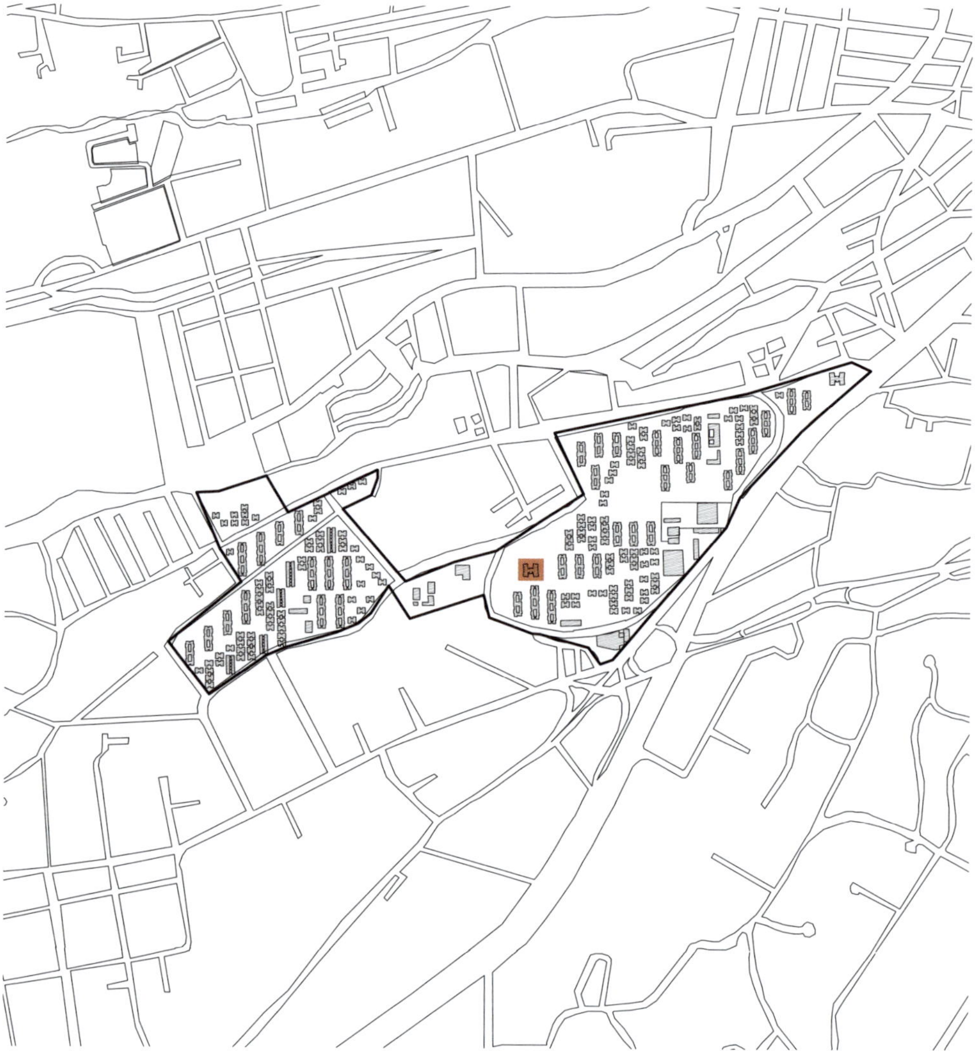

1960, Unidad Independencia complex, Alejandro Prieto, José María Gutiérrez, Pedro Miret, Manuel Santiago, Manuel San Román, Carlos Villaseñor and Leonel Pérez

1964, Urban Complex Presidente López Mateos de Nonoalco-Tlatelolco, Mario Pani, Luis Ramos Cunningham, Enrique Molina, Domingo García Ramos, Víctor Vila and Hilario Galguera

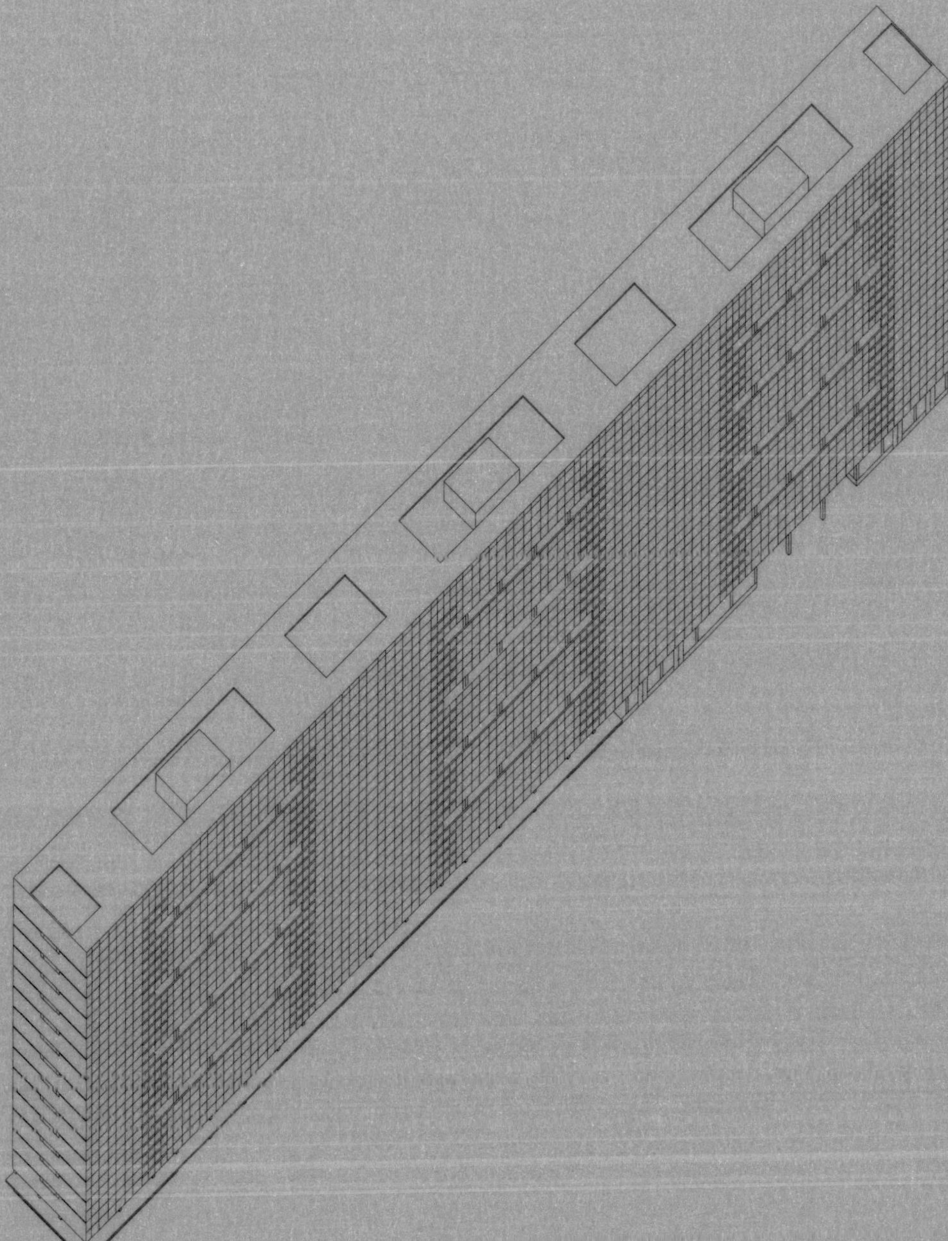

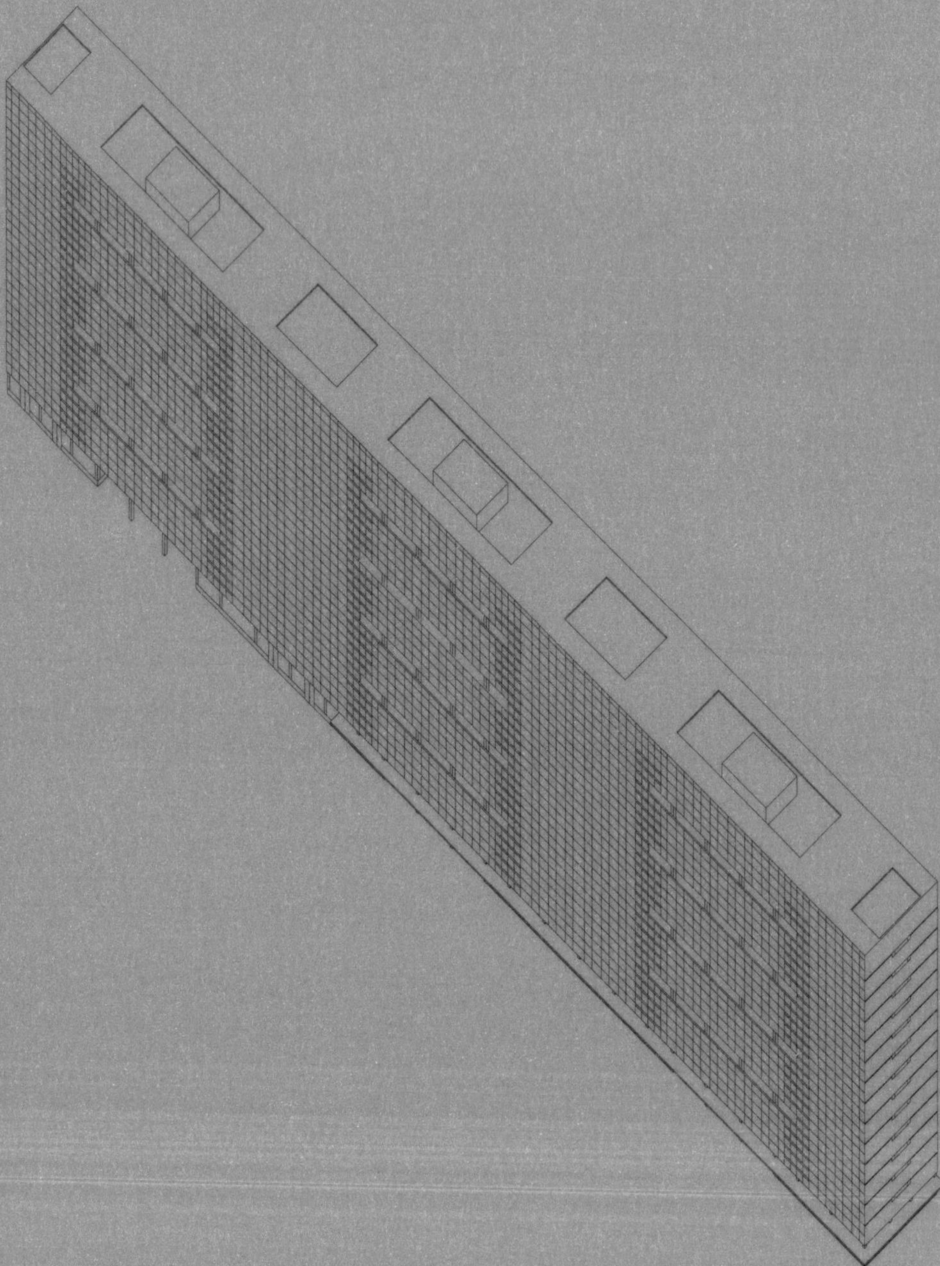

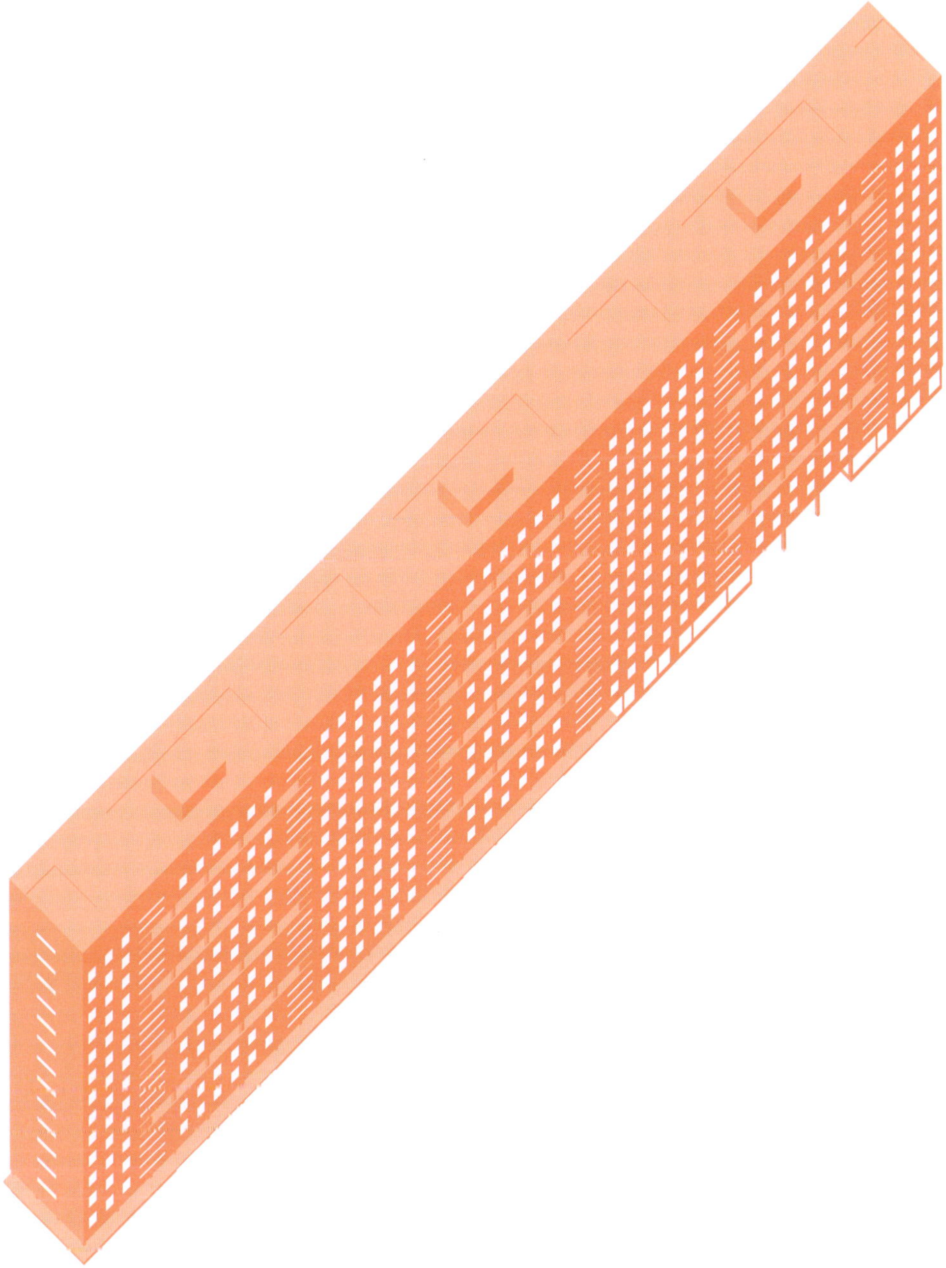

"Thoughts on urban planning must necessarily have an impact on affordable housing themes, and vice versa."[40]

Alberto T. Arai, 1956

"Better housing that takes us less space, in better conditions, and with ample green zones for the greatest possible number of people."[41]

Mario Pani, 1956

"This chaos, this hodgepodge of shades, colors, forms, scales, tastes, and whims among social groups contributes to the perception that our communities do not have the clean, uniform serenity that characterizes residential complexes in Sweden, Denmark, Germany, England, or North America –though perhaps that is their greatest asset."[42]

Félix Sánchez Baylón, 1956

"If we did a survey in Mexico City [...] for every 100 people asked, 110 [sic] would answer that they prefer their little house, with a garden, patio, and plants."[43]

Félix Sánchez Baylón, 1956

"An architect should never impose highbrow forms on affordable housing without consideration for the genuine feelings of the residents."[44]

Alberto T. Arai, 1956

40 Alberto T. Arai, "La casa mexicana", op. cit., p. 8.
41 *Arquitectura México*, vol. XII, no. 53, March 1956, 3.
42 Félix Sánchez Baylón, "Aspectos del problema de la casa habitación en México", lecture given to the Society of Mexican Architects, July 3, 1956, Mexico City: Sociedad de Arquitectos Mexicanos/El Colegio Nacional de Arquitectos Mexicanos, n. d., op. cit., p. 9.
43 Ibid.
44 Alberto T. Arai, "La casa mexicana", op. cit., 46.

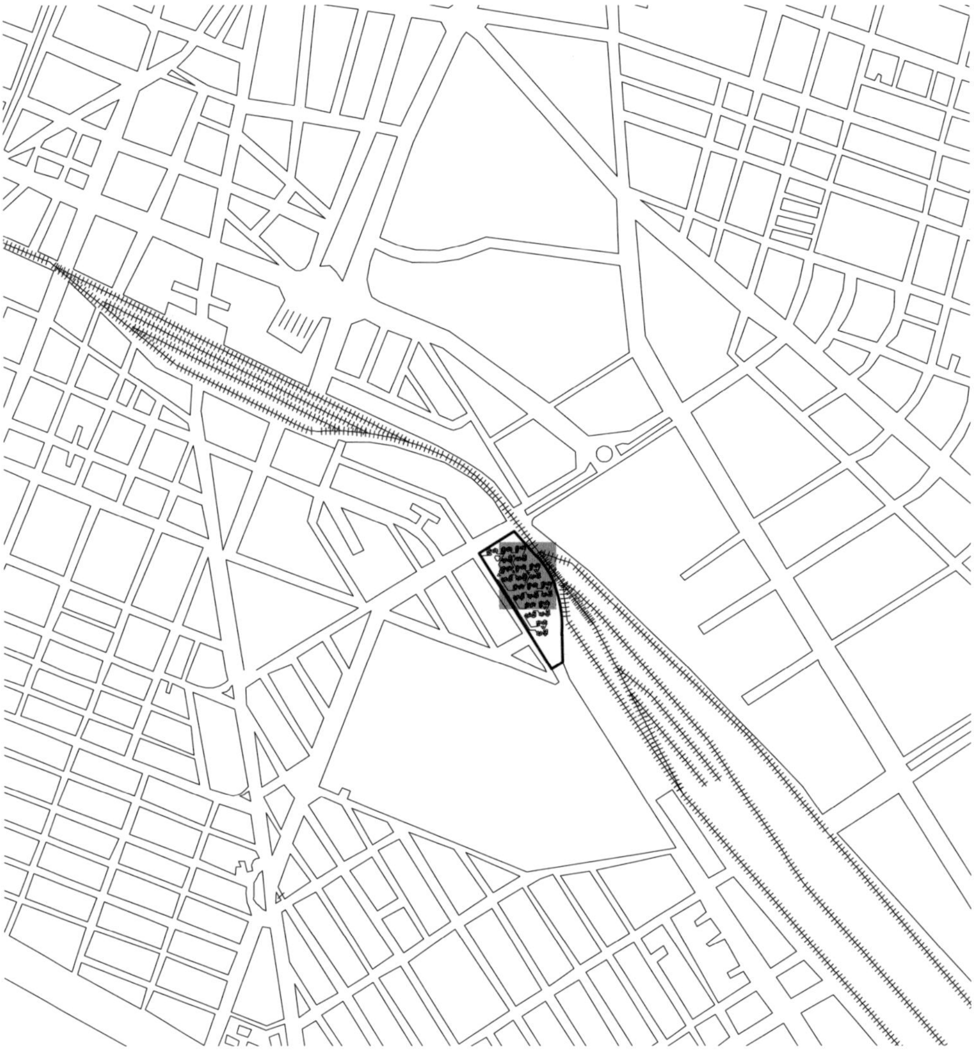

1964, Railway Workers complex, Pascual Broid, Óscar Urrutia, Benjamín Méndez and Carlos Ortega

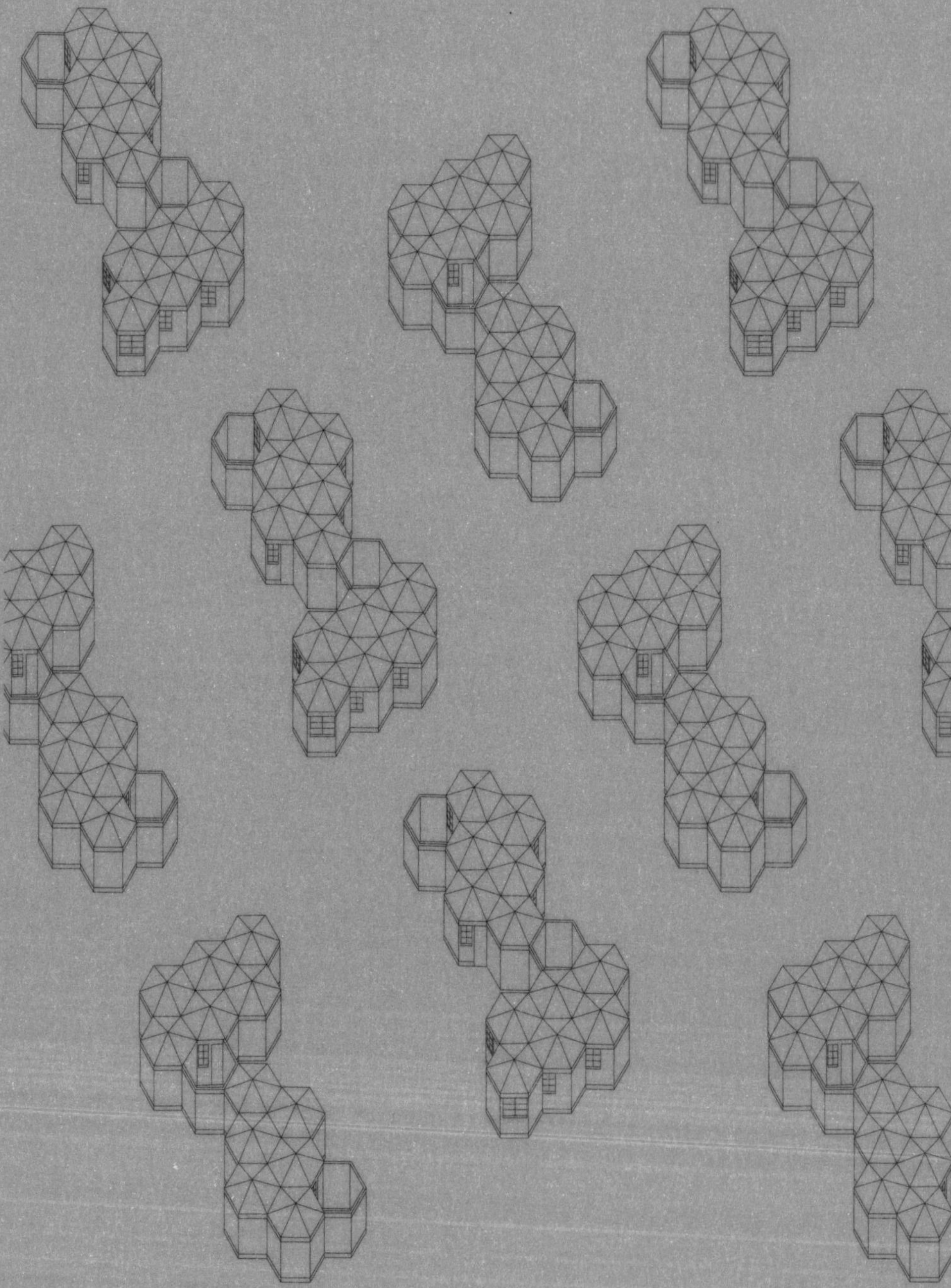

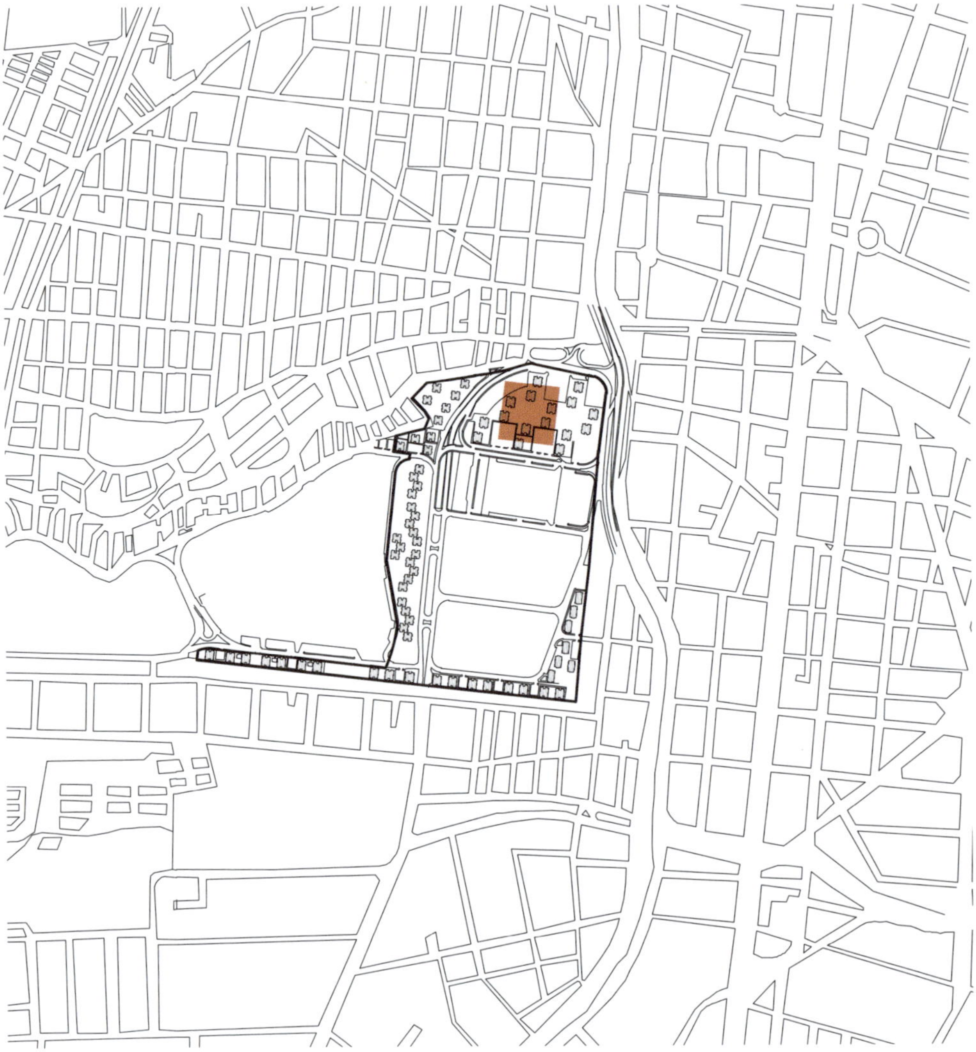

1968, Mixcoac Towers, Abraham Zabludovsky and Teodoro González de León

1968, Olympic Villa, Agustín Hernández, Manuel González, Ramón Torres, Héctor Velázquez and Carlos Ortega

"Applying that engineering principle to architecture has proved insufficient, because the place where man dwells is not just mechanically useful."[45]

Juan O'Gorman, c. 1957

"Houses have become clubs where people can no longer be alone."[46]

Luis Barragán, 1958

"They build thousands of apartment blocks and multifamily units. They use the best architects. They issue publications and write articles and books. But they do not go to the root of the problem. While Le Corbusier was right when he said that having a dwelling should be considered every man's right, those who give that man any dwelling are wrong."[47]

Vladimir Kaspé, 1958

"It is more costly to solve the housing problem with vertical buildings, properly conceived in terms of urban planning, than with horizontal structures, if you consider that the residential cores in vertical buildings need to be surrounded by open spaces in proportion to the density of occupation, and that these spaces must be large enough to provide smooth circulation, recreation, and cleanliness."[48]

Luis Barragán, 1959

"The only way to obtain a large quantity of dwellings for the masses is to forget about architectural aesthetics for a moment and scientifically plan a healthy living environment."[49]

Juan O'Gorman, c. 1960

45 Juan O'Gorman, "Más allá del funcionalismo", lecture given at Unidad Profesional Zacatenco ca. 1957, printed in Ida Rodríguez Prampolini, op. cit., 108.

46 Selden Rodman, *Mexican Journal: The Conquerors Conquered*, New York: The Devin Adair Co., 1958, 96-97; Spanish version: Antonio Riggen, Madrid: El Croquis Editorial, 2000, op, cit., 71.

47 *Arquitectura México*, vol. XIV, no. 61, March 1958, p. 53.

48 Luis Barragán, "Cómo deben desarrollarse las grandes ciudades modernas: el crecimiento de la Ciudad de México", in *Zócalo*, October 12, 1959, published in Antonio Riggen, op. cit., 50.

49 Israel Katzman, op. cit., 156.

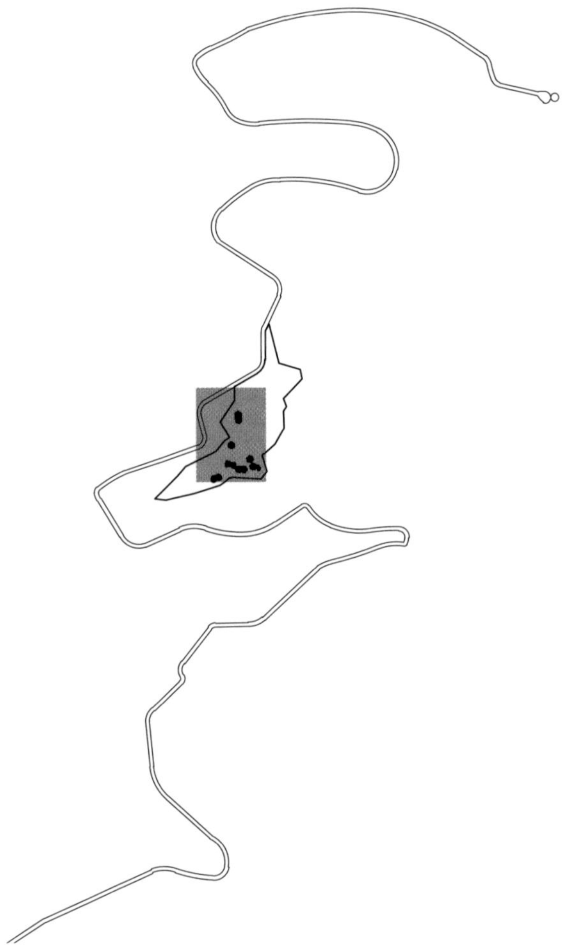

1969, Kalikosmia, Juan José Díaz Infante

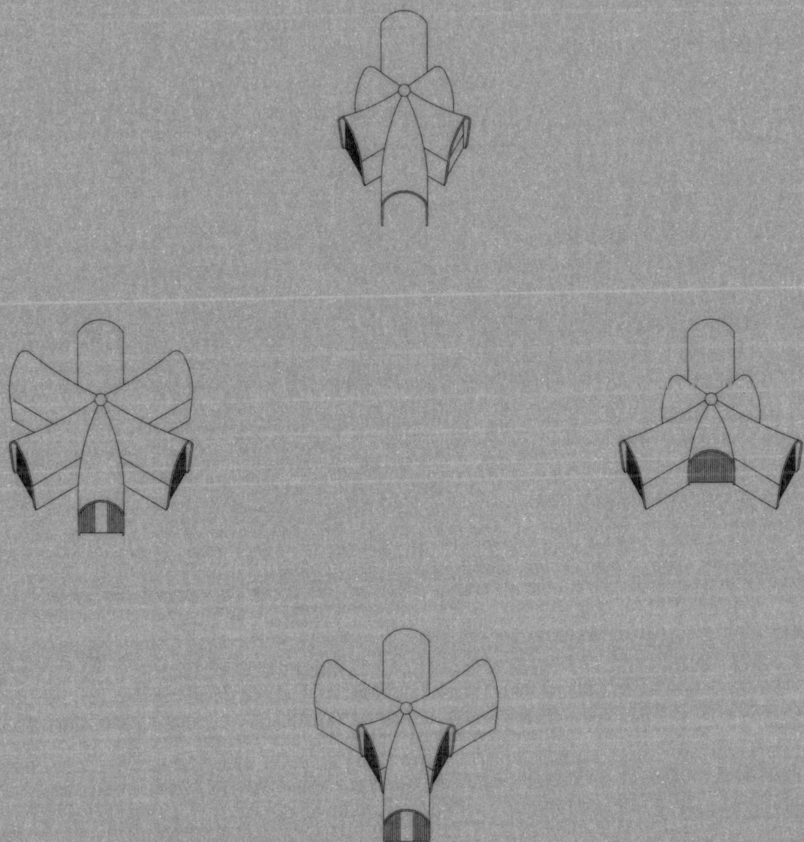

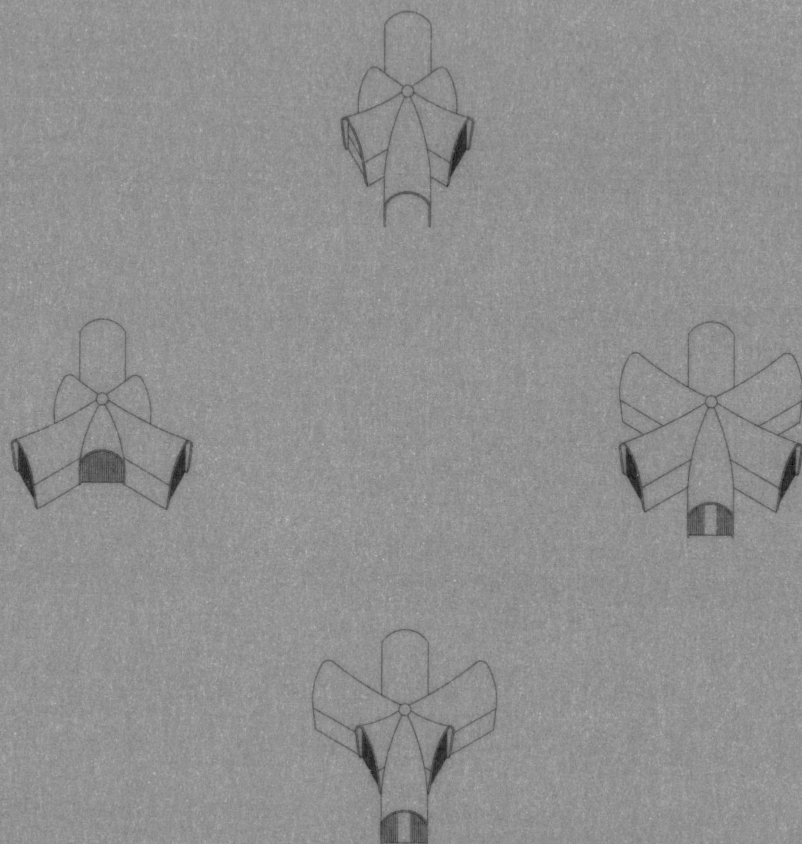

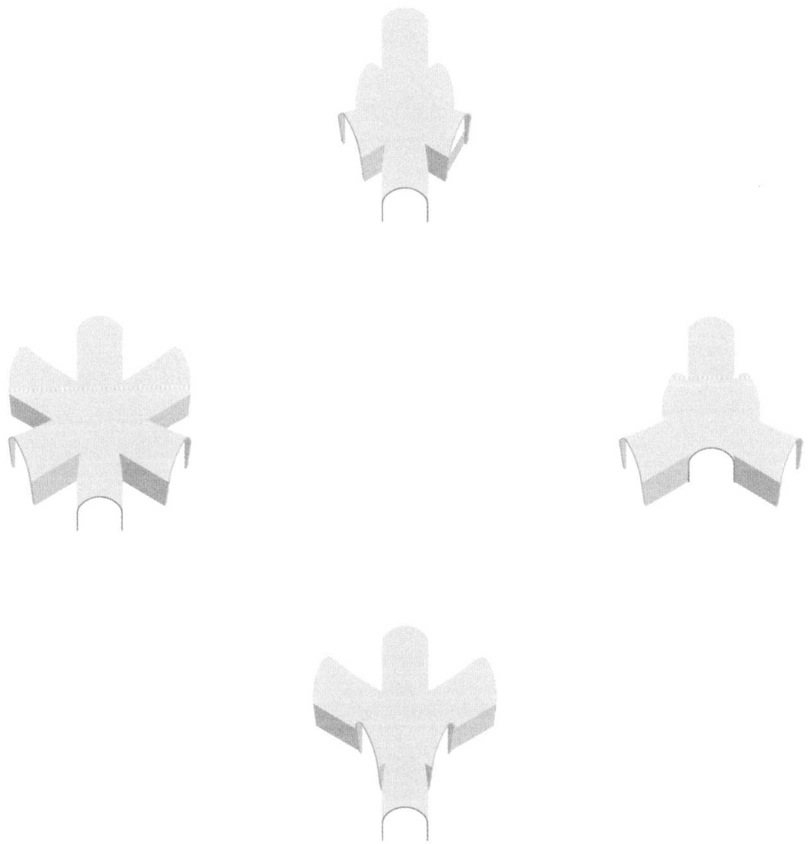

1973, Unidad Iztacalco complex, Imanol Ordorika, J. Francisco Serrano and José R. Nava Requesens

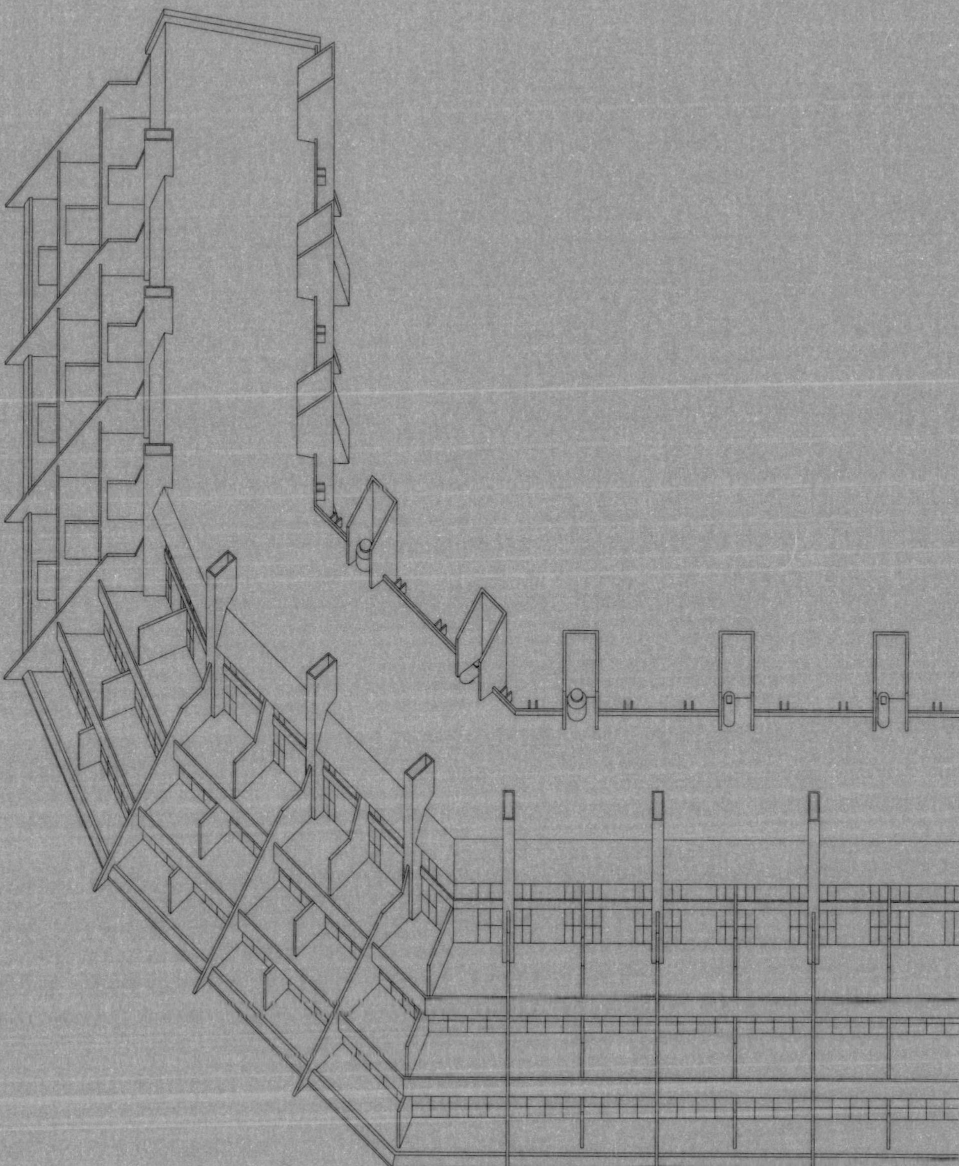

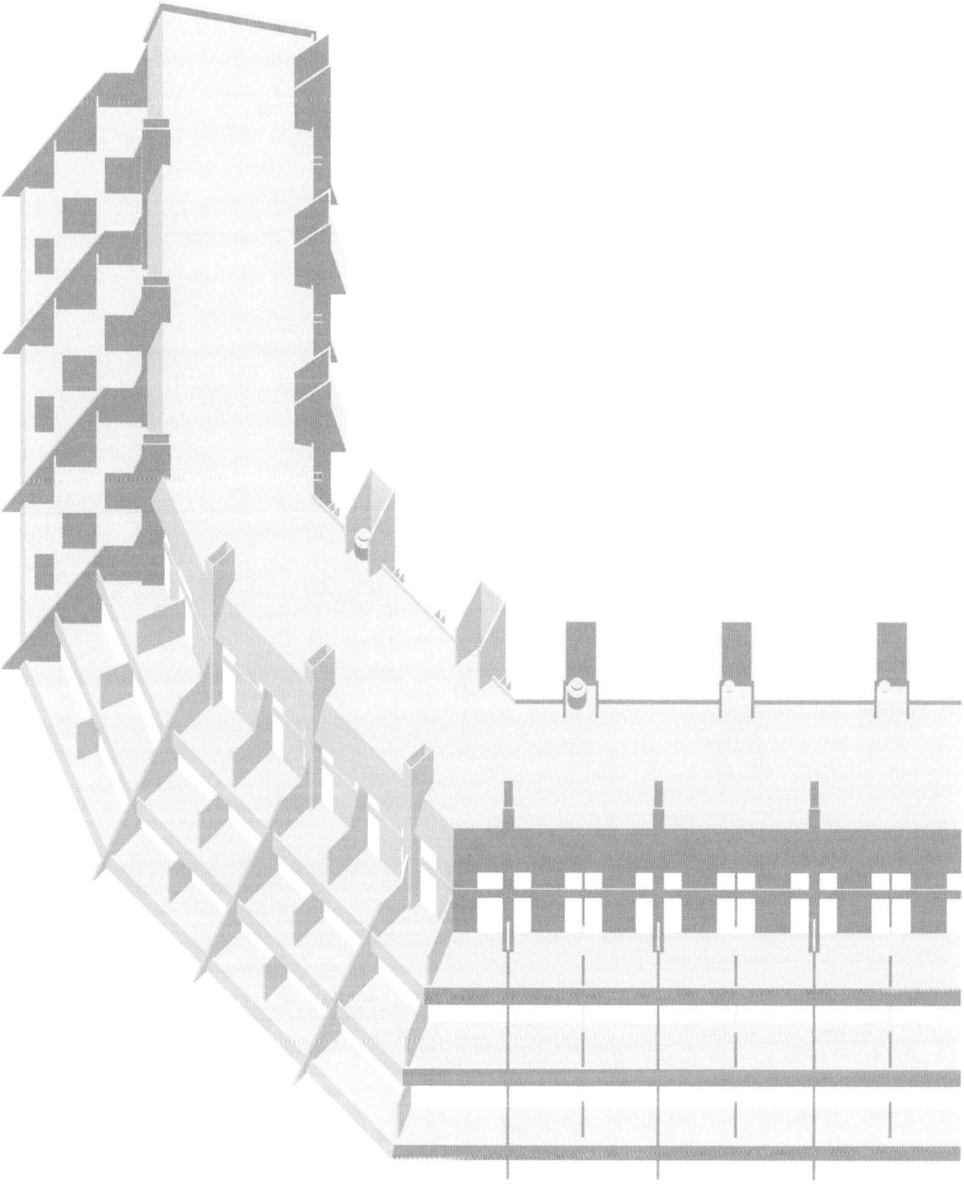

"House and city come under the category of beliefs when they define our sense of reality and unconsciously influence our daily lives."[50]

Carlos Mijares, 1960

"It is the daunting task of finding housing for three hundred thousand people each year and, at the same time, regenerating 60% of the city in poor living conditions."[51]

Mario Pani, 1960

"Contemporary Mexico's great endeavor began with the hospital-building campaign in 1943, the school-building campaign a few years later [and] the Presidente Alemán and Presidente Juárez apartment blocks."[52]

Mauricio Gómez Mayorga, 1961

"The architect identifies the house by its shape, the urban planner by the number of people who live in it. Architecture is necessarily individualistic, but urbanism is collectivist and sociological."[53]

Domingo García Ramos, 1961

"A dwelling is more than just a physical residence [...] it extends to the aspects that are now necessary services, such as municipal drinking water, drainage, paved roads [...] energy, transportation [...] and generally everything that should be directly connected to the residence."[54]

Domingo García Ramos, 1961

50 Carlos Mijares, "El fenómeno arquitectónico", in *Calli*, no. 1, July-August 1960, p. 23.
51 Mario Pani, "Habitaciones colectivas", in *Calli*, no. 1, July-August 1960, p. 24.
52 Mauricio Gómez Mayorga, "Notas polémicas", in *Artes de México*, year IX, no. 36: *La arquitectura contemporánea en México*, 1961, p. 3.
53 Domingo García Ramos, "Definiciones y conceptos generales: iniciación al urbanismo", Escuela Nacional de Arquitectura-Universidad Nacional Autónoma de México, México, 1961, p. 21.
54 Ibid., p. 123.

1976, Mexicali Housing, Christopher Alexander

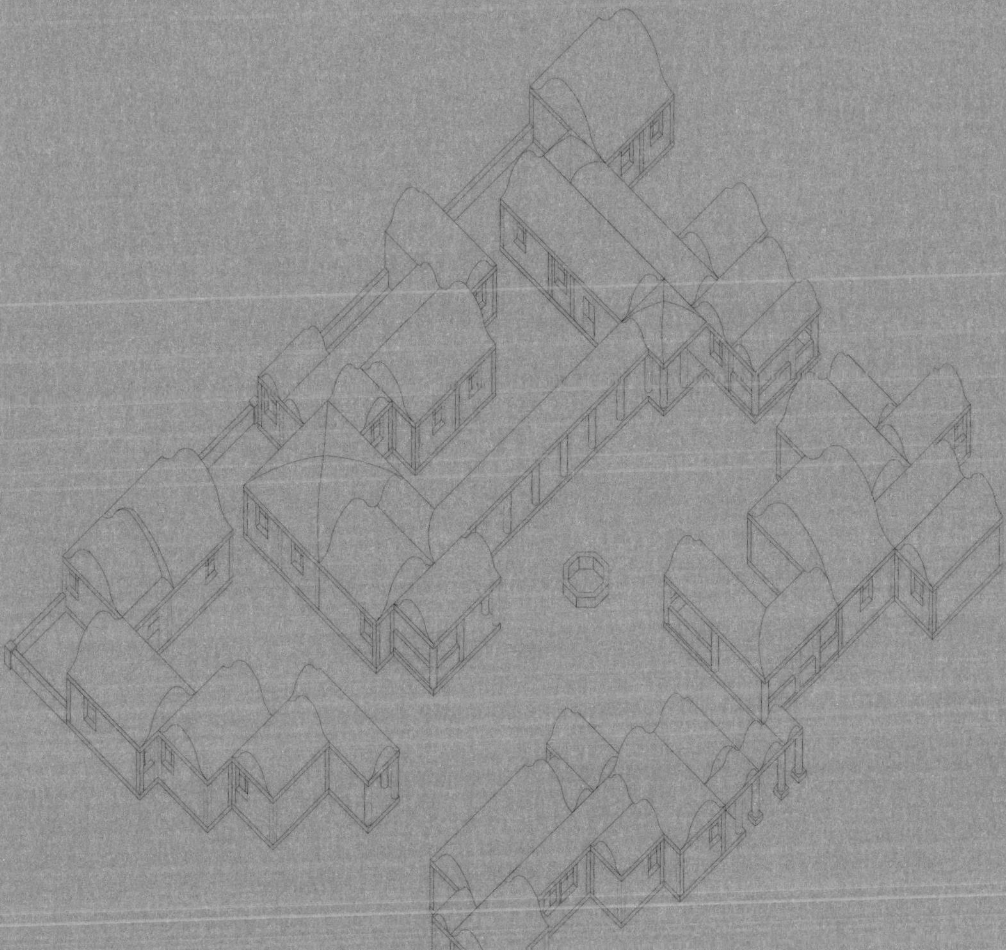

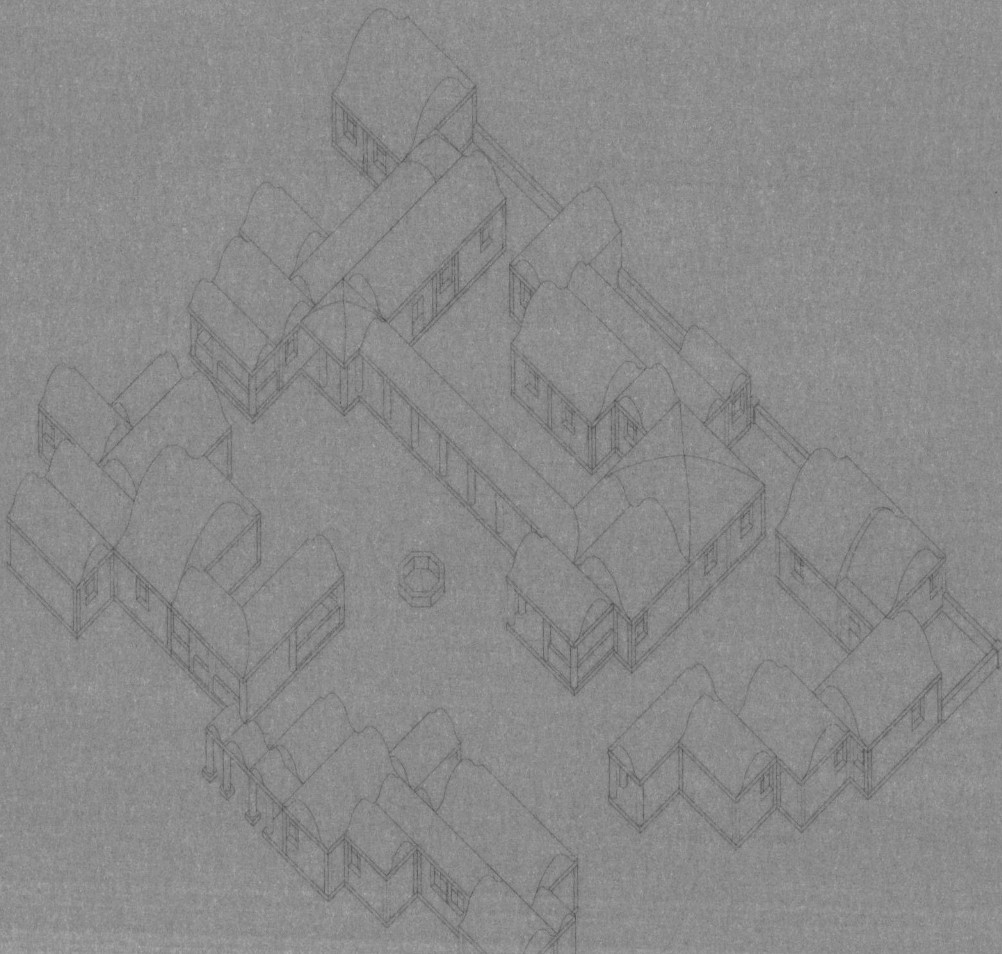

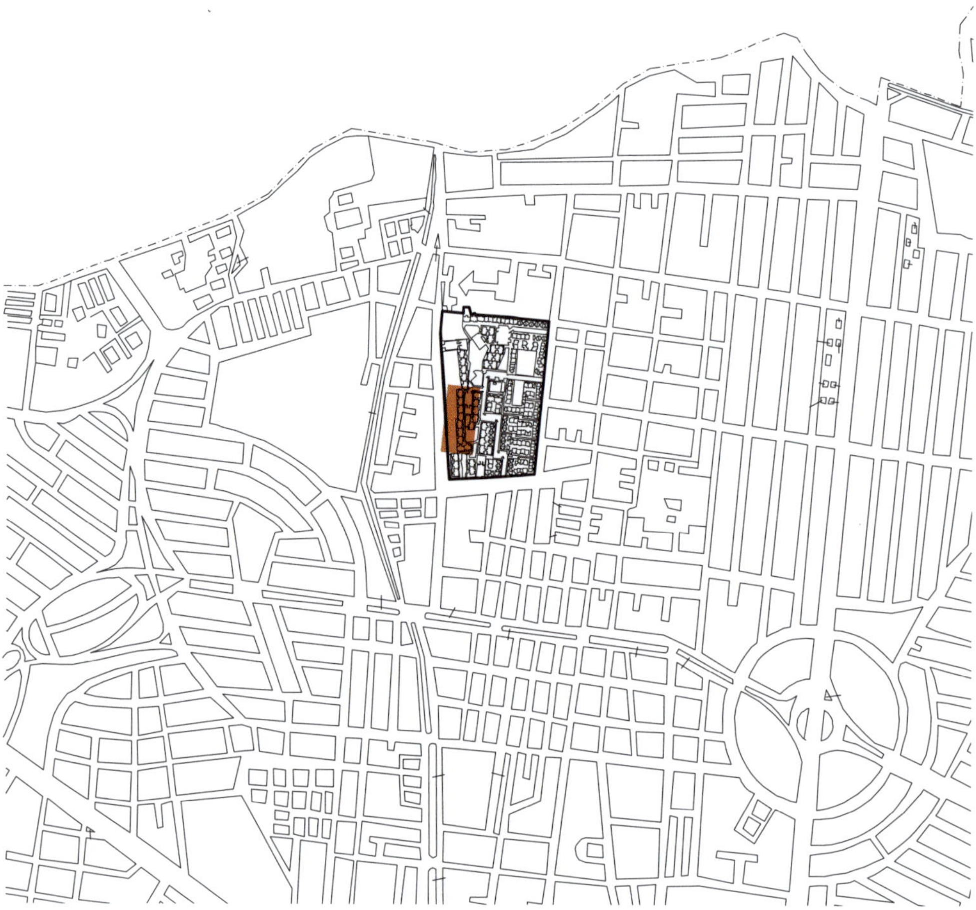

1977, CTM-Atemajac Housing complex, Alejandro Zohn

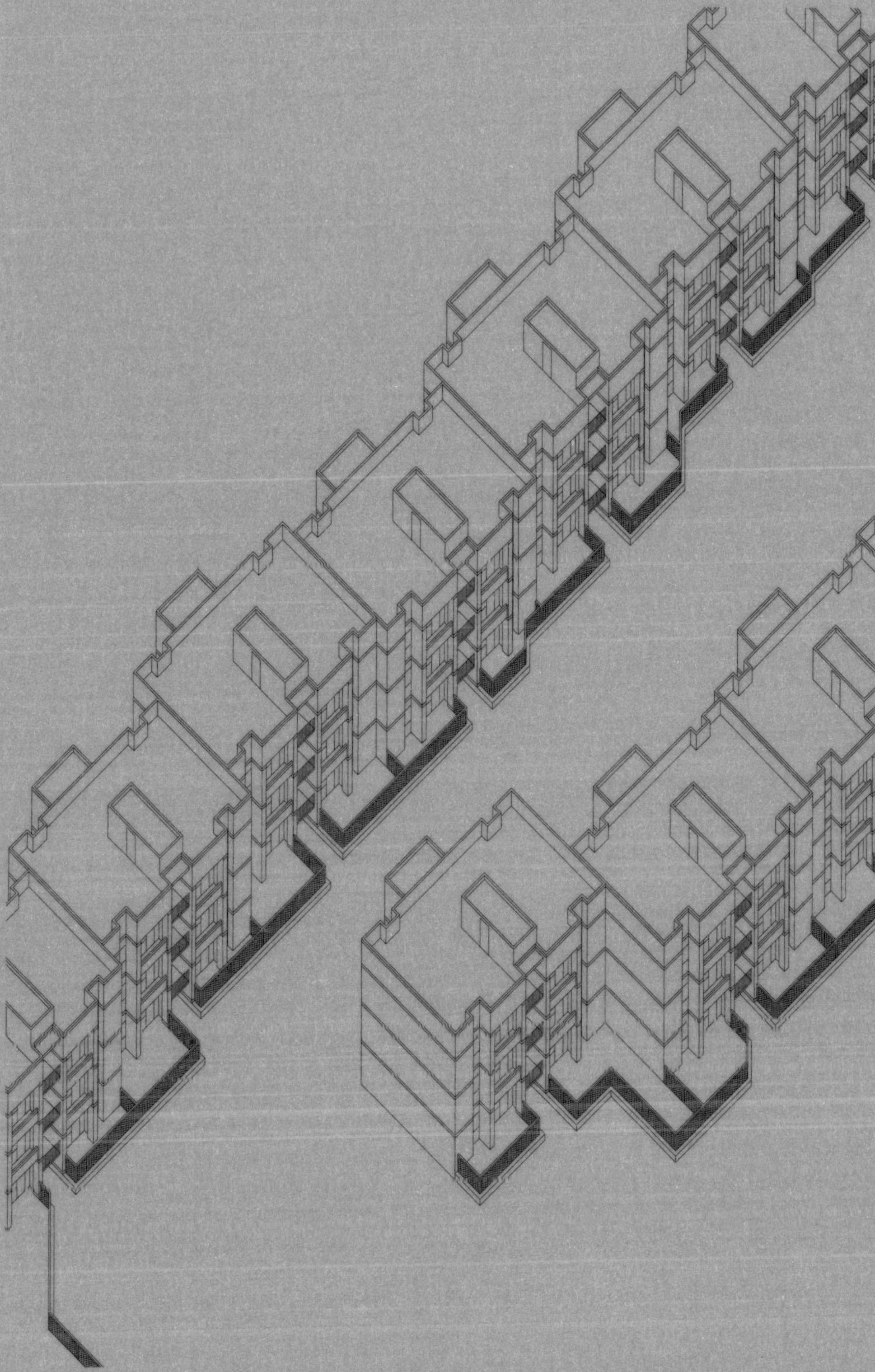

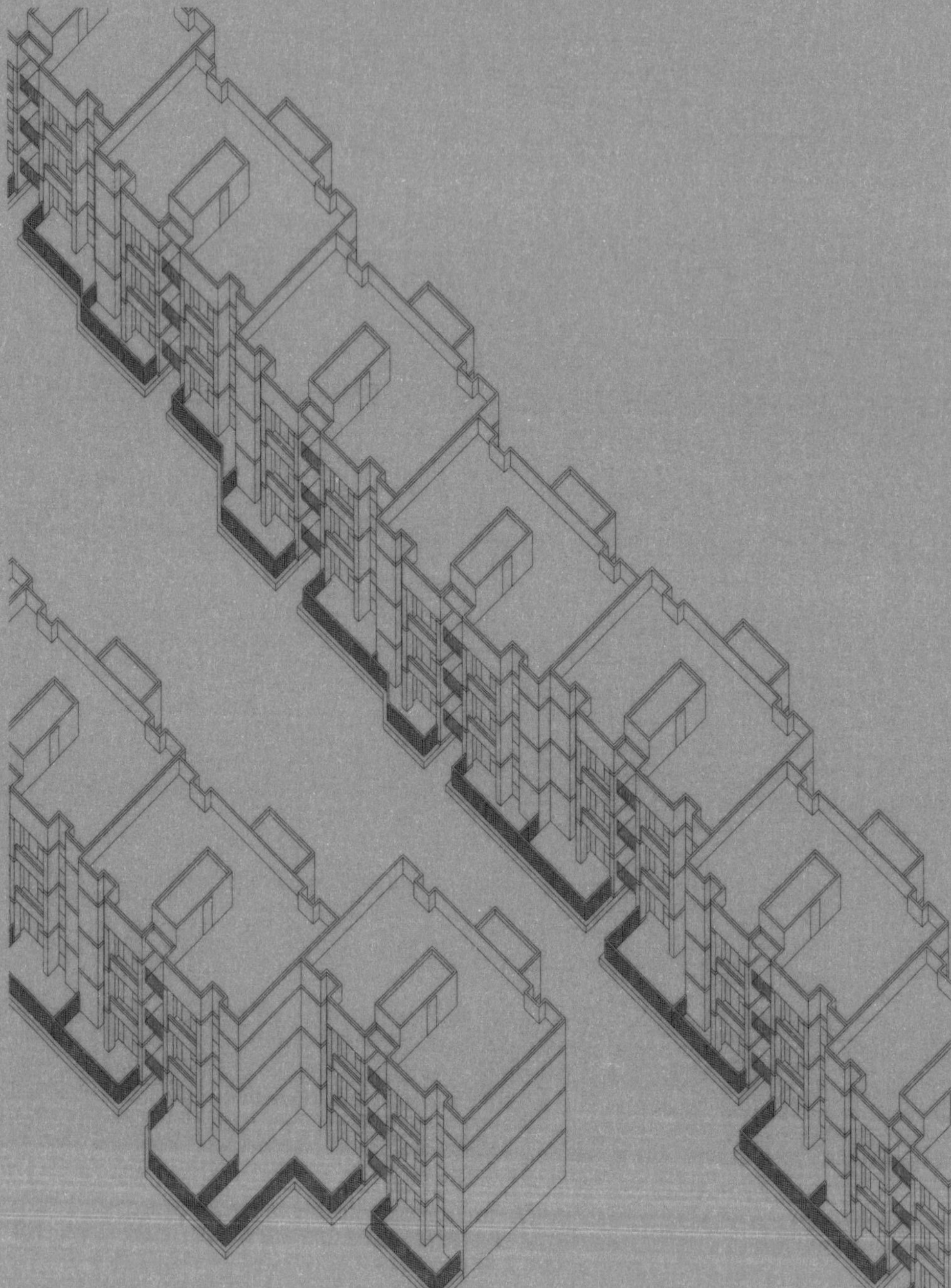

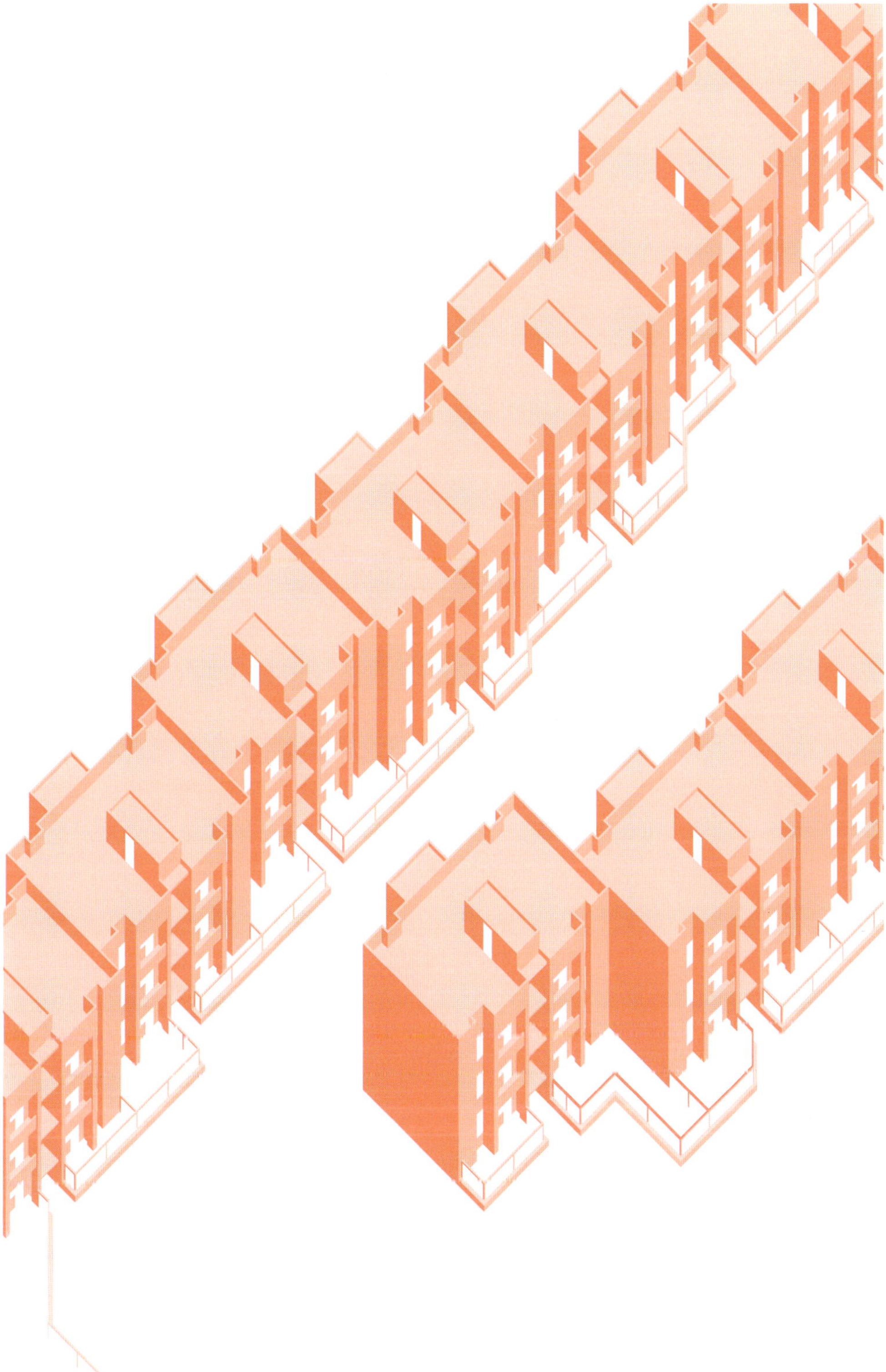

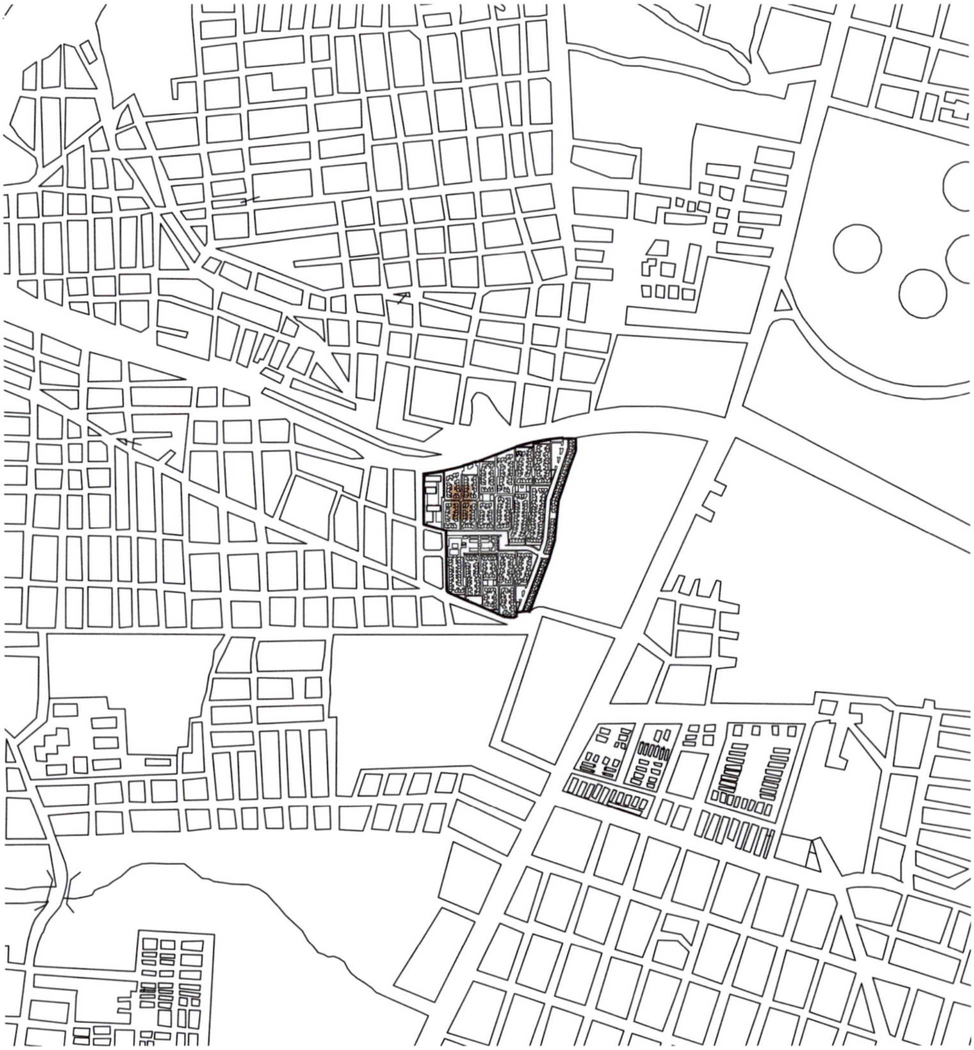

1977, Ricardo Flores Magón Housing complex, Alejandro Zohn

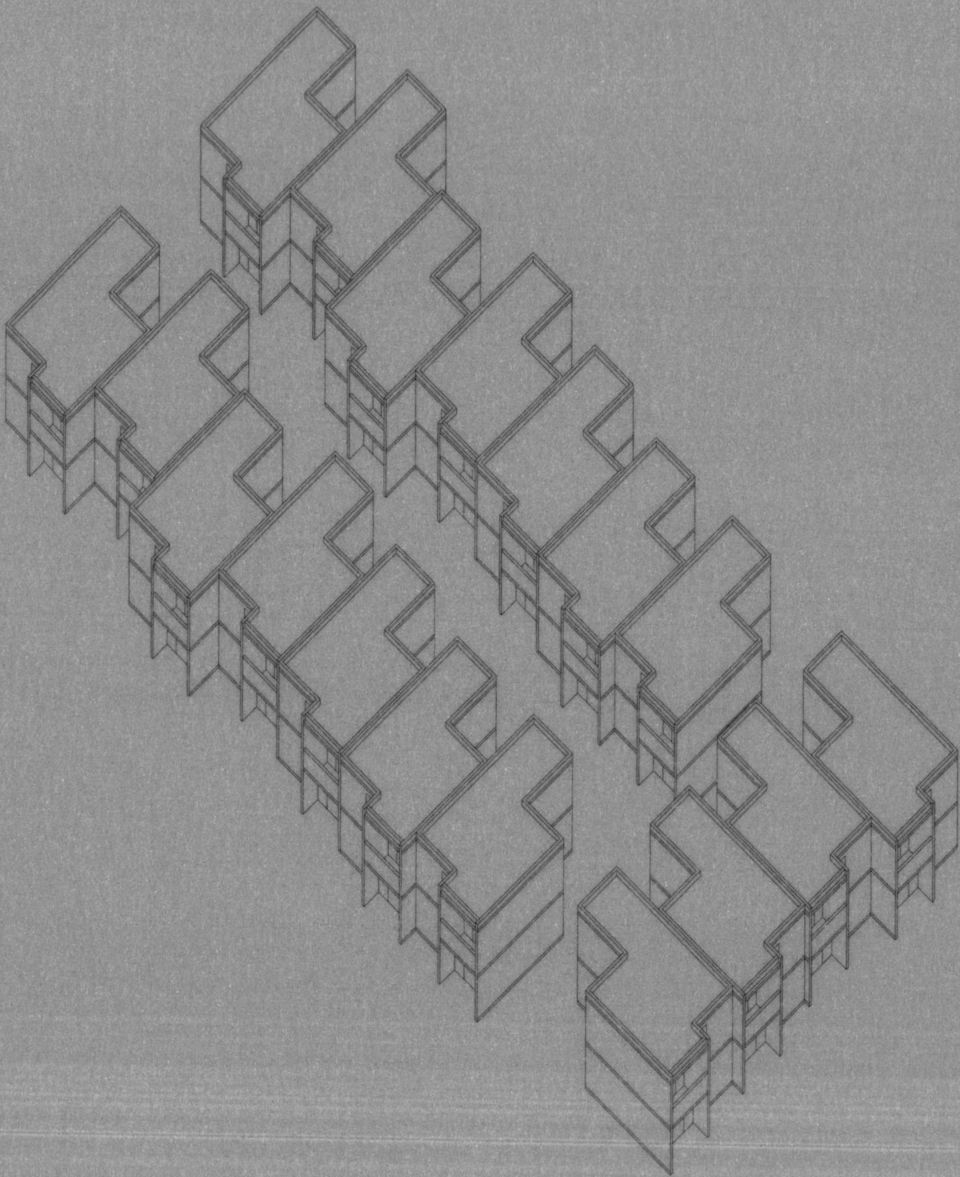

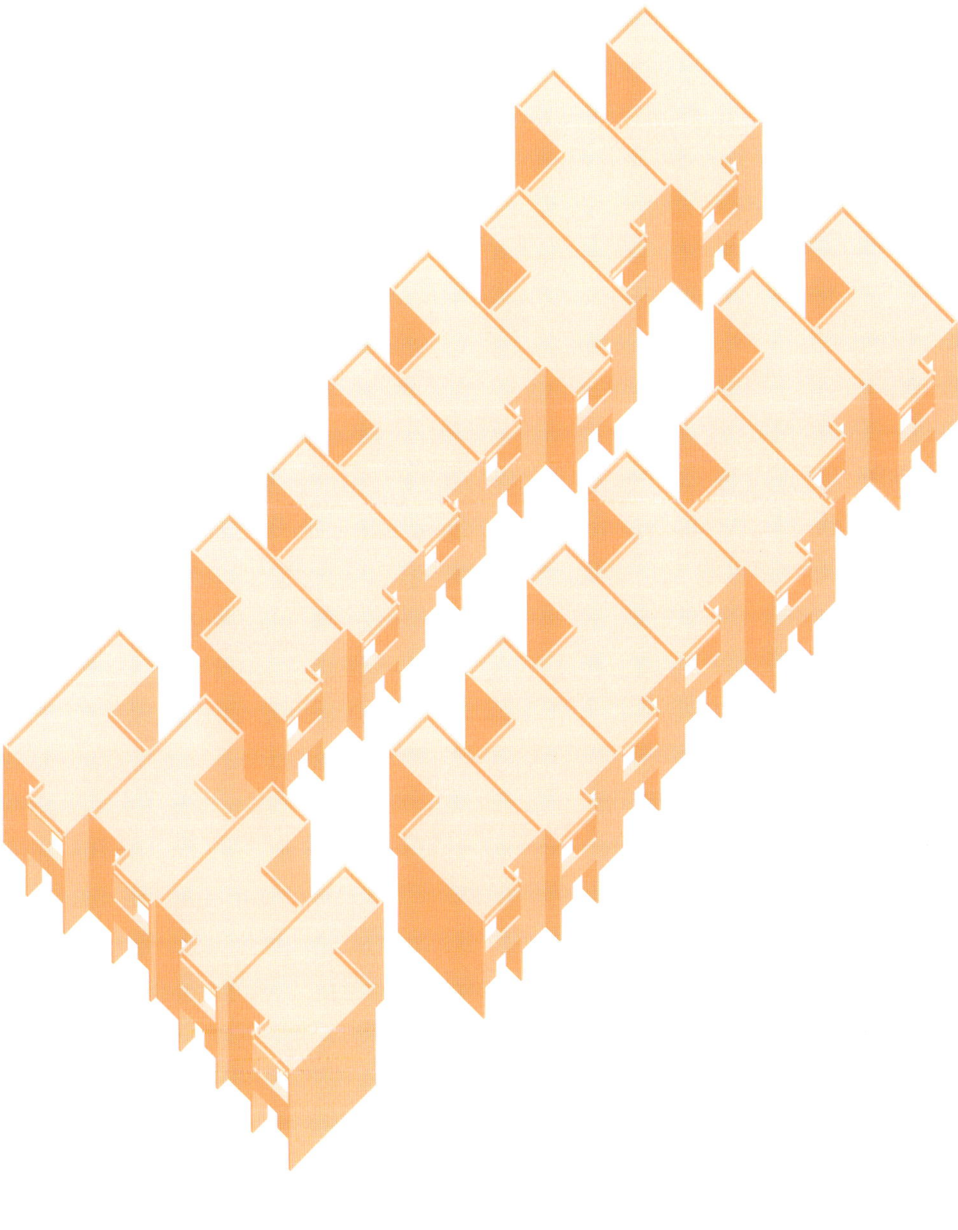

"Dwellings and structures for the people's individual use in general, comprise a de facto infra-architecture."[55]

Reinaldo Pérez Rayón, 1962

"In the schools and in the drawing studios, we will work to hasten the coming of an architecture that will allow us to meet the human dwelling needs of our people."[56]

Reinaldo Pérez Rayón, 1962

"In 1957, the Instituto de la Vivienda conducted a study of those working-class slums and obtained the following statistics: 30.6% of families living there needed to be moved out due to their dreadful housing conditions, 63.2% required substantial improvements, and only 5.2% lived in suitable conditions [...]. 84.20% of the houses that needed improvements were lacking a bathroom."[57]

Raúl Cacho, 1963

"[Pani was] the first visionary to see the true scale of the housing problem."[58]

Óscar Urrutia, 1963

"Living is not merely being, but living, feeling, sleeping –in short, living complexly and individually, and complexly and collectively."[59]

José Villagrán, 1963

"Pedro Ramírez Vázquez posited the parallel growth of the family and the home [...] which he called the democratization of architecture because it allows everyone to receive the same thing in the same conditions, and develop it freely according to their own needs."[60]

Óscar Urrutia, 1963

55 Reinaldo Pérez Rayón, "La enseñanza del funcionalismo en la ESIA. 30 años de funcionalismo en la ESIA. 25 años del IPN", in Cuadernos de Arquitectura, no. 6., Departamento de Arquitectura-Instituto Nacional de Bellas Artes, July 1962, XXX.
56 Ibid., XXIX-XL.
57 Raúl Cacho, *La vivienda. México: 50 años de Revolución,* Mexico City: Fondo de Cultura Económica, 1963, op, cit., 172.
58 Óscar Urrutia, "Veinticinco años de arquitectura moderna en México", *Arquitectura México*, year XXV, vol. XX, no. 83, September 1963, op, cit., 179.
59 José Villagrán García, course on "Estructura teórica del programa arquitectónico", El Colegio Nacional, August 1963, printed in Ramón Vargas Salguero and J. Víctor Arias Montes (eds.), *Ideario de los arquitectos mexicanos*, vol. II: *Los olvidados,* Mexico City: Instituto Nacional de Bellas Artes, 2010, 116.
60 Óscar Urrutia, op. cit., p. 179.

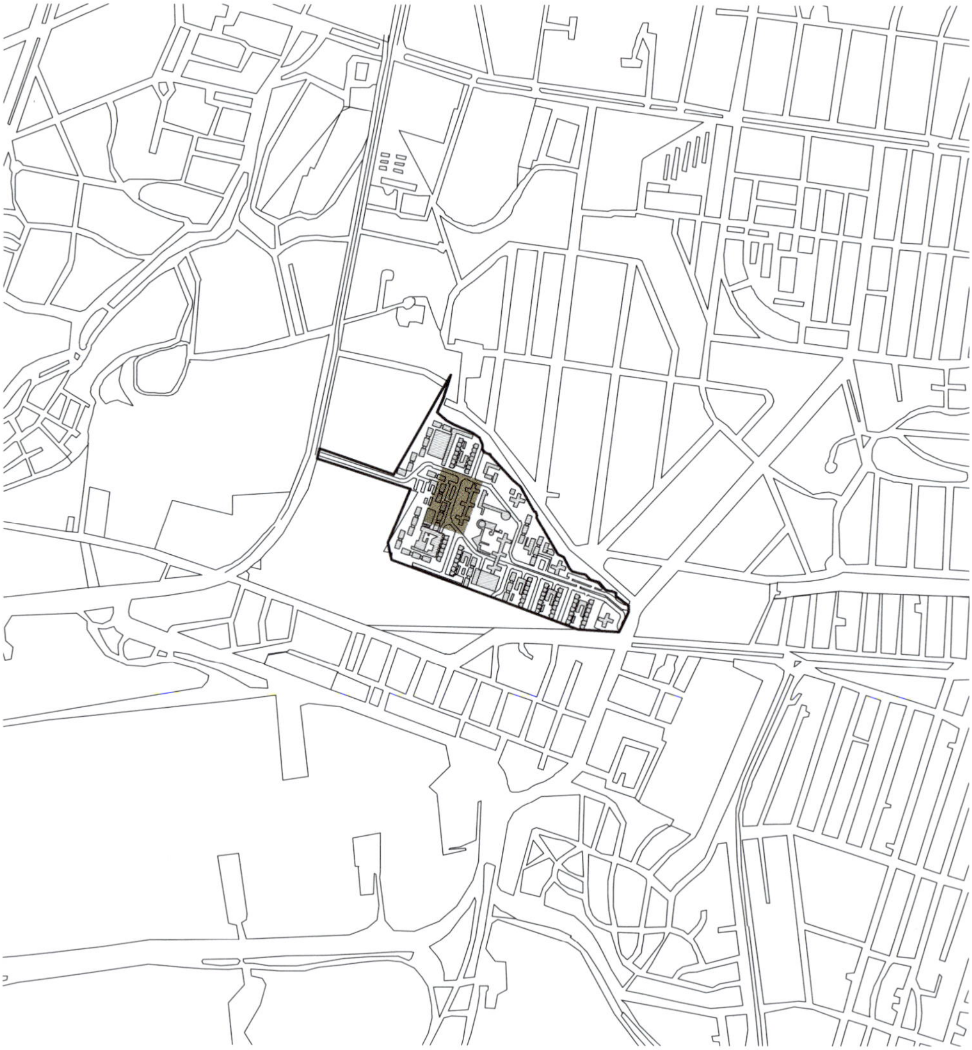

1978, Integración Latinoamericana, Sánchez Arquitectos y Asociados-Félix Sánchez, Luis Sánchez Renero, Gustavo López Padilla, Fernando Mota, Humberto Ricalde and Héctor Meza

1986, Fuentes Brotantes (II), Teodoro González de León and J. Francisco Serrano

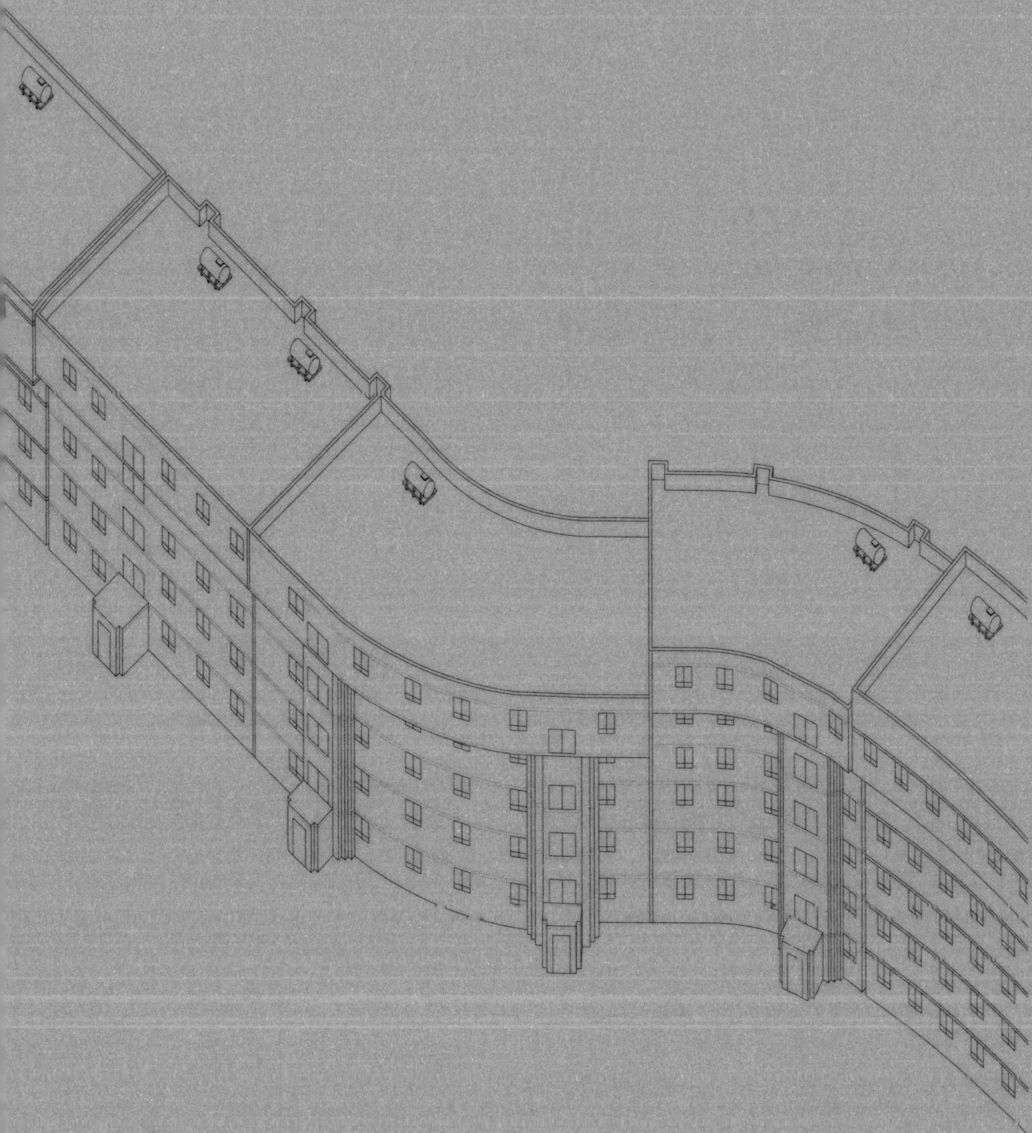

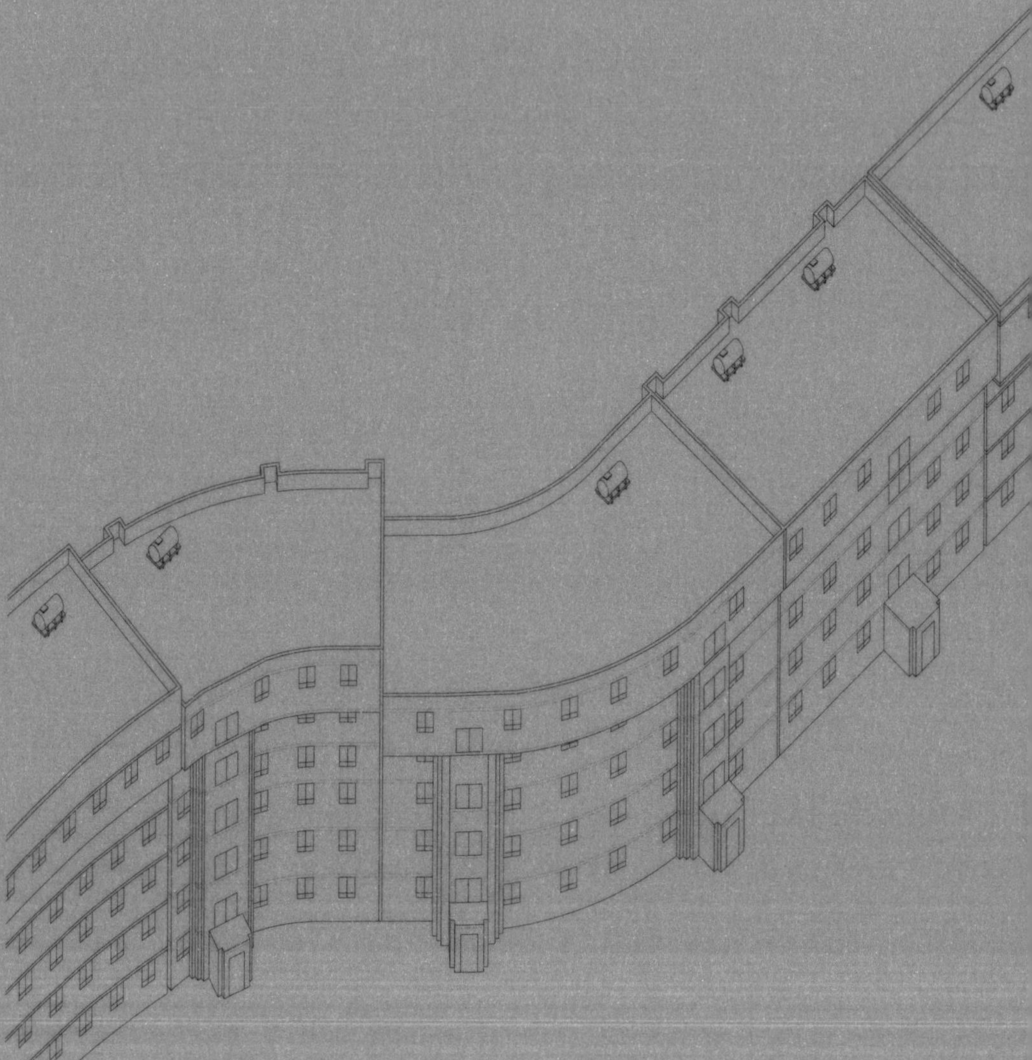

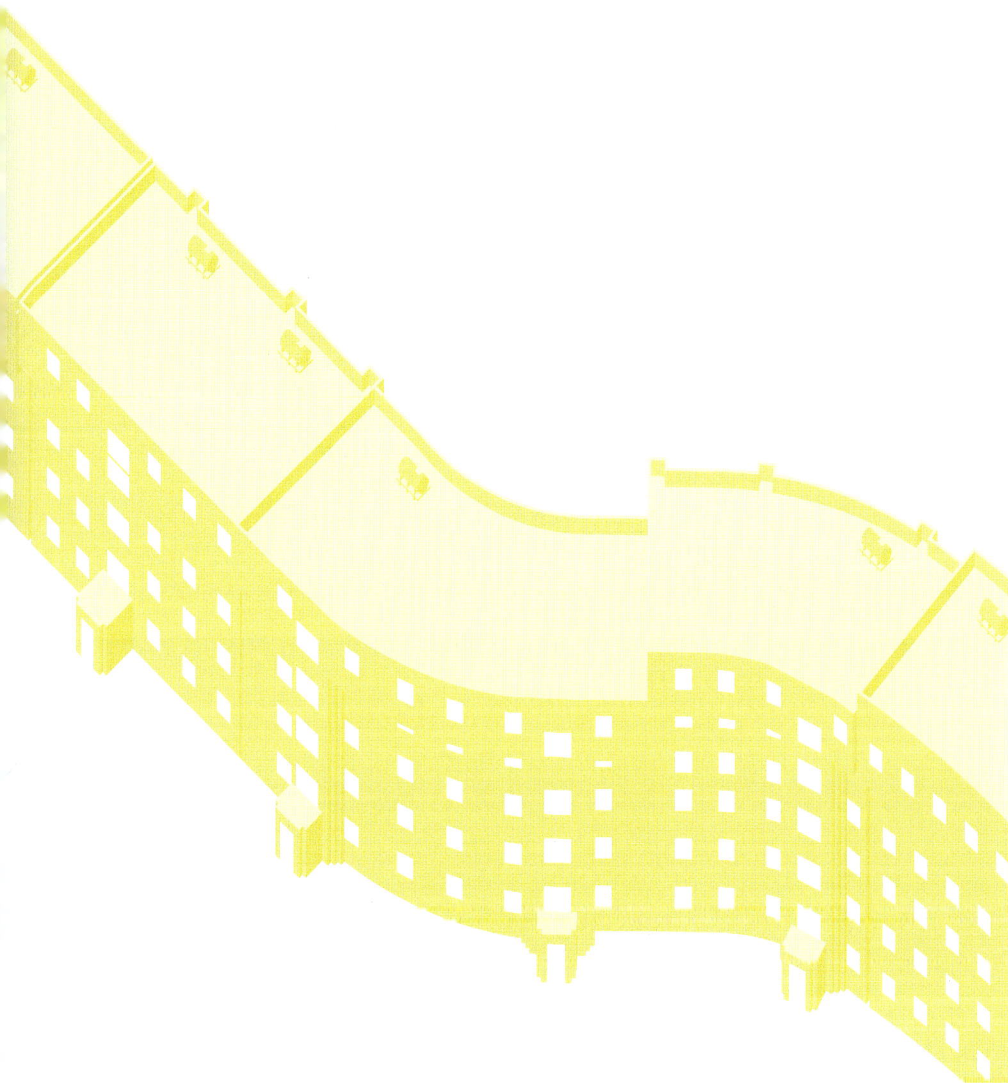

"The best response is that of the tenants of Balbuena: in the four blocks of homes he [Juan Legarreta] built, only three apartments maintain the original façade; the rest have been transformed by the occupants to suit *their tastes.*"[61]

Israel Katzman, 1963

"[Juan Legarreta] was practically blinded by a single idea: that housing had to be provided for the homeless masses."[62]

Israel Katzman, 1963

"No other nation presents such a strong tendency towards the variations that give each home a distinctive, personal, original signature; each house must be truly different from the one next door, the one further down the street, and even the one that is nowhere nearby."[63]

Óscar Urrutia, 1963

"Perhaps a new and individual aesthetic will be achieved at a later time, determined by new production methods. But this belongs to the future, which unfortunately we will not see and can only imagine, hoping that someday there will come a time when it is possible to provide shelter and housing for everyone."[64]

Juan O'Gorman, 1967

61 Israel Katzman, *Arquitectura contemporánea Mexicana,* Mexico City: Instituto Nacional de Antropología e Historia/Secretaría de Educación Pública, 1963, op. cit., 152.

6 Ibid., 151.

63 Óscar Urrutia, op, cit., 179.

64 Juan O'Gorman, "Acerca de la arquitectura en México", op. cit., 211.

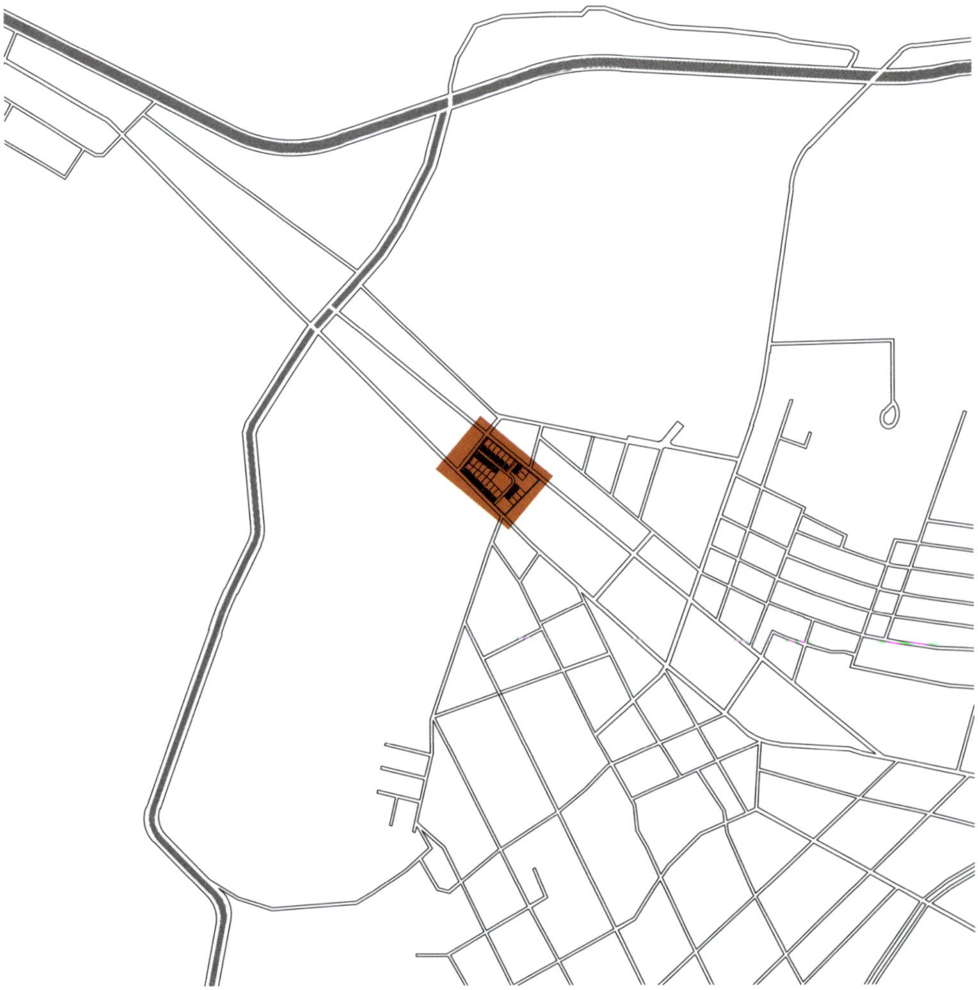

1991, Las Crucesitas, Carlos González Lobo and María Eugenia Hurtado

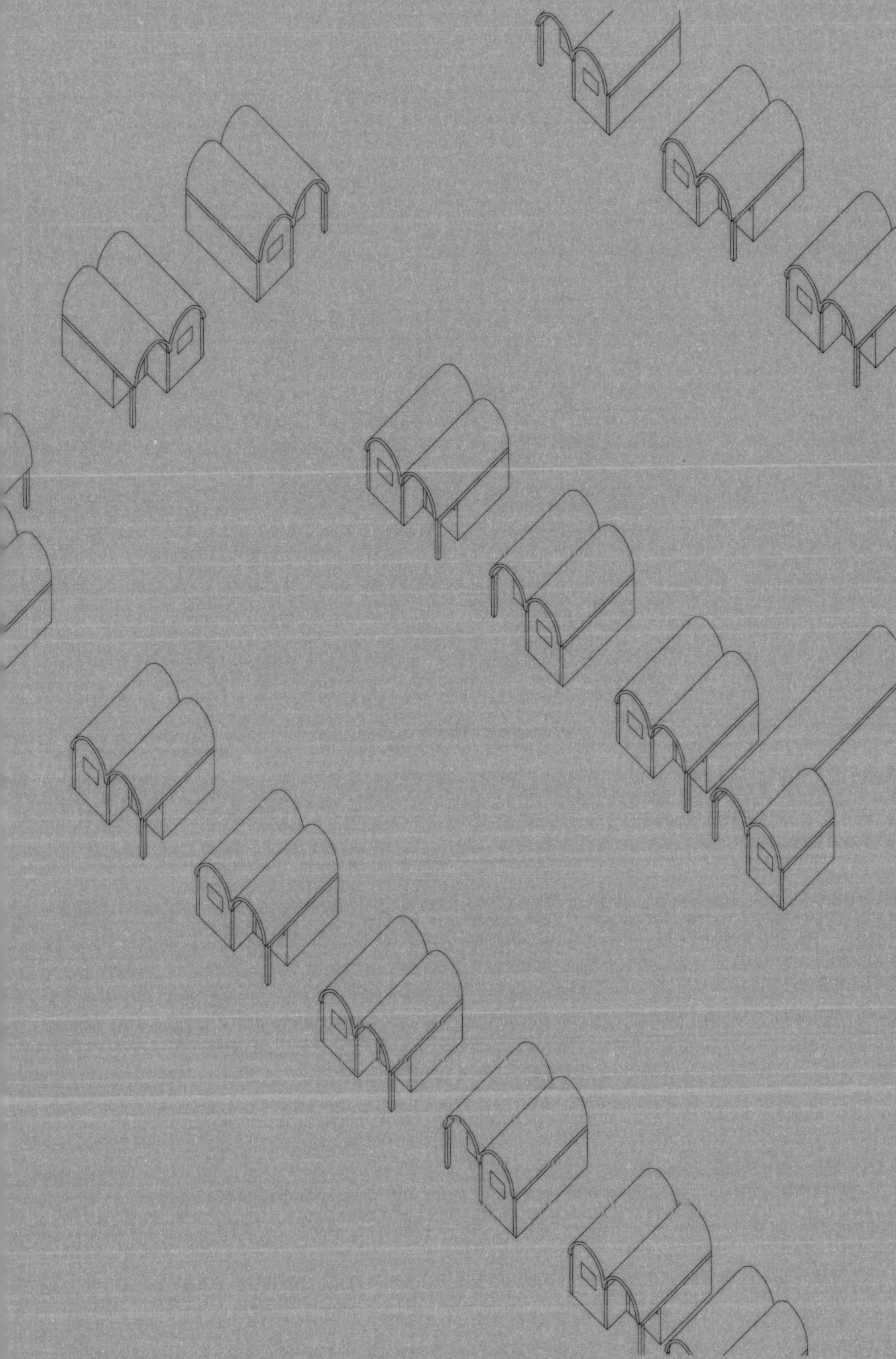

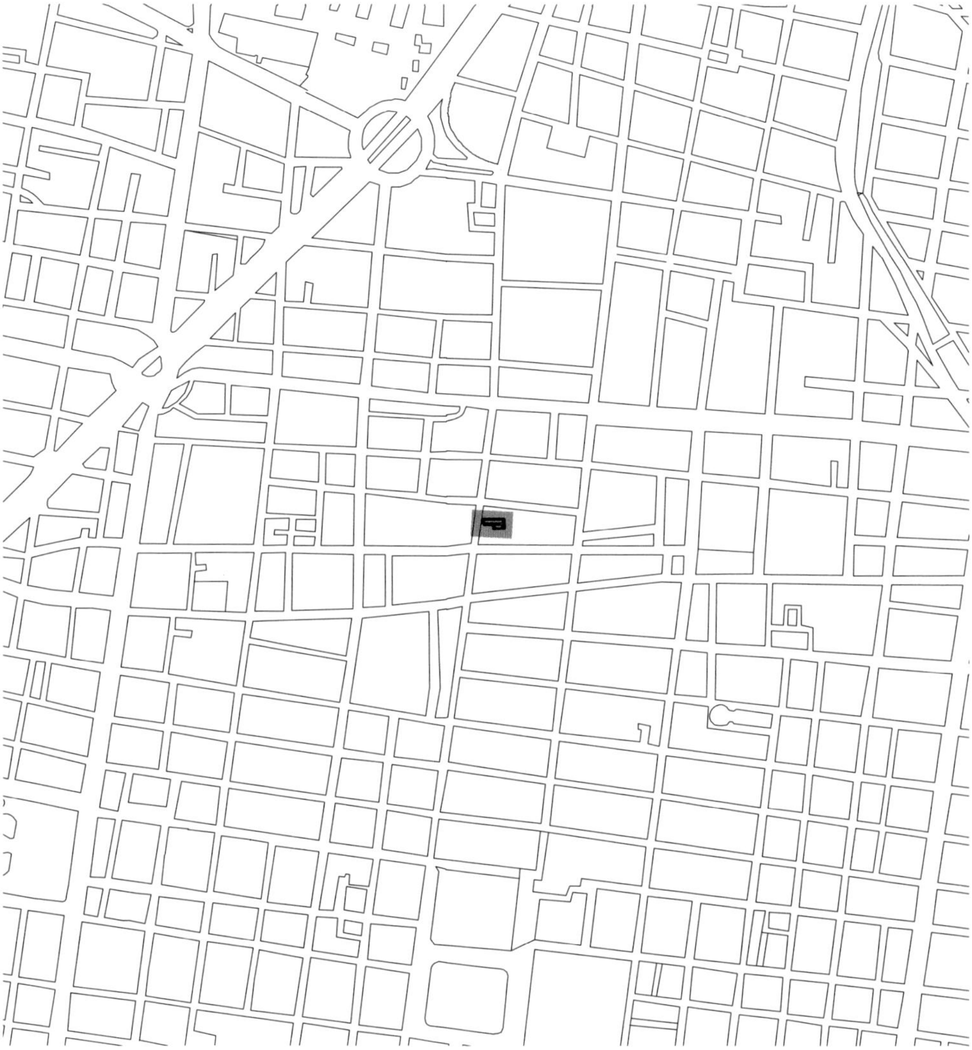

1992, Brasil 75, Enrique Norten and Bernardo Gómez-Pimienta

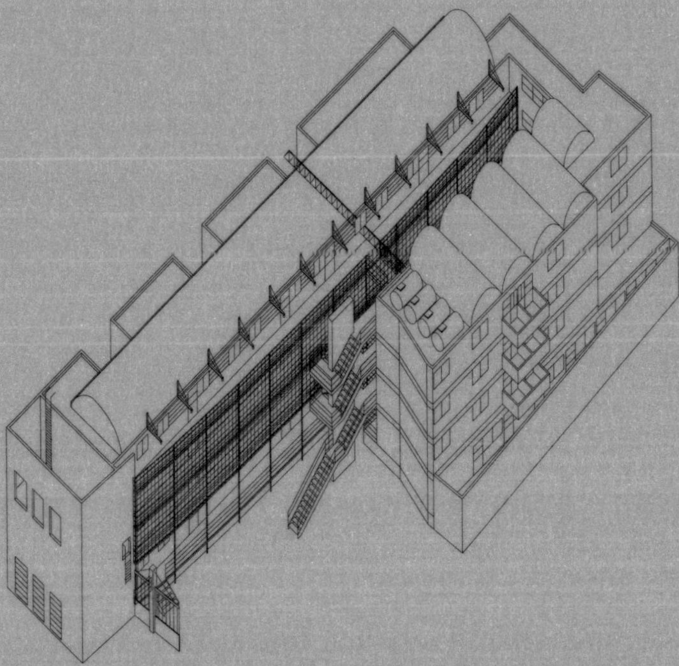

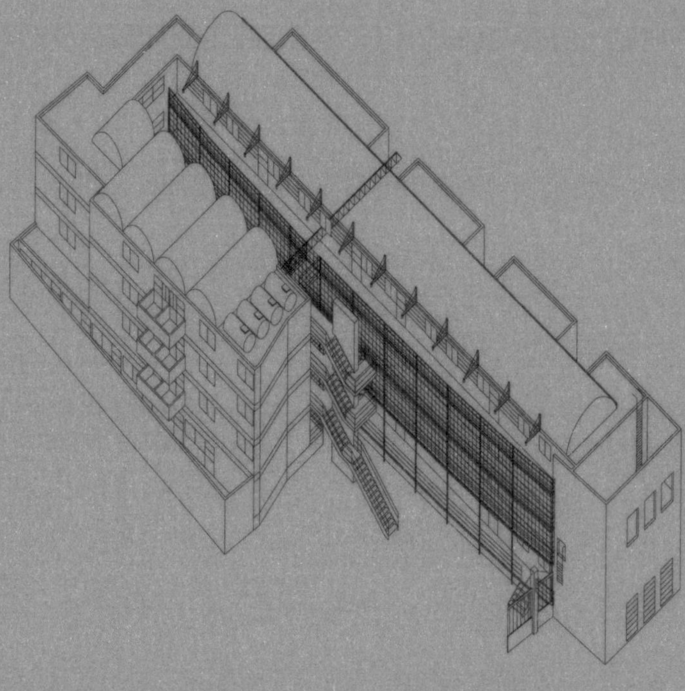

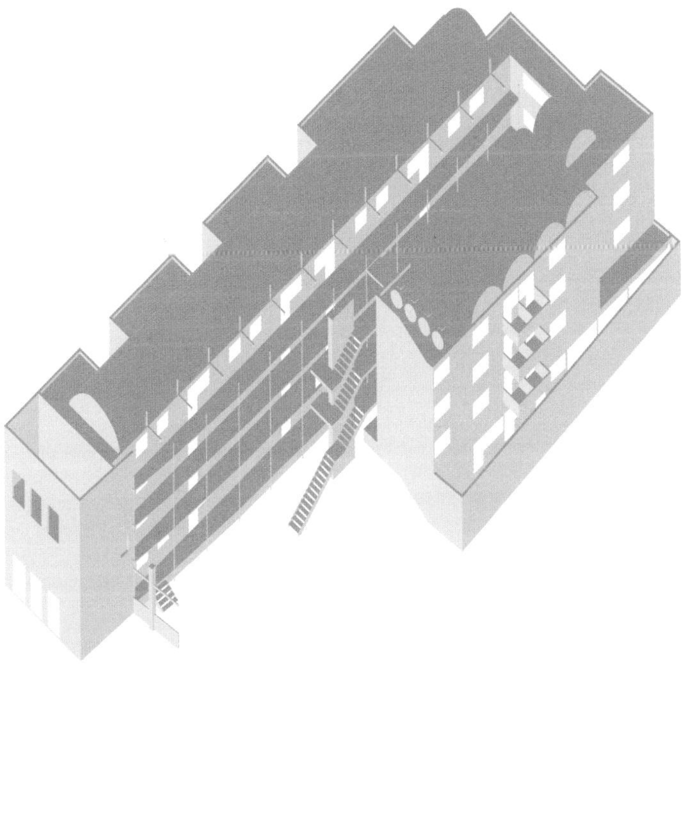

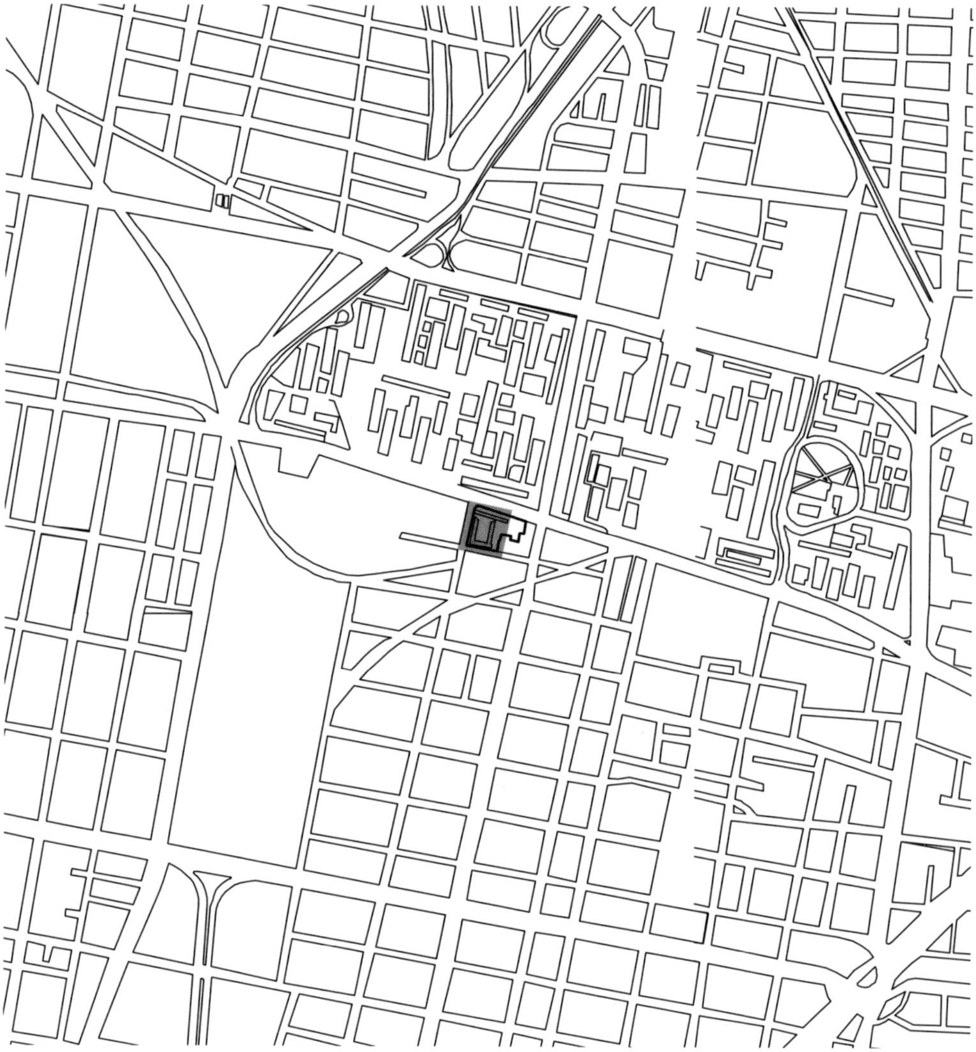

1994, Tláloc complex, Alberto Kalach, Daniel Álvarez, Axel Arañó, Felipe Buendía, Rebeca Cotera, Salvador Ferreiro, Julio González and Moisés Miserachi

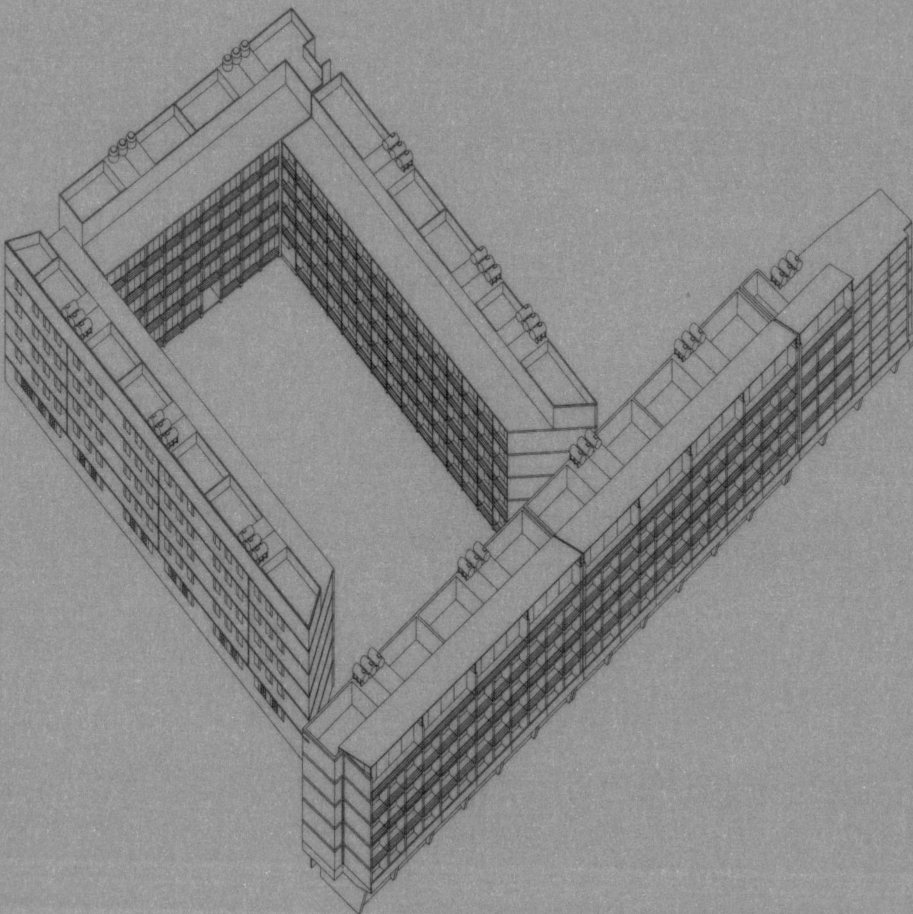

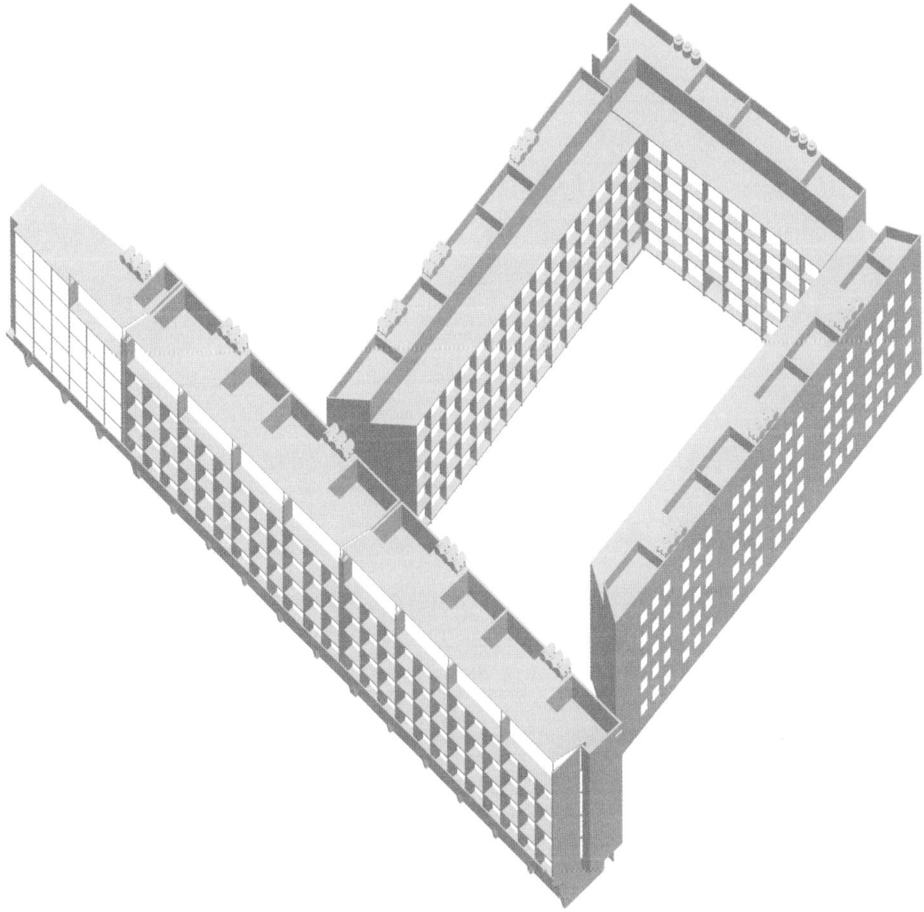

"On the eastern fringes of Mexico City, on and around the dry bed of Lake Texcoco, a million people somehow exist, without sanitation, without proper shelter [...]. Another three hundred thousand people crouch in caves in the lava that is part of the Pedregal, at the opposite end of the city. They're waiting for a home, a room, inside the city, and they multiply while they wait."[65]

Mario Pani, 1967

"Mankind must build, in the next thirty-five years, more homes than it has built in the past five thousand years."[66]

Mario Pani, 1967

"My home is my refuge, an emotional work of architecture, not a cold work of convenience."[67]

Luis Barragán, 1976

"What must technicians who made a space capsule habitable think of the earth-bound architect who cannot even achieve a comfortable temperature in a room?"[68]

Mauricio Gómez Mayorga, 1977

"In the days of General Obregón [president from 1920 to 1924], they discovered that there was a huge demand for housing in Mexico because our population jumped from a half million to one million! And back then there were hardly any houses..."[69]

Francisco J. Serrano, 1979

65 Clive Bamford Smith, *Builders in the Sun: Five Mexican Architects*, New York: Architectural Book Publishing, 1967, Book Publishing, 1967, 176.

66 Ibid.

67 Emilio Ambasz, *The Architecture of Luis Barragan,* New York: Museum of Modern Art, 1976, 8.

68 Mauricio Gómez Mayorga, *Ensayos críticos de arquitectura,* Guadalajara: Universidad Autónoma de Guadalajara, 1977, 138.

69 Interview with Juan F. Serrano, October 9, 1979, in *Testimonios vivos*, Cuadernos de Arquitectura y Conservación del Patrimonio Artístico, nos. 15-16, Mexico City: Secretaría de Educación Pública/Instituto Nacional de Bellas Artes, 1981, 60.

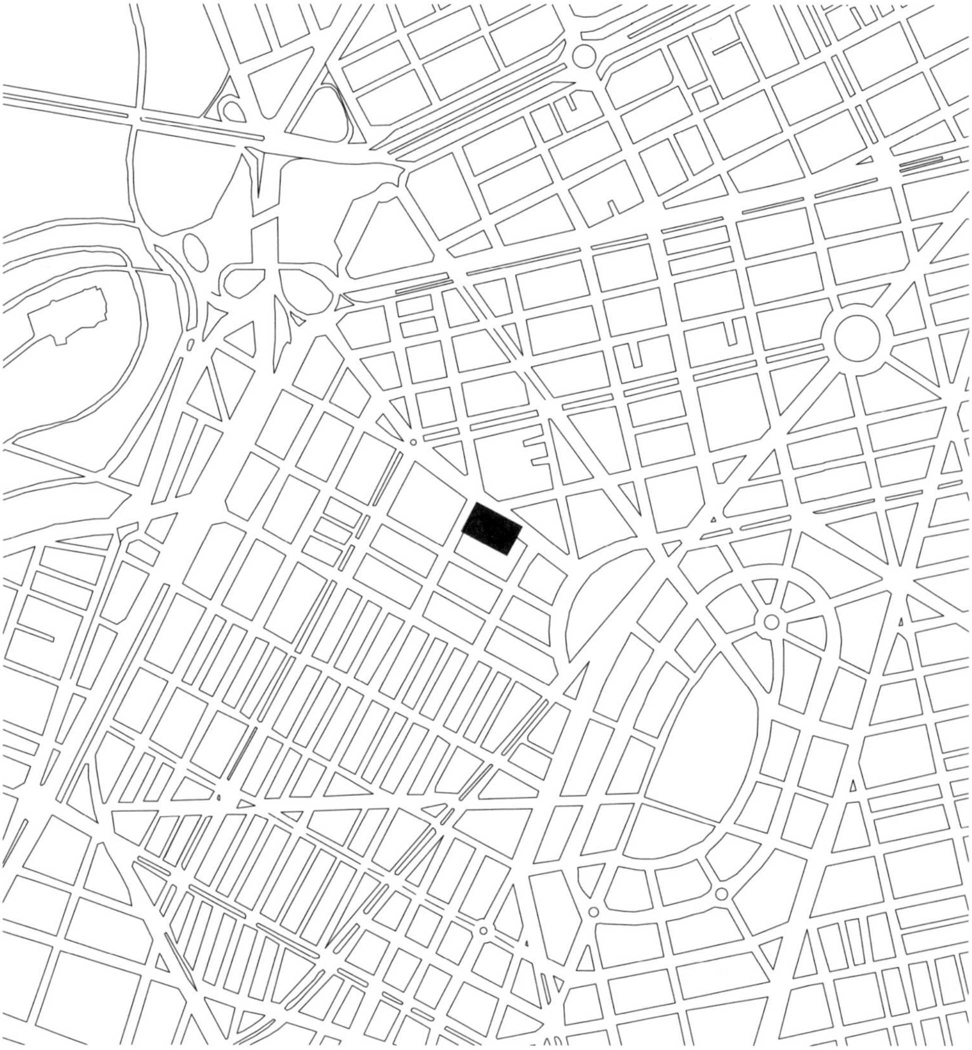

1996, Veracruz complex, Javier Sánchez, Ernesto Sánchez and Lorenzo Farfán

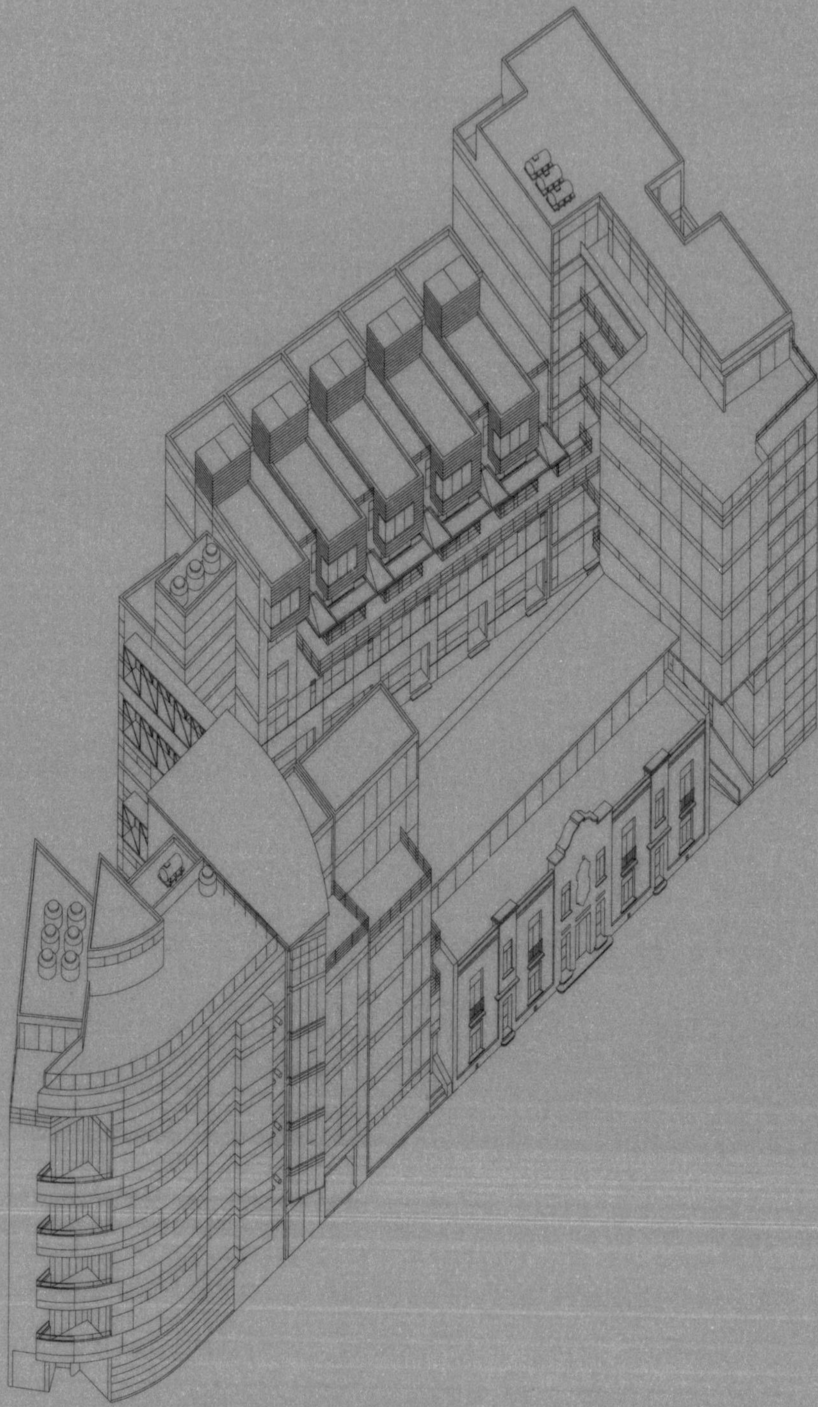

1998, Portal Bretaña, Gonzalo Gómez-Palacio and Gustavo Eichelmann

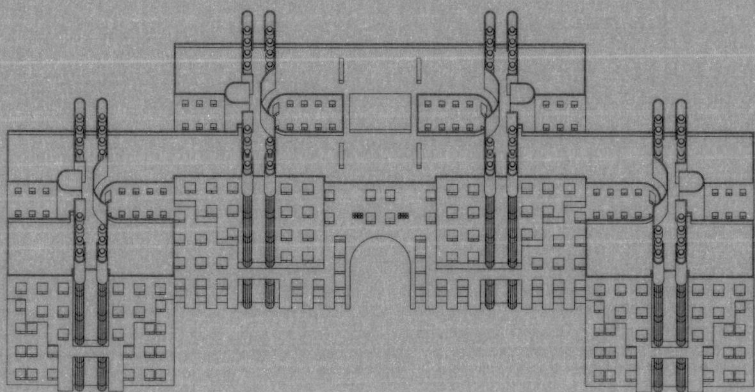

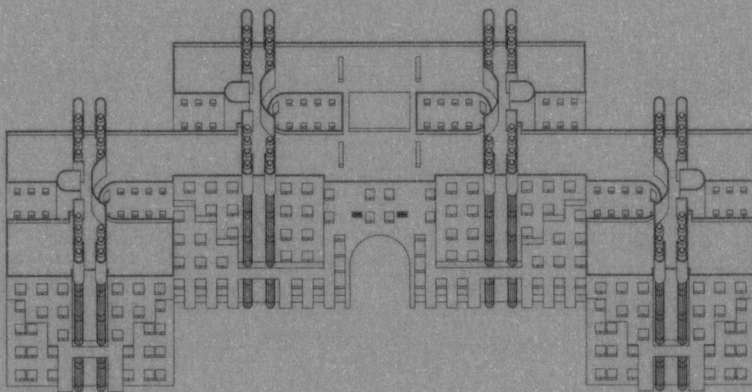

"I see all the housing projects in magazines [...] and not one addresses the concept of flexibility in the home. In other words, architecture has no response to the changing dynamic of family life."[70]

Manuel Teja, 1979

"80% of homes built today are DIY [...] I feel that this is a sign of our failure."[71]

Manuel Teja, 1979

"The single-family home [...] is a business for the developer, an anti-cultural business, a business that is making people unprepared to live in a community, to live better, with much more modern systems."[72]

Manuel Teja, 1979

"People say no, Mexicans aren't ready to live in collective housing blocks, and I say that they are not prepared to live, period. They have to learn first, they need to be taught how to live better, [whether] in an apartment block [or] a single-family home."[73]

Manuel Teja, 1979

"A room in a house can also elicit strong emotion."[74]

Luis Barragán, 1981

70 Interview with Manuel Teja, October 4, 1979, in Pablo Quintero (ed.), *Modernidad en la arquitectura mexicana: 18 protagonistas*, Mexico City: Universidad Autónoma Metropolitana-Xochimilco, 1990, 168.
71 Ibid., 170.
72 Interview with Manuel Teja, October 4, 1979, in *Testimonios vivos*, Cuadernos de Arquitectura y Conservación del Patrimonio Artístico, nos. 15-16, Mexico City: Secretaría de Educación Pública/Instituto Nacional de Bellas Artes, 1981, 166.
73 Interview with Manuel Teja, October 4, 1979, op. cit., 166.
74 Marie-Pierre Colle, "Luis Barragán: 'La buena arquitectura es bella'", *House and Garden*, New York, September 1981, interview published in Antonio Riggen, op. cit., 134.

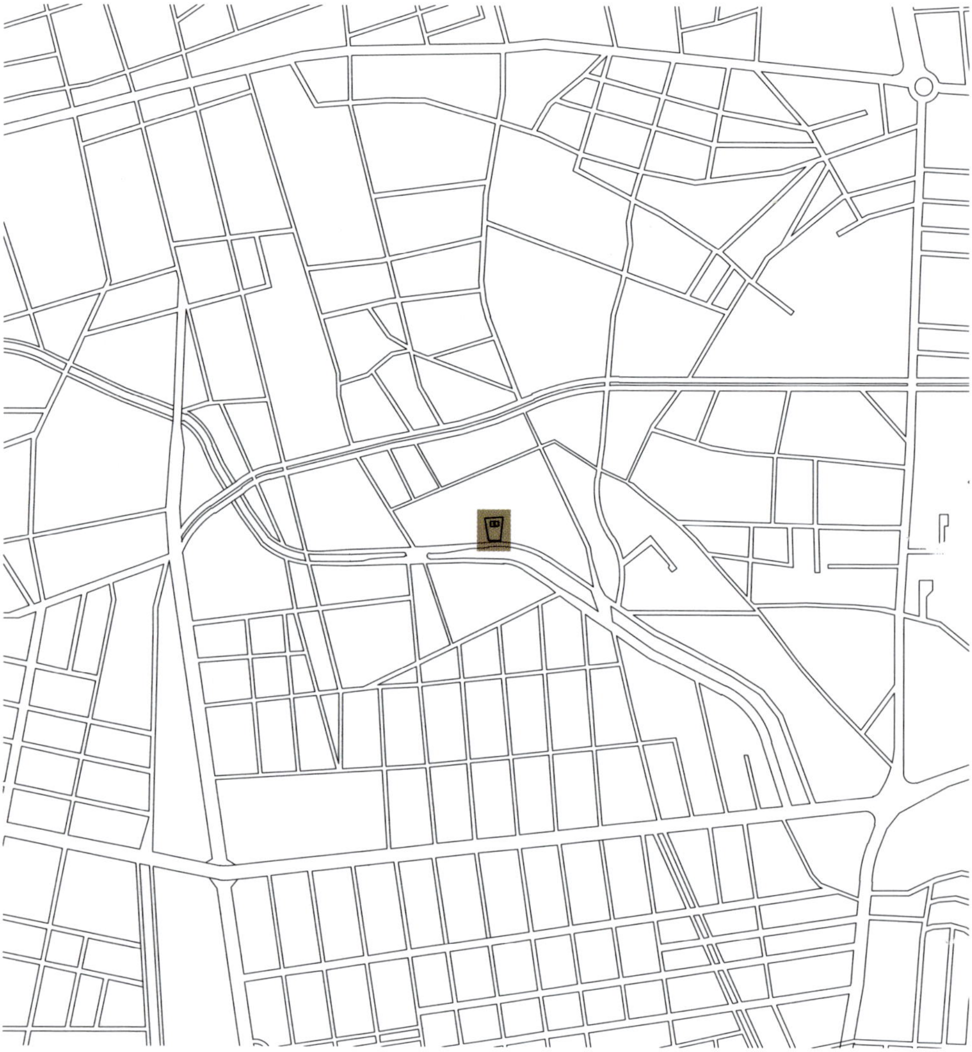

1999, Stacked housing, Reinaldo Pérez Rayón

2000, Ámsterdam Building, Isaac Broid, Fernando Donis, Benjamín Campos and Alfredo Hernández

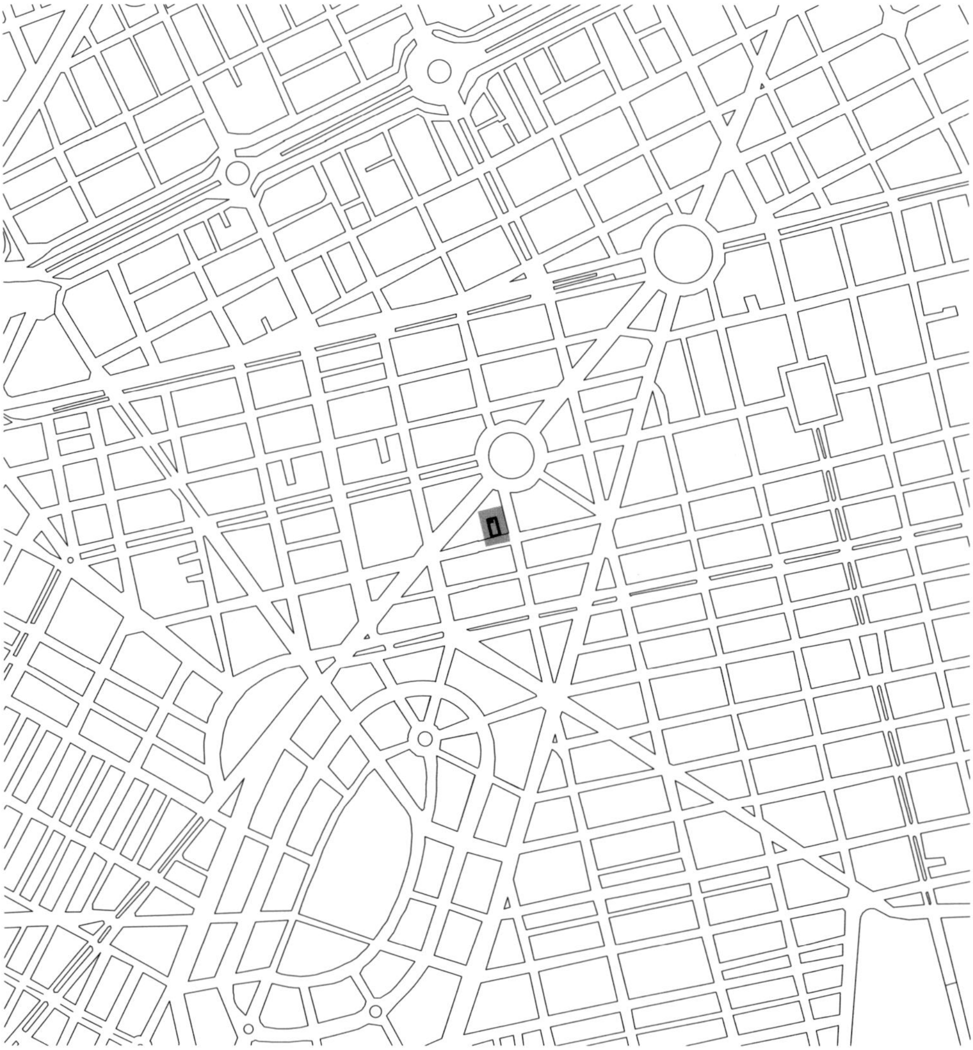

2001, Housing for artists, Fernando Romero, Juan Pablo Maza, Gerardo Asali, Pablo Quiroga, Víctor Jaime and Adriana Lara

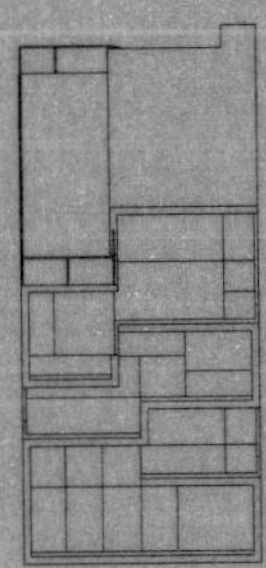

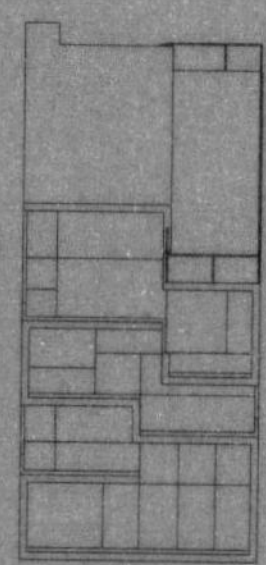

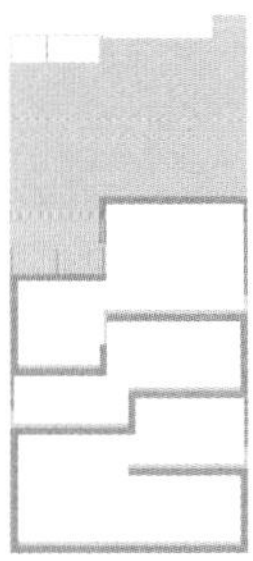

"When devising these large complexes, Infonavit did not plan for an adequate communal management and maintenance system (security, traffic, provisions, waste disposal) [...], overlooking all the social and urban integration aspects that should be the primary goal of an institution of this size."[75]

Humberto Ricalde and Gustavo López Padilla, 1982

"Certain apartment blocks, like Unidad Independencia, are magnificent examples of ways of life to which the working class should aspire, but precisely because of their excellent conditions, healthy, uncongested environment, and all sorts of supplementary services –academic, sports, medical, and social– offered with admirable quality, in our time they can only be a demonstration of what might be accomplished with tremendous difficulty in a socialist regime."[76]

Enrique Yáñez, 1982

"That is why all those bureaucratic and official 'social welfare' housing developments fail so miserably. Before packing people into rooms they don't know how to use (and poorly designed to boot), they need to be taught how to live."[77]

Mauricio Gómez Mayorga, 1982

"Pani brought a new element of urban culture to Mexico, the multi-family apartment block or *multifamiliar*, whose name has also enriched Mexico's architectural vocabulary"[78]

Manuel Larrosa, 1985

75 Humberto Ricalde and Gustavo López Padilla, "Arquitectura en México, 1960-1980", in *Apuntes para la historia y crítica de la arquitectura Mexicana del siglo xx: 1900-1980*, vol. 2, Cuadernos de Arquitectura y Conservación del Patrimonio Artístico, nos. 22-23, Mexico City: Secretaría de Educación Pública/Instituto Nacional de Bellas Artes, 1982, 170.

76 Enrique Yáñez, *Arquitectura, teoría, diseño, contexto,* Mexico City: Limusa, 2006, 223.

77 Mauricio Gómez Mayorga, *Al rescate de México,* Mexico City: Editores Asociados Mexicanos, 1982, 112.

78 Manuel Larrosa, *Mario Pani, arquitecto de su época,* Mexico City: Universidad Nacional Autónoma de México, 1985, 54.

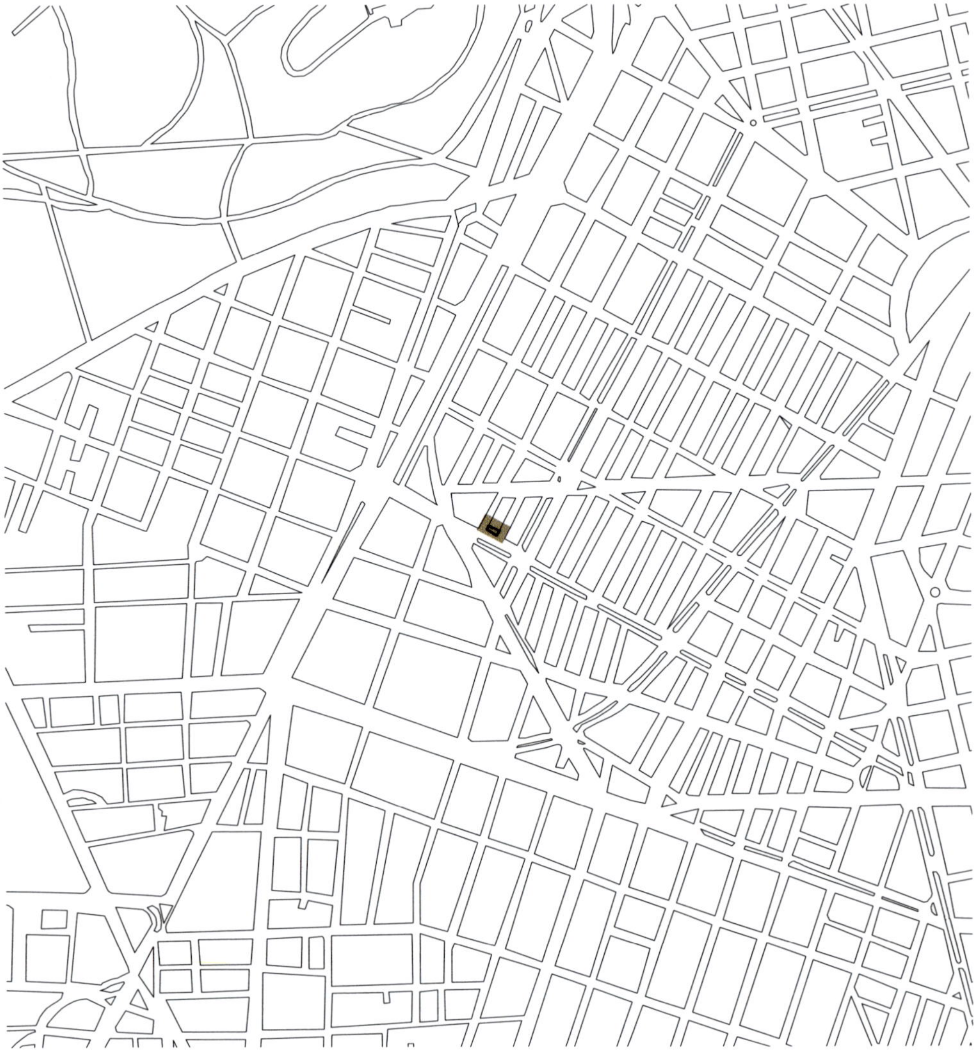

2003, AR58, Derek Dellekamp

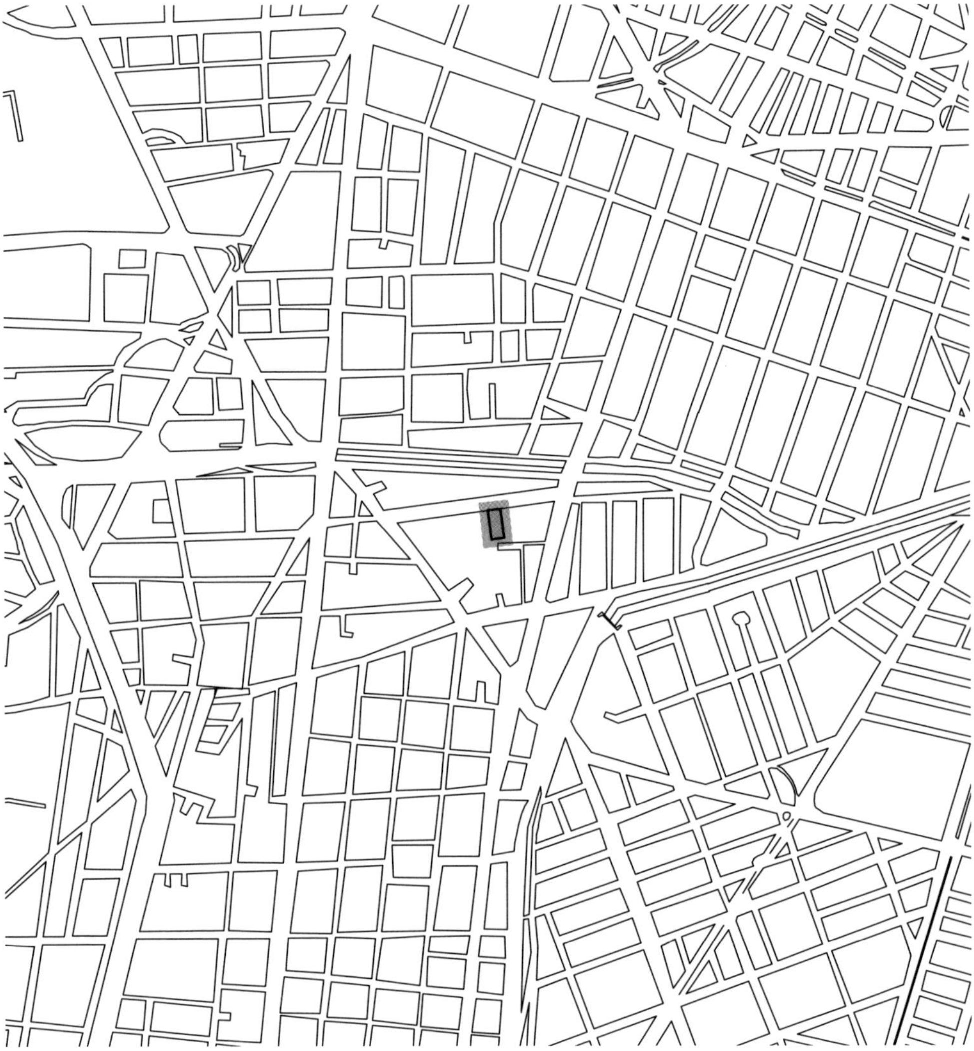

2004, 13 de Septiembre, Javier Sánchez, Juan Reyes, Iris Sosa, Mariana Mas and María Elena Reyes

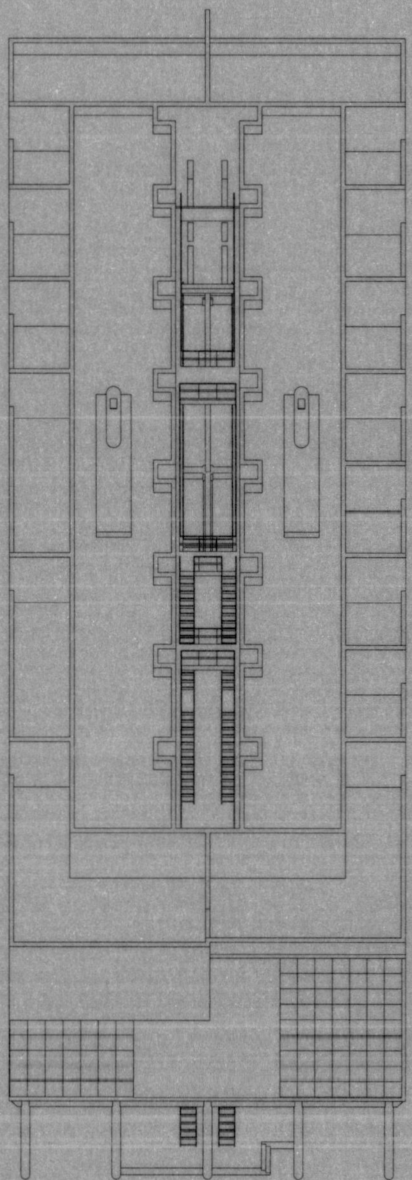

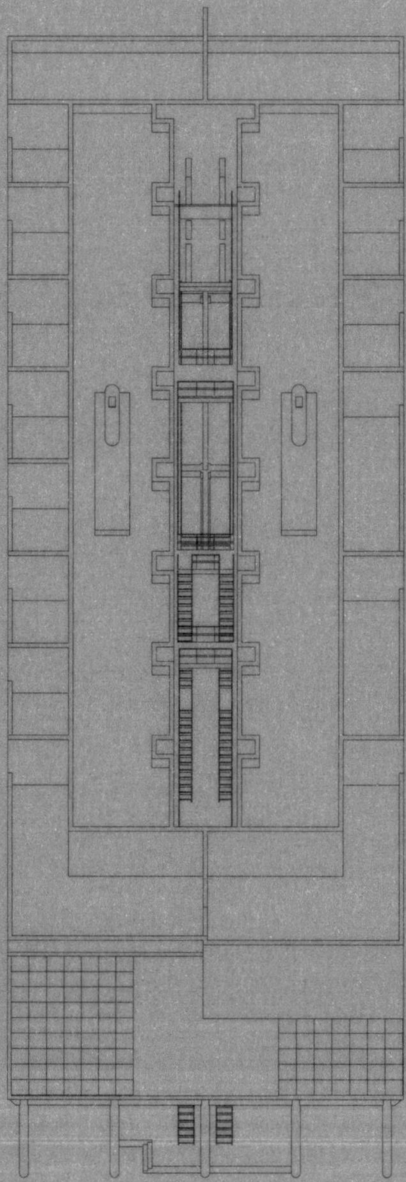

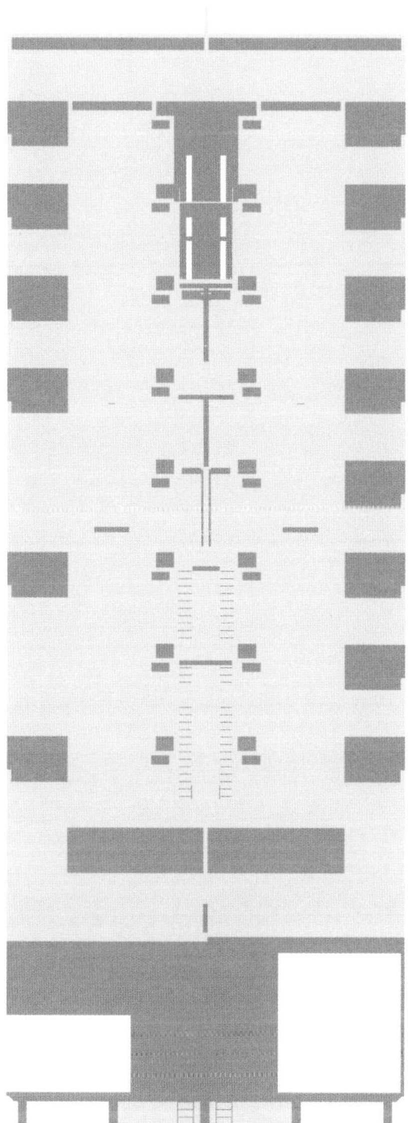

"[After the 1985 earthquake] we saw the consequences of leaving many great government projects in the hands of private developers who sought only their own profit. Nowhere is this more apparent than in the housing developments."[79]

Fernando González Gortázar, 1985

"During that half century, architects were ousted from programmatic planning processes related to housing, as financial mechanisms emerged to regulate it. Then came the *housologists*, very financially-minded financiers who only managed to create new financing costs that doubled the price of housing and, in collusion with the banks, thwarted all attempts at spatial innovation in mass-produced housing."[80]

Manuel Larrosa, 1990

"Our capital has grown via the proliferation of residential subdivisions comprising isolated houses on small lots, with disastrous results."[81]

Reinaldo Pérez Rayón, 1990

"The housing problem is not just about homes [...] for it also extends to buildings that provide complementary services for residents in the fields of education, health care, recreation, commerce, etc."[82]

Enrique Yáñez, 1990

79 Fernando González Gortázar, "México y sus alfileres", *La Jornada*, October 12, 1985. *Escritos reunidos*, Cuadernos de Arquitectura, nos. 11-12, Mexico City: Consejo Nacional para la Cultura y las Artes/Instituto Nacional de Bellas Artes, 2004, 254-255.

80 Manuel Larrosa, "Vivienda en renta: congelación y deshielo", in *Periodismo arquitectónico*, Cuadernos de Arquitectura, no. 13, Mexico City: Consejo Nacional para la Cultura y las Artes/Instituto Nacional de Bellas Artes, 2006, 22-23.

81 Roberto Olvera Camacho (ed.), *Reinaldo Pérez Rayón: ideas y obras*, Mexico City: Roc, 1990, 48.

82 Enrique Yáñez, *Del funcionalismo al post-racionalismo: ensayo sobre la arquitectura contemporánea en México*, Mexico City: Limusa, 1990, 107.

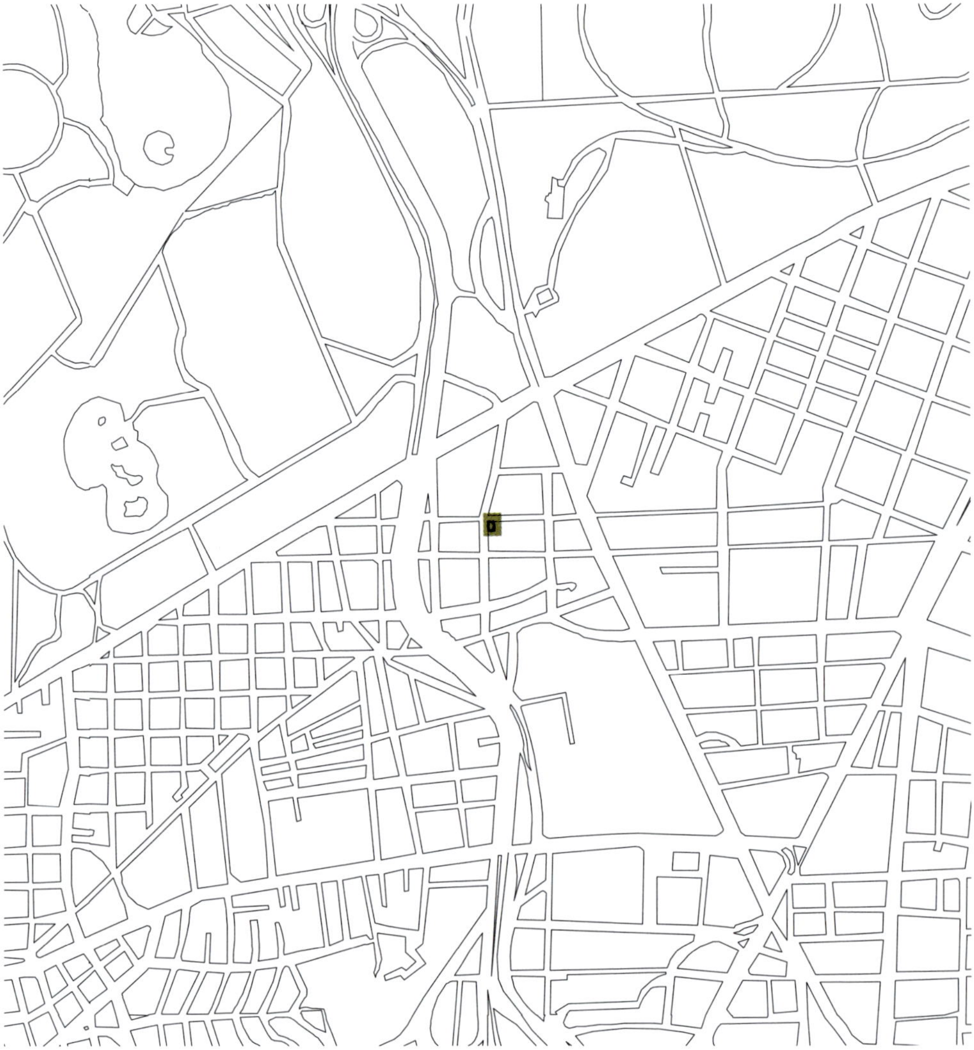

2008, FR43, Juan Carral and Juan Pablo Valdés

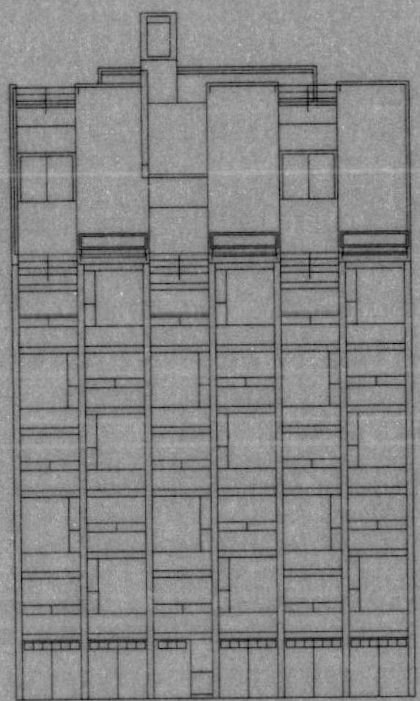

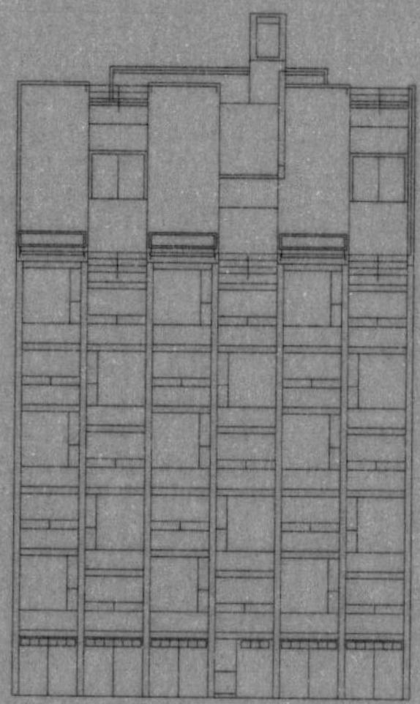

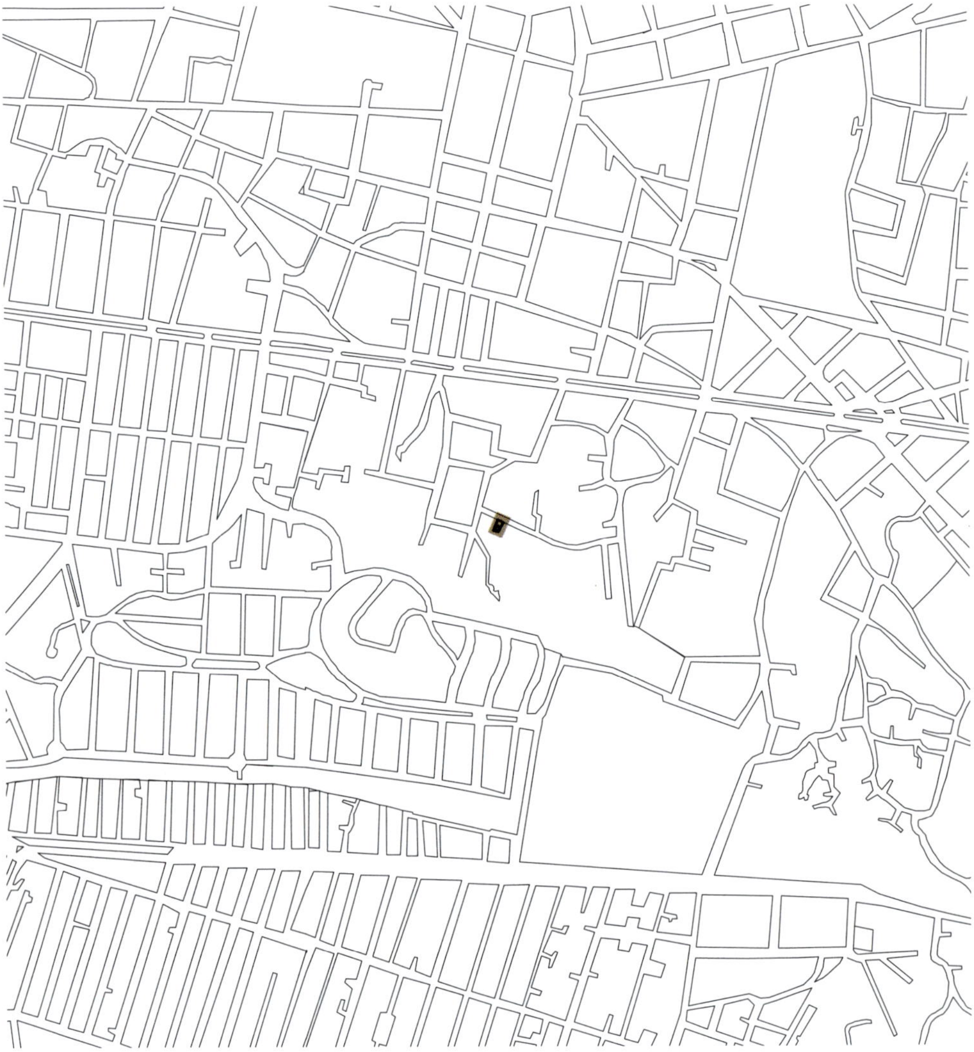

2009, Atrio de San Francisco Apartments, Mauricio Rocha and Gabriela Carrillo

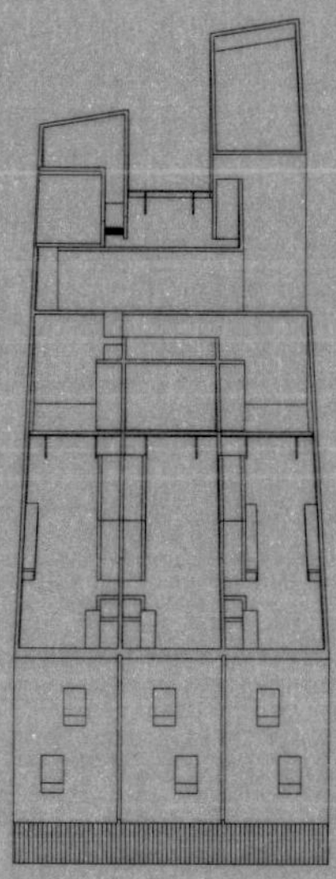

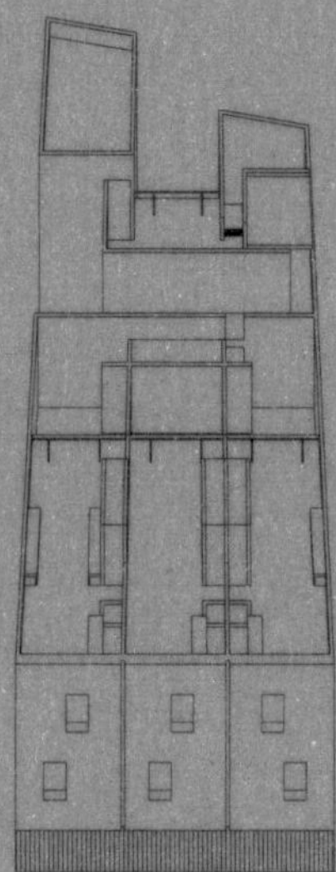

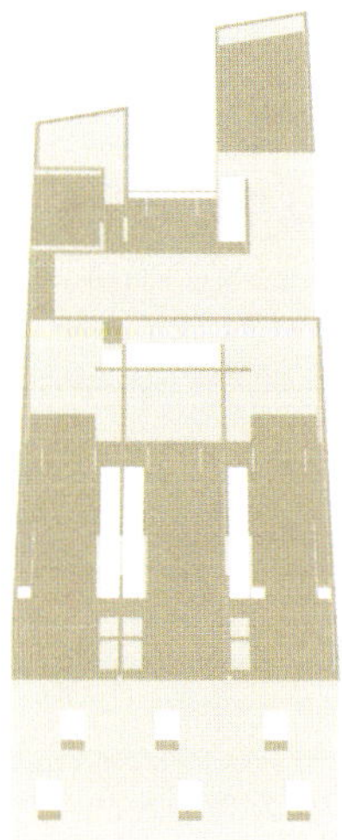

2010, Tlacolula 11H, Derek Dellekamp

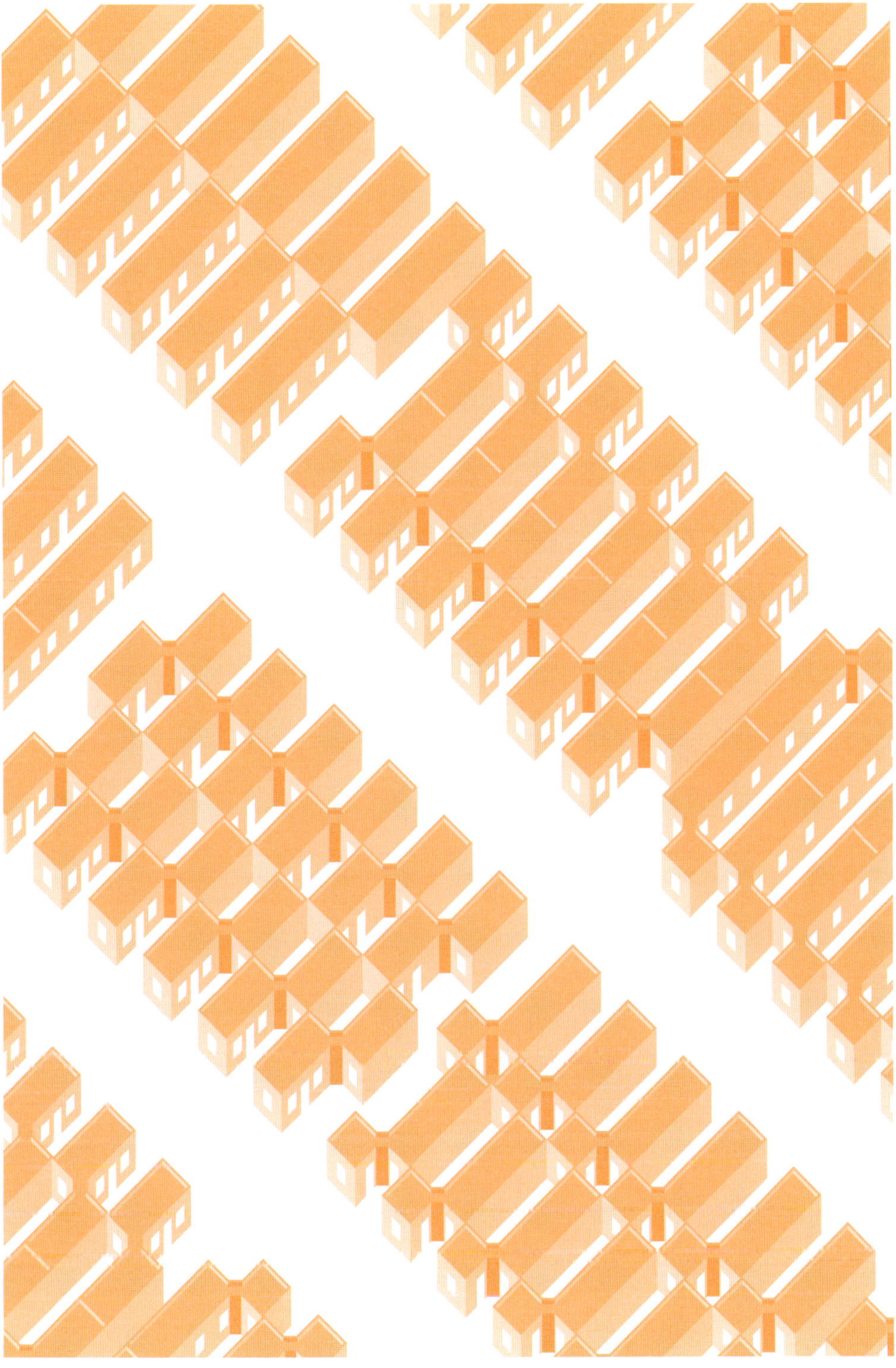

"If I could dedicate the rest of my life to something, it would be the design of social welfare housing. Unfortunately, the housing problem is very complex. It's not an architectural problem, but a social, political and economic one."[83]

Ricardo Legorreta, 1990

"Apartment buildings are, quite possibly, the most important elements in a city's development [...] the fact that we have good models, scarce as they may be, proves the feasibility of creating environments conducive to wellbeing and happiness."[84]

Alejandro Zohn, 1997

"It's baffling that mass housing has not benefitted from the contributions Barragán so clearly made to the two elements that converge in apartment blocks: homes and public spaces (plazas, gardens, walkways, and parking spaces)."[85]

Manuel Larrosa, 1992

"Decent housing means decent spaces both inside and outside the home."[86]

Pedro Ramírez Vázquez, 1995

"The apartment building is an urban ashlar; it is the partition wall for building the great architectural work that is the city [...]. An isolated building means nothing; it must be woven into the urban fabric."[87]

Teodoro González de León, 1996

"Infonavit's big projects were copies that were applied without questioning whether the principle of the new towns in England was adaptable to the Mexican reality."[88]

José Aldrete-Haas, 1991

83 Wayne Attoe (ed.), *The Architecture of Ricardo Legorreta,* Austin: University of Texas Press, 1990, 127.
84 Alejandro Zohn, *Entorno e identidad,* Mexico City: Menhir, 1997, 19-20.
85 Manuel Larrosa, "La vivienda enajenante. Cultura sin casas", in *Periodismo arquitectónico,* Cuadernos de Arquitectura no. 13, Mexico City: Consejo Nacional para la Cultura y las Artes/Instituto Nacional de Bellas Artes, 2006, 24.
86 Beatrice Trueblood (ed.), *Ramírez Vázquez en el urbanismo: conversaciones con José Antonio Aguilar Narváez,* Mexico City: Studio, 1995, 40.
87 Teodoro González de León, *Retrato de arquitecto con ciudad,* Mexico City: Artes de México, 1996, 81.
88 José Aldrete-Haas, *La deconstrucción del Estado mexicano: políticas de vivienda, 1917-1988,* Mexico City: Alianza, 1991, 99.

2010, Elemental Monterrey, Alejandro Aravena, Gonzalo Arteaga and Fernando García-Huidobro

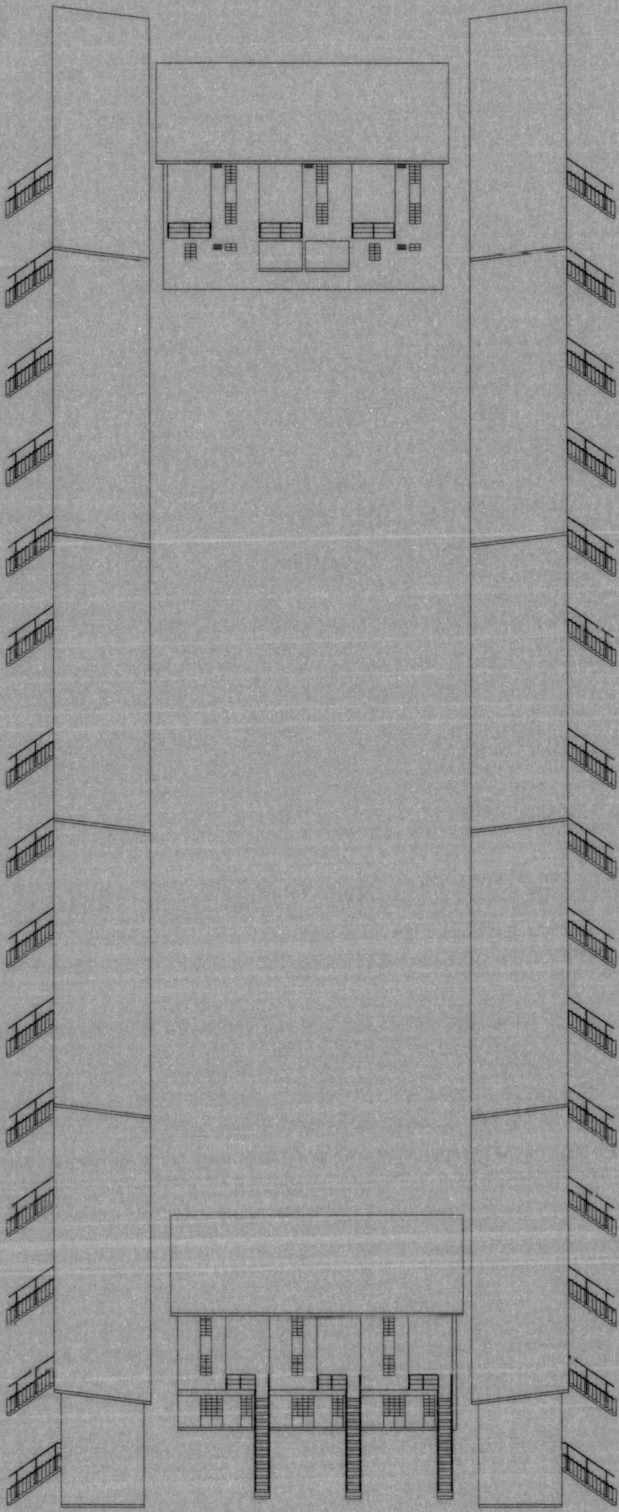

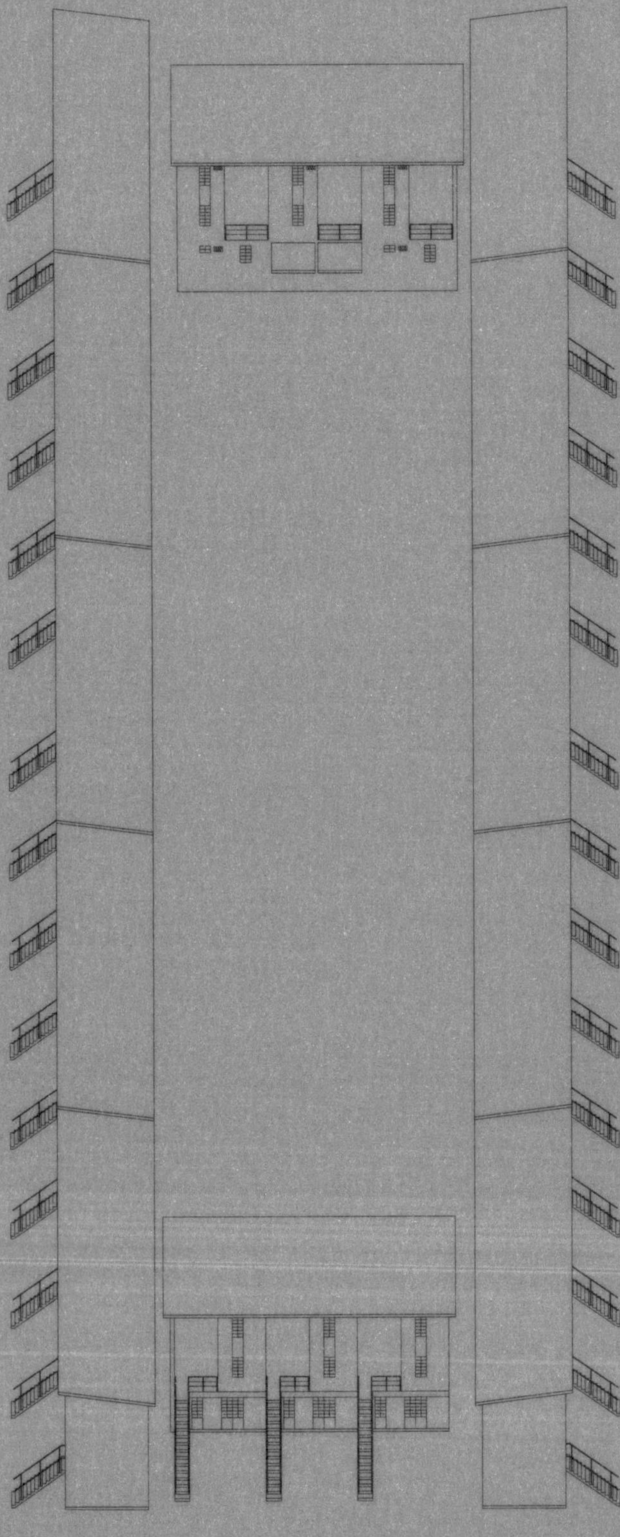

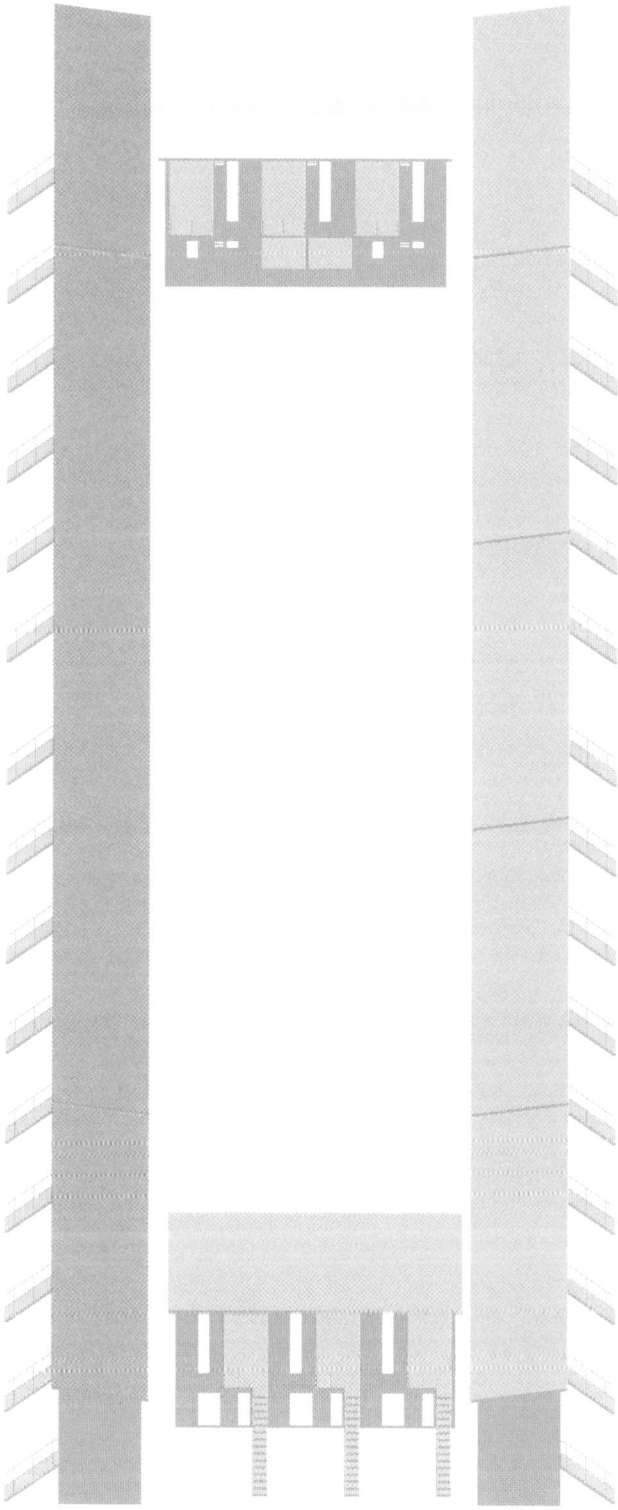

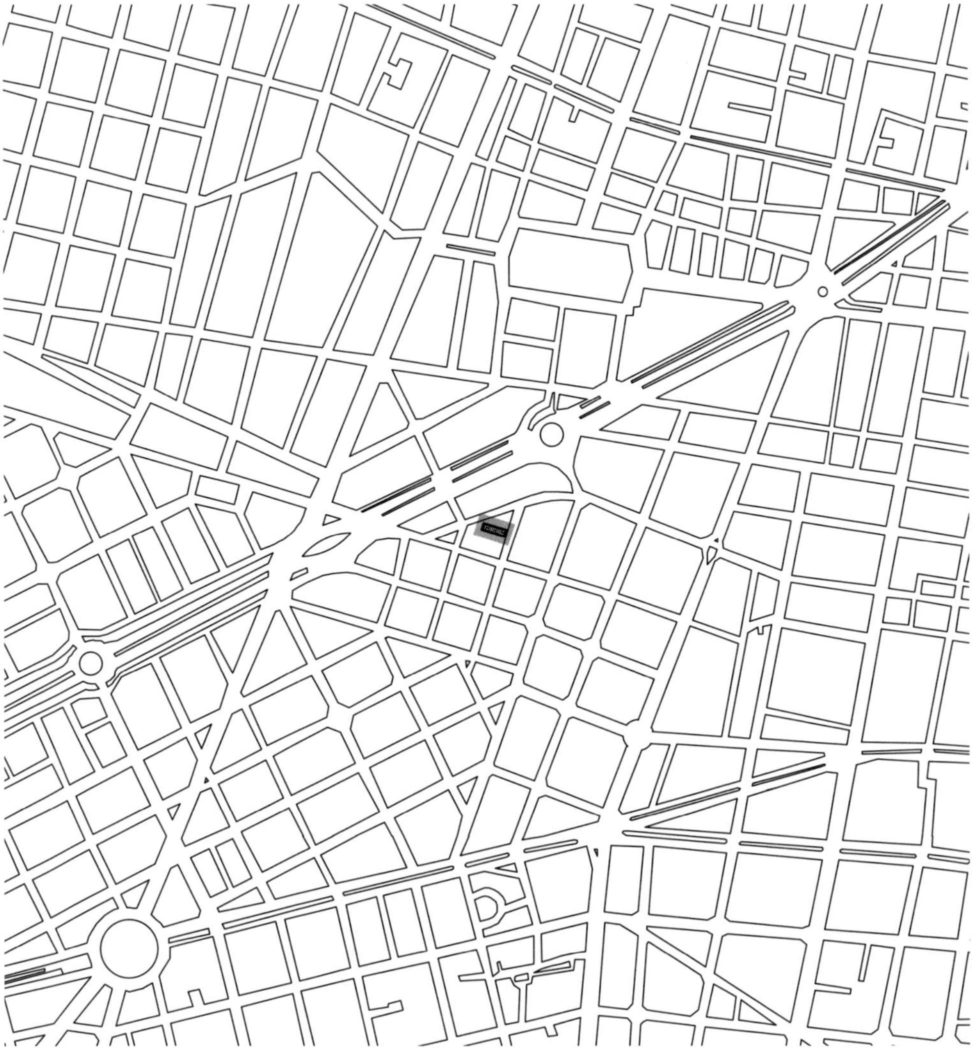

2010, Lisboa 7, Francisco Pardo and Julio Amezcua

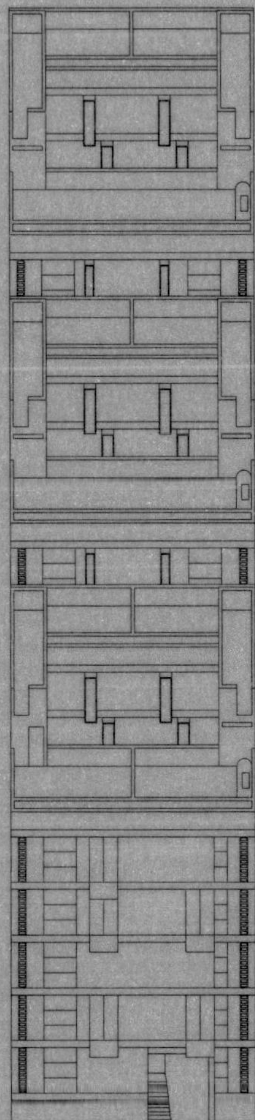

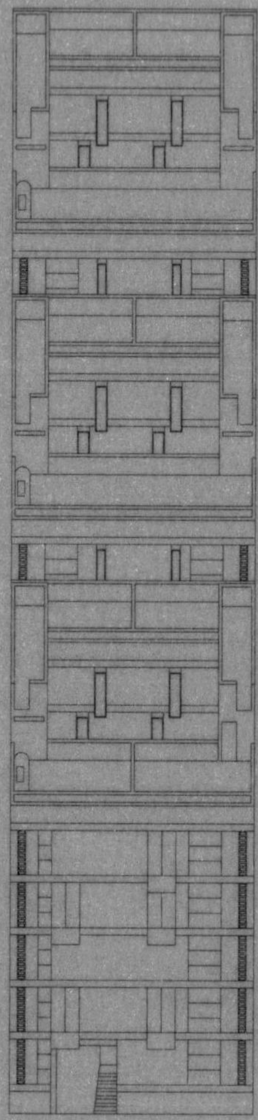

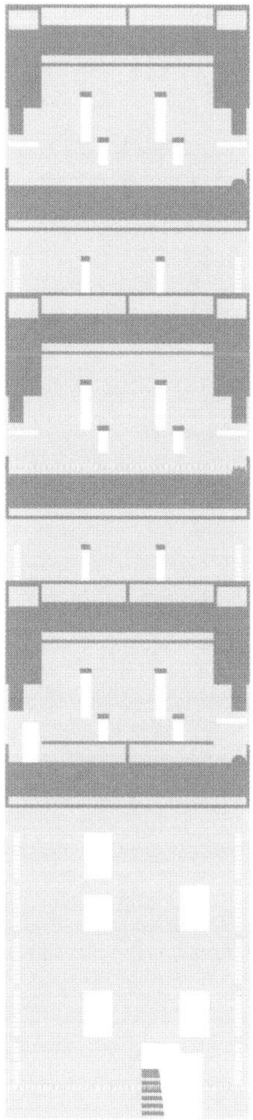

"Given the necessary permanence of certain parts of a home, a reduction in size does not imply a proportional reduction in cost. For example, the cost of a 30 square-meter house would be approximately 80% of a 60 square-meter house."[89]

Reinaldo Pérez Rayón, 1998

"It is disconcerting to realize that many of the works which cemented the reputations of architects now in vogue incorporate highly specialized technology and require extremely sophisticated representation, calculation, and building systems, making them not just costly but exorbitant [...]. We cannot ignore the fact that those inflated costs could be used to build hundreds of homes or improve dozens of neighborhoods where thousands of people live in precarious conditions."[90]

Carlos Mijares, 2002

"This house on this street. This street in this neighborhood. This neighborhood in this city. This city in this landscape. This landscape in this region. Space within space... within space... a specific structure contained within another... specific as well."[91]

Carlos Mijares, 2002

"When a new family is born a new home should be born, and as it grows, so too in proportion should the home [...]. Welfare housing programs frequently assume that the answer is to reduce spaces: but I insist that the home is not a package for containing the family, and there are minimum requirements for human life."[92]

Pedro Ramírez Vázquez, c. 2000

89 Reinaldo Pérez Rayón, lecture "El problema de la habitación", 1998.
90 Carlos Mijares Bracho, *Tránsitos y demoras: esbozos sobre el quehacer arquitectónico*, Universidad Nacional Autónoma de México, México, 2008, p. 70, first edition: Instituto Superior de Arquitectura y Diseño, México, 2002.
91 Carlos Mijares Bracho, *Tránsitos y demoras: esbozos sobre el quehacer arquitectónico,* Mexico City: Universidad Nacional Autónoma de México, 2008, ibid 168; first edition: Mexico City: Instituto Superior de Arquitectura y Diseño, 2002.
92 Pedro Ramírez Vázquez, "Arquitectura para la vivienda", *Arquitectura: Pedro Ramírez Vázquez,* Mexico City: Porrúa, 2013, 31-32.

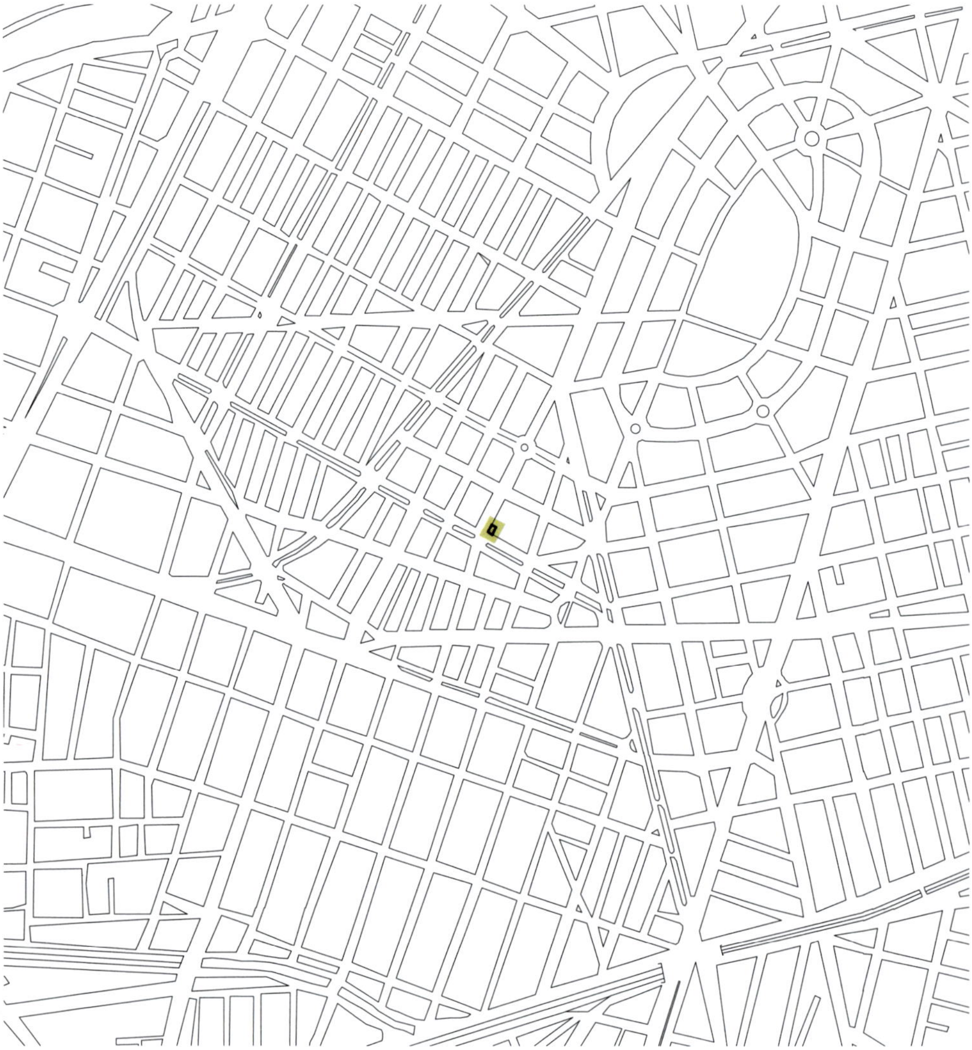

2012, Alfonso Reyes 200, Jorge Ambrosi and Gabriela Etchegaray

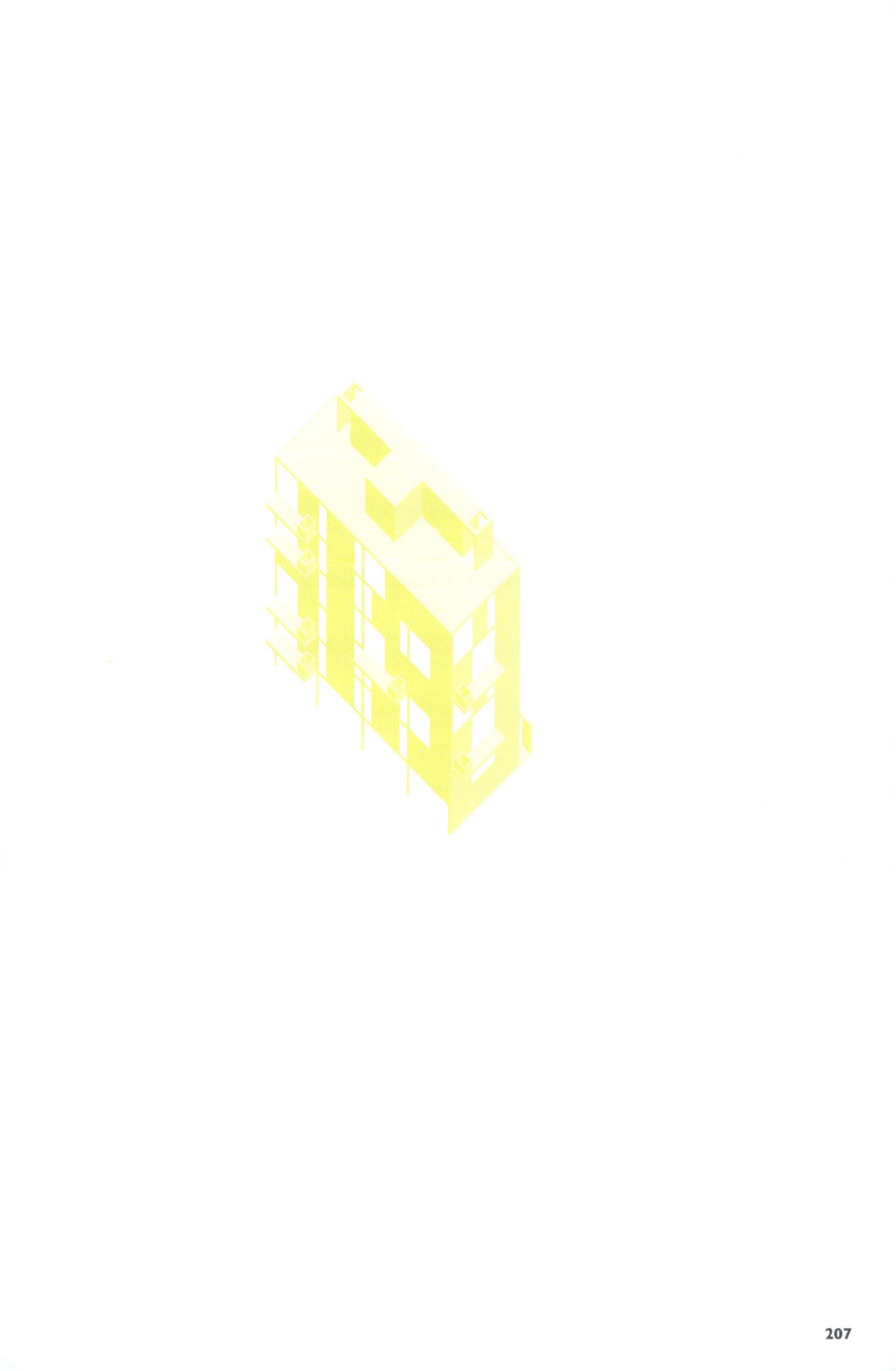

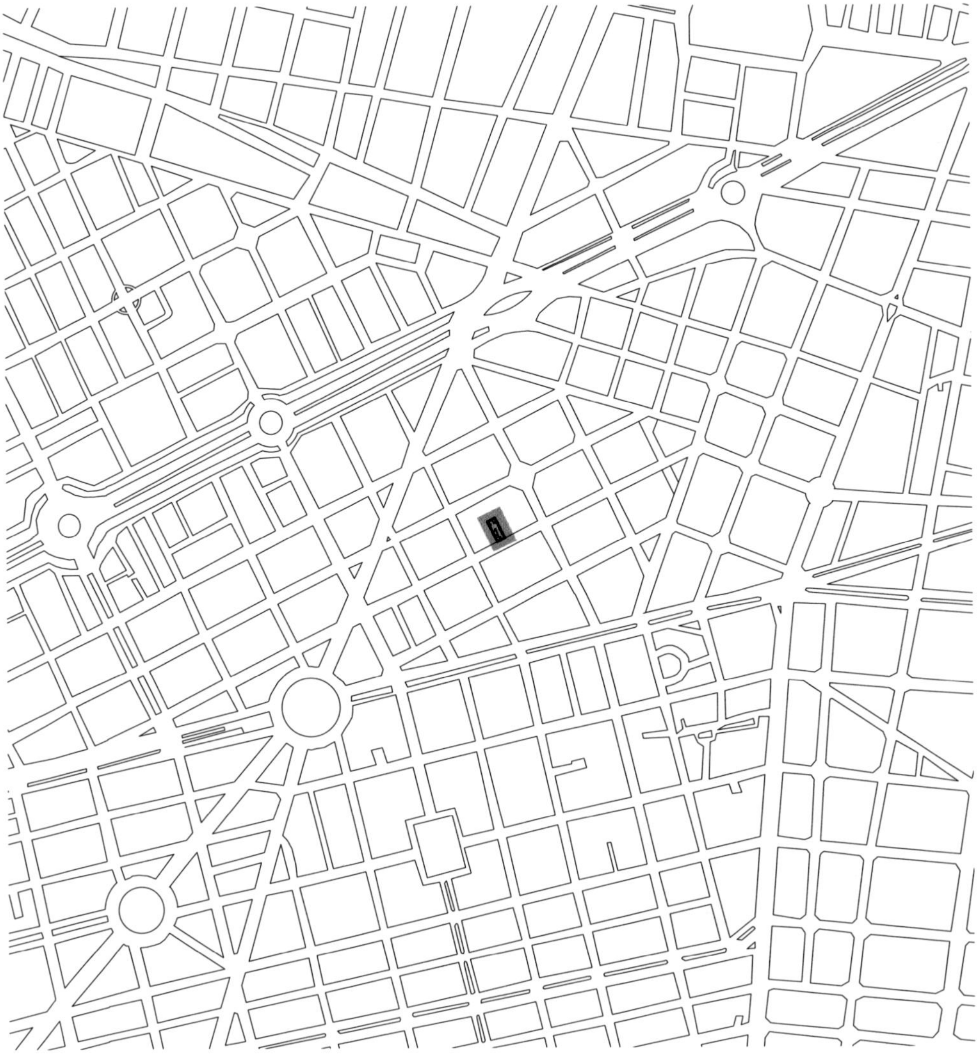

2012, Liverpool 61, Jorge Arvizu, Ignacio del Río, Emmanuel Ramírez, Diego Ricalde and Olga Romano

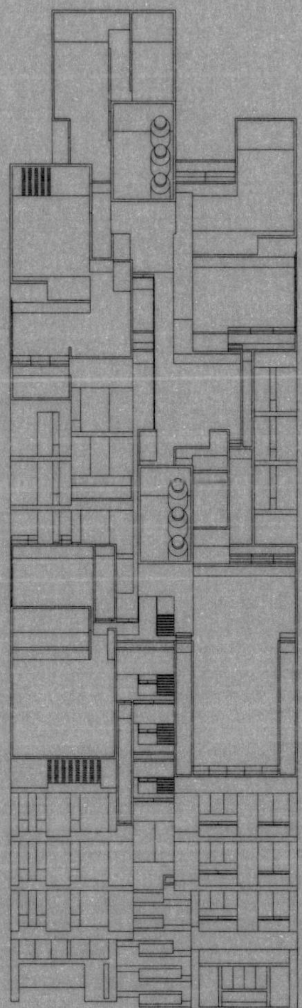

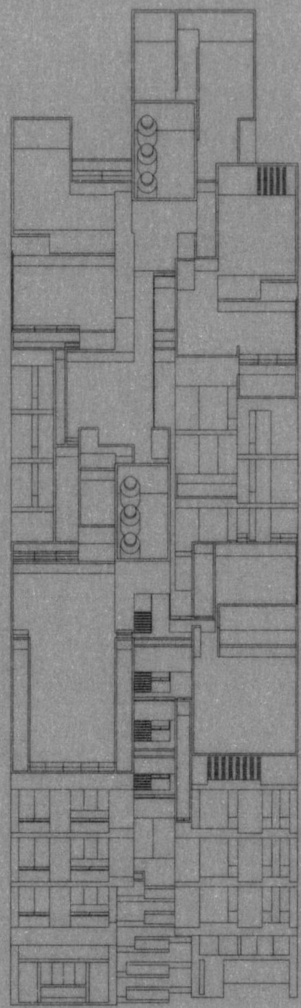

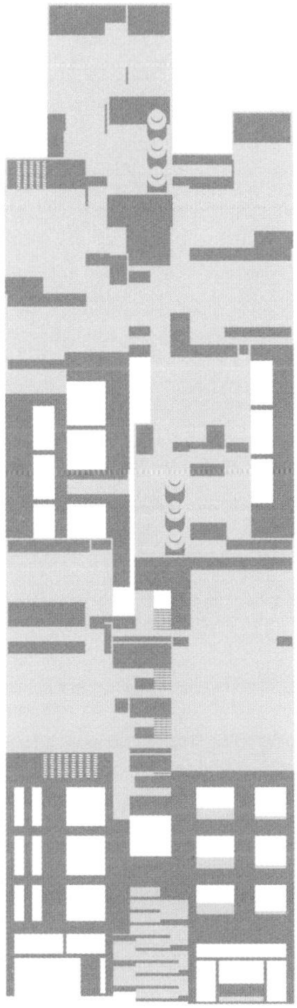

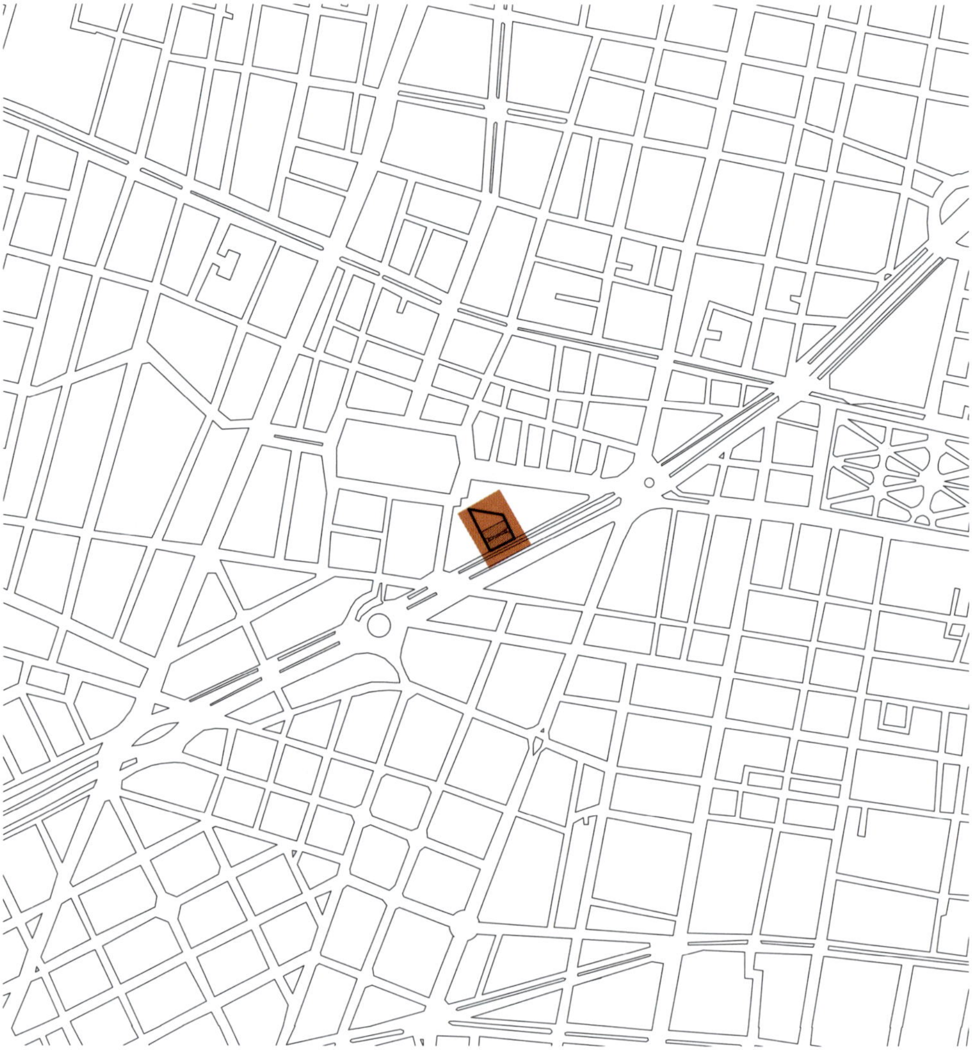

2012, Reforma 27, Alberto Kalach

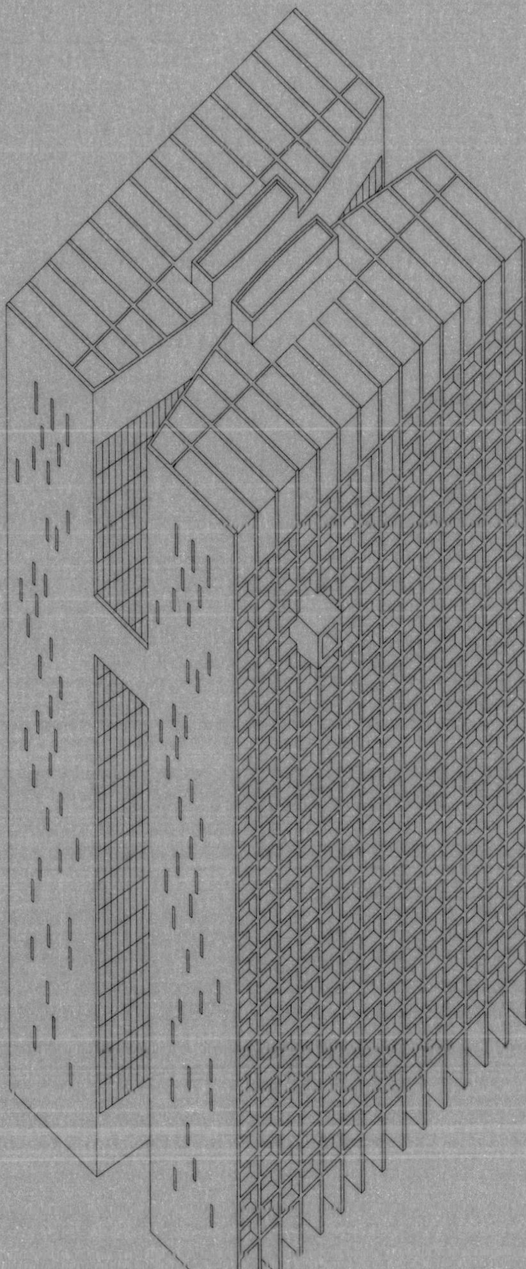

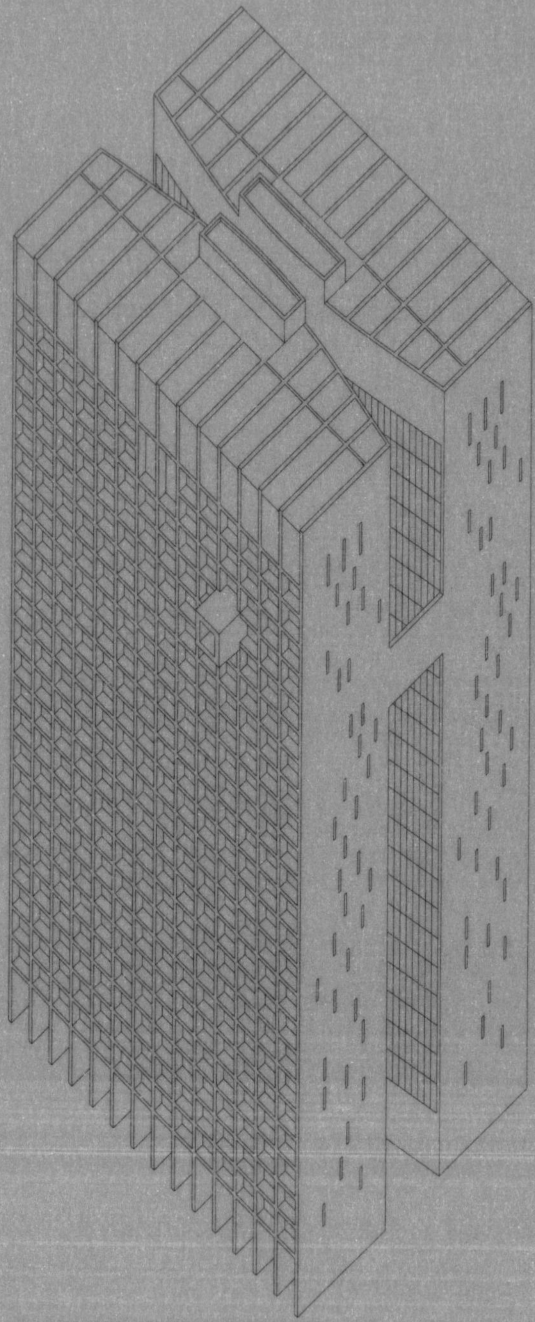

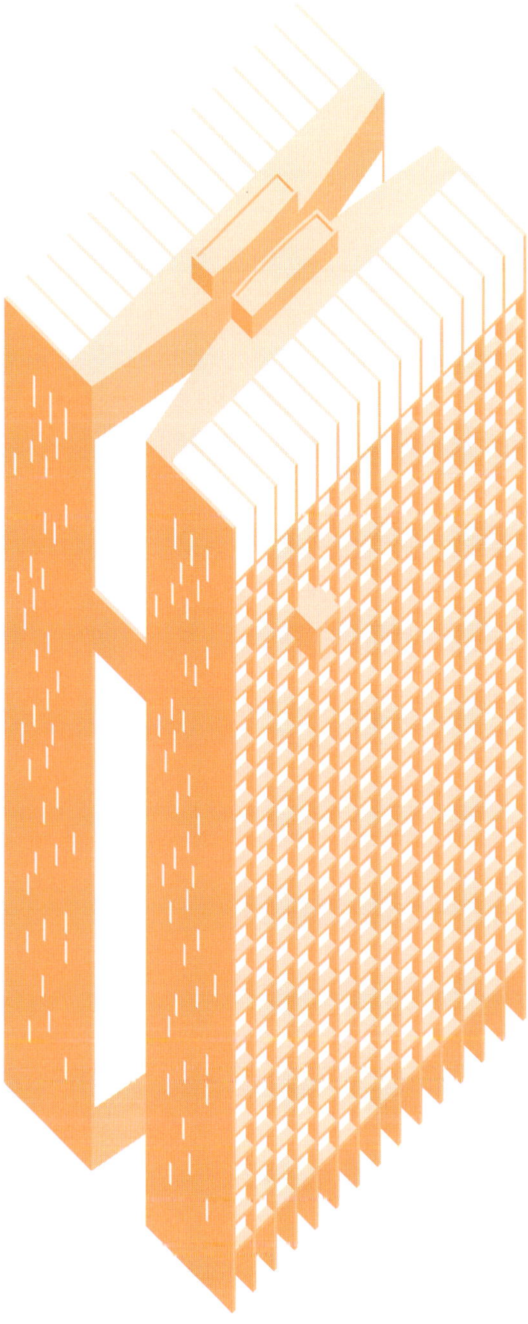

"The relevant debates of our time revolve around affordable housing."[93]

Javier Sánchez, 2005

"Throughout the 19th century, the vast majority lived in the traditional *casa de vecindad*, which consisted of a long, spacious central patio with stairs at the end and homes opening onto it. The outward-facing units, with separate entrances, were larger and had a secondary space, for retail or business, while the inward-facing apartments were smaller. At the back, practically in the dark, there might be other smaller, humbler units called *cuartos redondos*, residences consisting of a single room where people cooked by day and slept by night [...]even using it as a small workshop during the day."[94]

Xavier Guzmán Urbiola, 2008

"Hannes Meyer considered that the patio was the essence of collective housing spaces for people with limited resources (the *casa de vecindad*)."[95]

Enrique X. de Anda, 2008

> "If we built only one house in this area, we were solving one set of problems for them but at the same time creating new ones."[96]
>
> Raúl Cárdenas (Torolab), 2008

> "They have the same horrible 34 square meters and awful materials that force you to spend more on electricity than necessary, while experiencing bitter cold in winter and suffocating heat in summer."[97]
>
> Raúl Cárdenas (Torolab), 2008

93 Julio Gaeta, "Fábrica: una conversación con Javier Sánchez", *Higuera + Sánchez*, Mexico City: Arquine/RM, 2005, 157.
94 Xavier Guzmán Urbiola, *Arquitectura mexicana: vivienda, escuela y hospitales*, Mexico City: Consejo Nacional para la Cultura y las Artes, 2008, 10.
95 Enrique X. de Anda, op. cit., 159.
96 Juan Herreros (ed.), *Vivienda y espacio doméstico en el siglo XXI*, Madrid: La Casa Encendida, 2008, 41.
97 Ibid, 40.

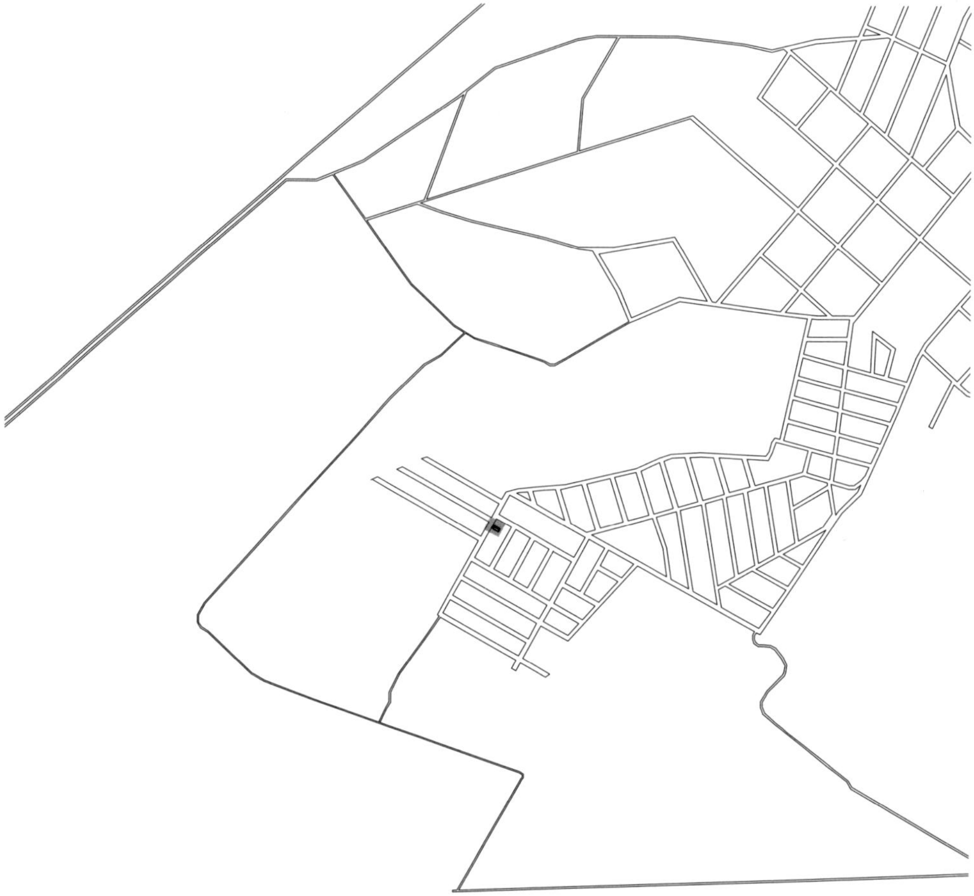

2014, Casa Caja, César Guerrero, Ana Cecilia Garza, Carlos Flores and María Sevilla

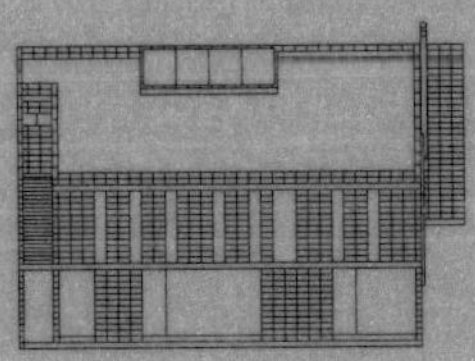

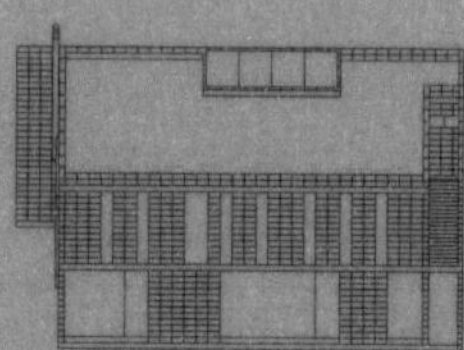

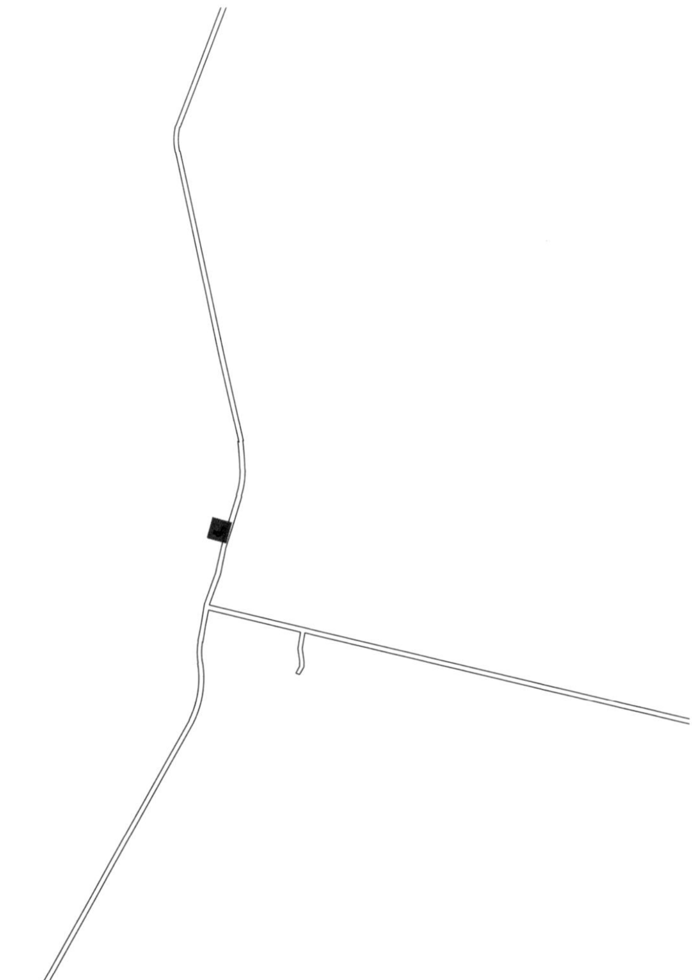

2014, Modular house, Óscar Hagerman and Xuxcab inhabitants

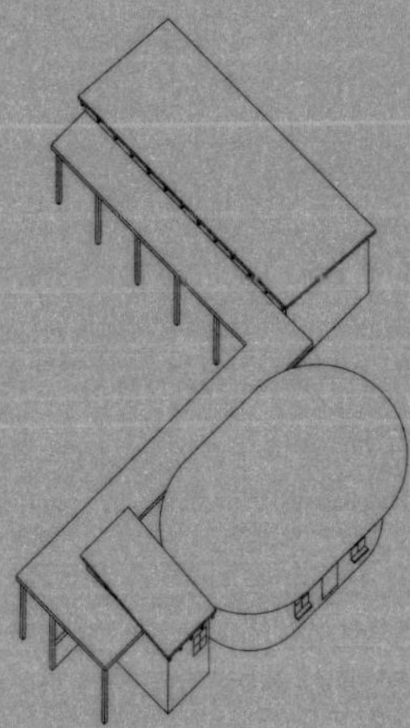

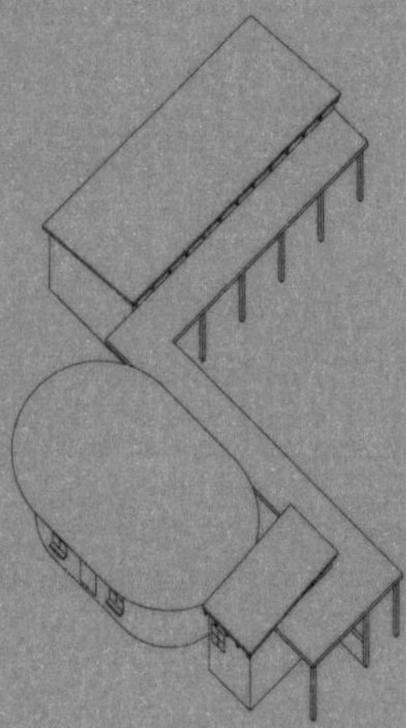

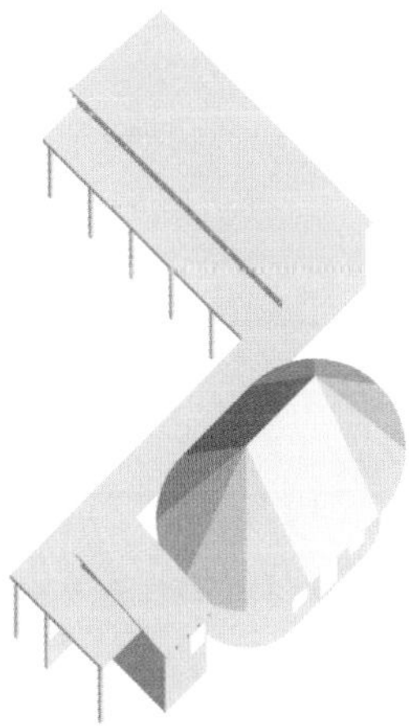

"The Mexican multi-family apartment block moved quickly in a direction that, unlike other architectural types, began at a level of excellence and ran out of steam in less than thirty years, entering the crisis period that continues to this day."[98]

Enrique X. de Anda, 2008

"The construction of apartment blocks changed not only the landscape of Mexico City, but also the dynamics of city life and expectations of appreciation and the capital's housing potential."[99]

Enrique X. de Anda, 2008

"The collective housing block did not rescue the masses from the squalor of the hovels, except in appearance."[100]

Alejandro Hernández Gálvez, 2011

"The relationship between residential architecture and urban architecture has not been resolved."[101]

Carlos Mijares, 2012

"I think Alberti's notion of the city as a great house and the house as a small city is a good simile, and one worth recovering."[102]

Alberto Kalach, 2012

98 Enrique X. de Anda, *Vivienda colectiva de la modernidad en México: los multifamiliares durante el periodo presidencial de Miguel Alemán, 1946-1952,* Mexico City: Instituto de Investigaciones Estéticas-Universidad Nacional Autónoma de México, 2008, op. cit., 21.

99 Ibid., 26.

100 Alejandro Hernández Gálvez, "Ubi? Quo? Unde? Qua?", June 8, 2011; available at otrootroblog.blogspot.mx, accessed December 13, 2015.

101 Alberto Kalach and Fernando Fernández (eds.), *Croquis: los dibujos de Carlos Mijares*, Mexico City: Consejo Nacional para la Cultura y las Artes/Contornos, 2015, 35.

102 Ibid., 163.

2014, Regional single housing, Alberto Kalach + TAX

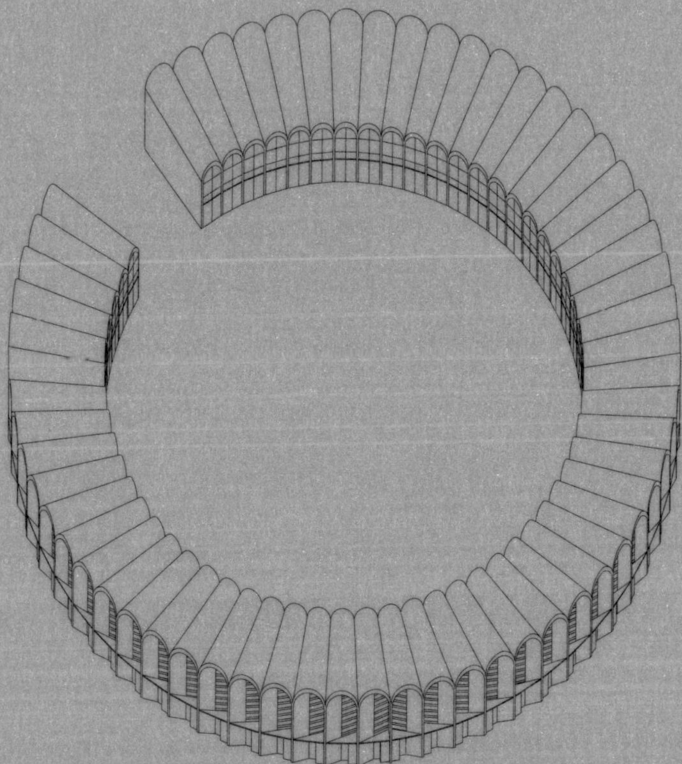

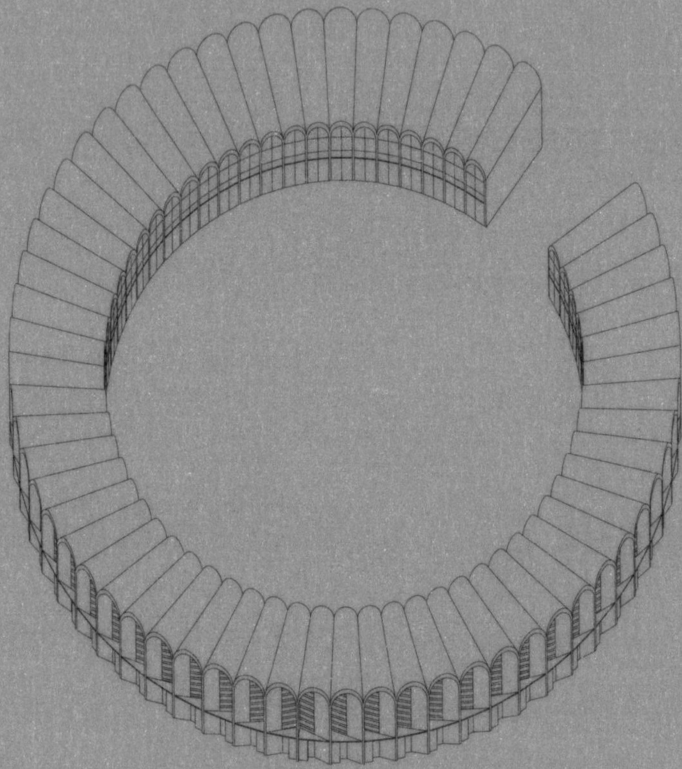

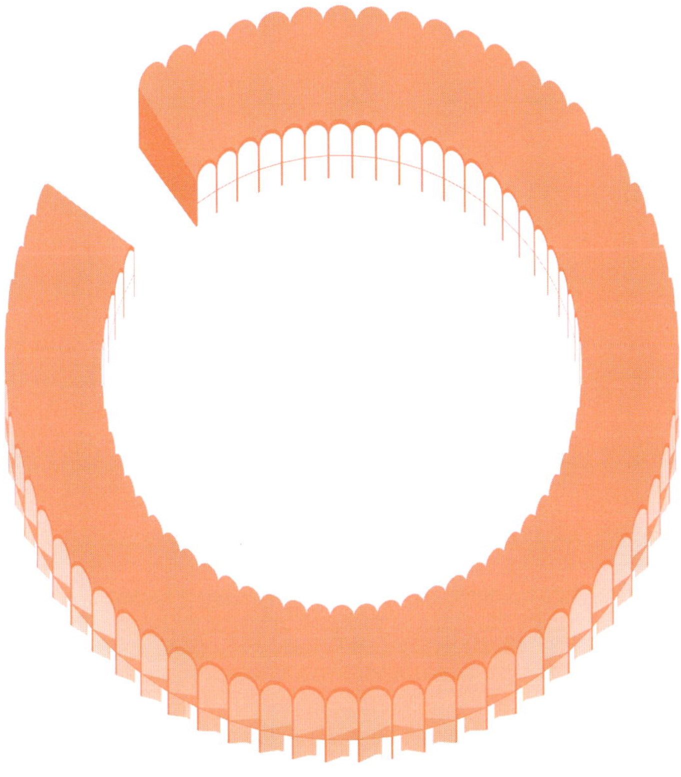

2014 Bosco Housing, Alberto Kalach + TAX

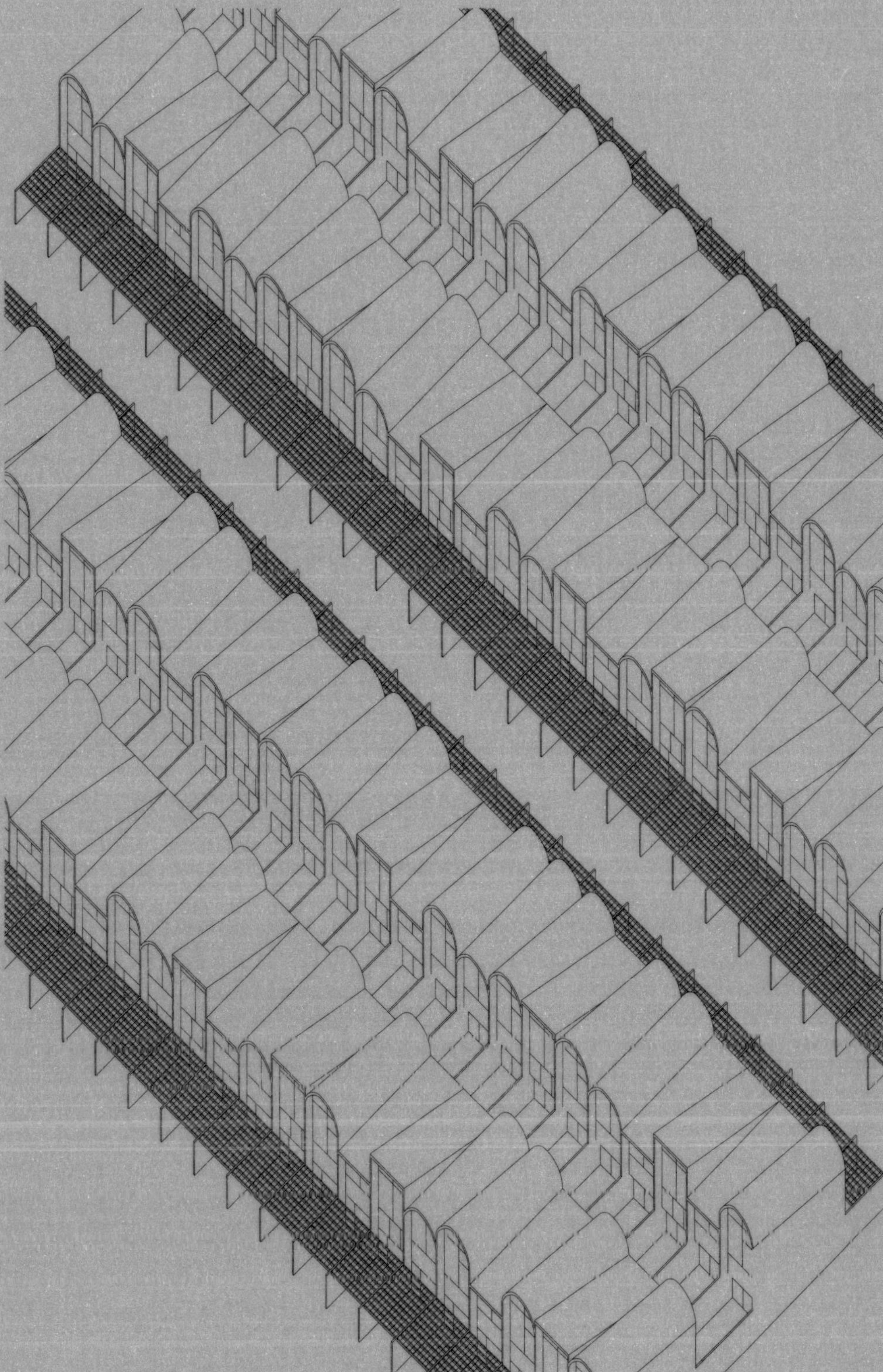

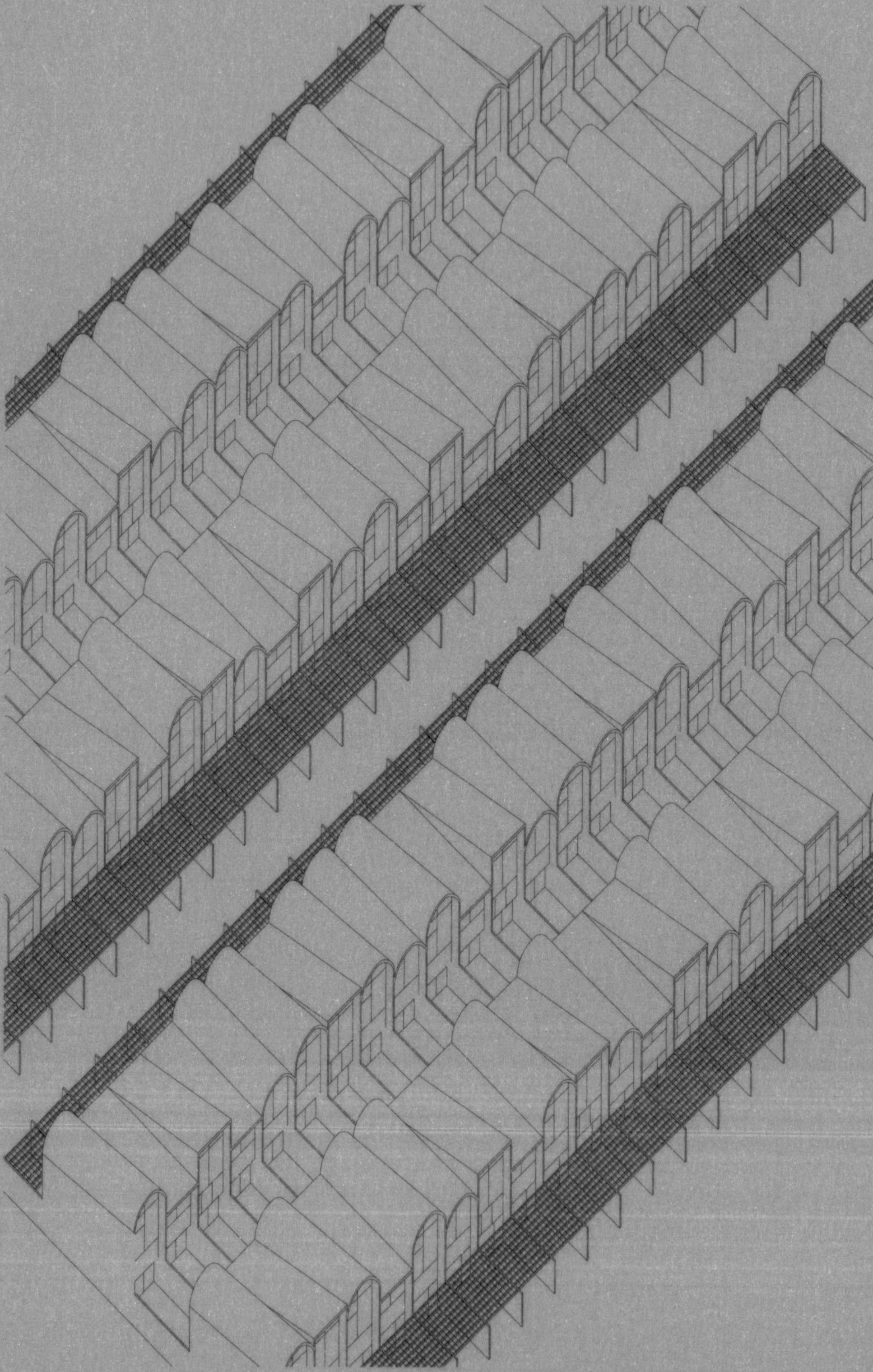

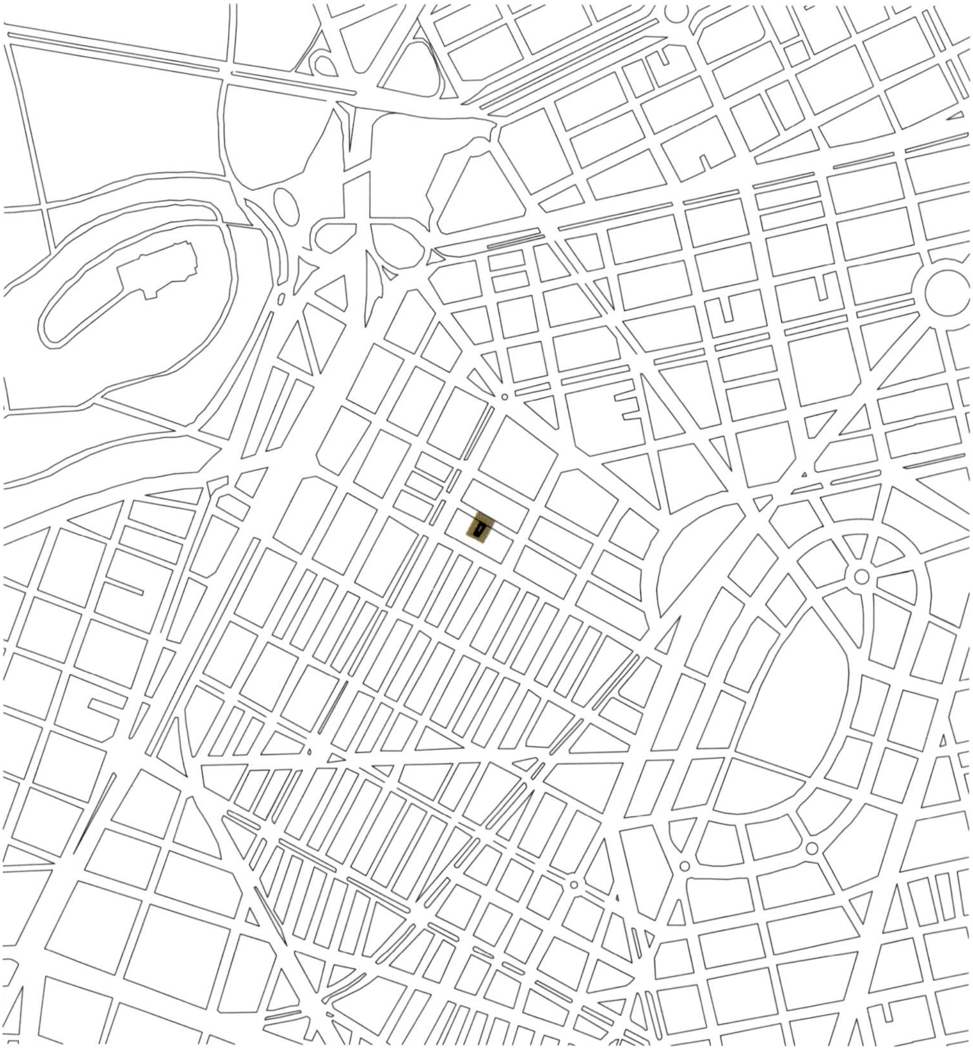

2014, Antonio Sola, Jorge Ambrosi, Gabriela Etchegaray and Gerardo Reyes

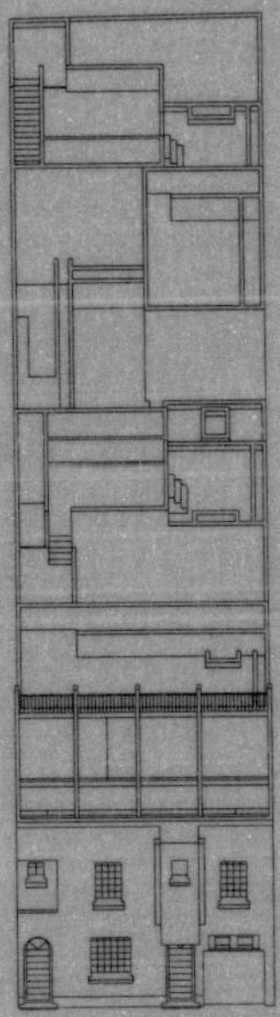

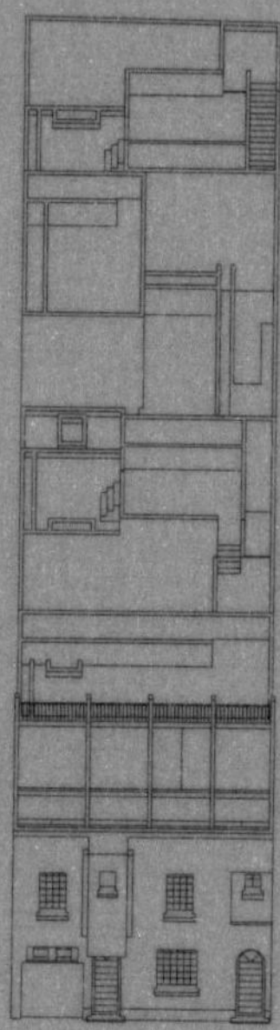

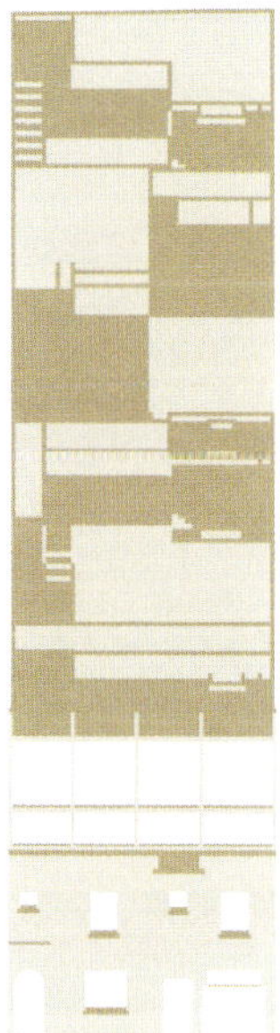

"Today, one hundred years later, we must make a fresh start; we urgently need another *new vision* for housing, this time inserted in the city."[103]

Félix Sánchez, 2013

"A new, modern society is not necessarily one that makes spectacular buildings, but rather one that helps people live with dignity and respects all human beings."[104]

Óscar Hagerman, 2014

"I've attempted to make housing simple, just as rural communities know how to do."[105]

Óscar Hagerman, 2015

"Through the lens of housing and its layout in the city, we can observe the persistence of social inequality."[106]

Félix Sánchez, 2013

"Collective housing is perhaps the most conventional and least evolved typology."[107]

Miquel Adrià, 2013

"Housing policy should be based on land use policy, an urban policy that brings order to the territory and growth of cities."[108]

Ernesto Alva, 2013

103 Félix Sánchez, *Vivienda adentro: la arquitectura (no) importa,* Mexico City: Arquine, 2013, 121.
104 Óscar Hagerman, *Arquitectura y diseño,* Mexico City: Arquine, 2014, 195.
105 Interview with Óscar Hagerman, January 19, 2015.
106 Félix Sánchez, op. cit., 122.
107 Miquel Adrià, "Vivienda colectiva", *Arquine*, no. 64, Summer 2013, 1.
108 Ernesto Alva, op. cit., 113.

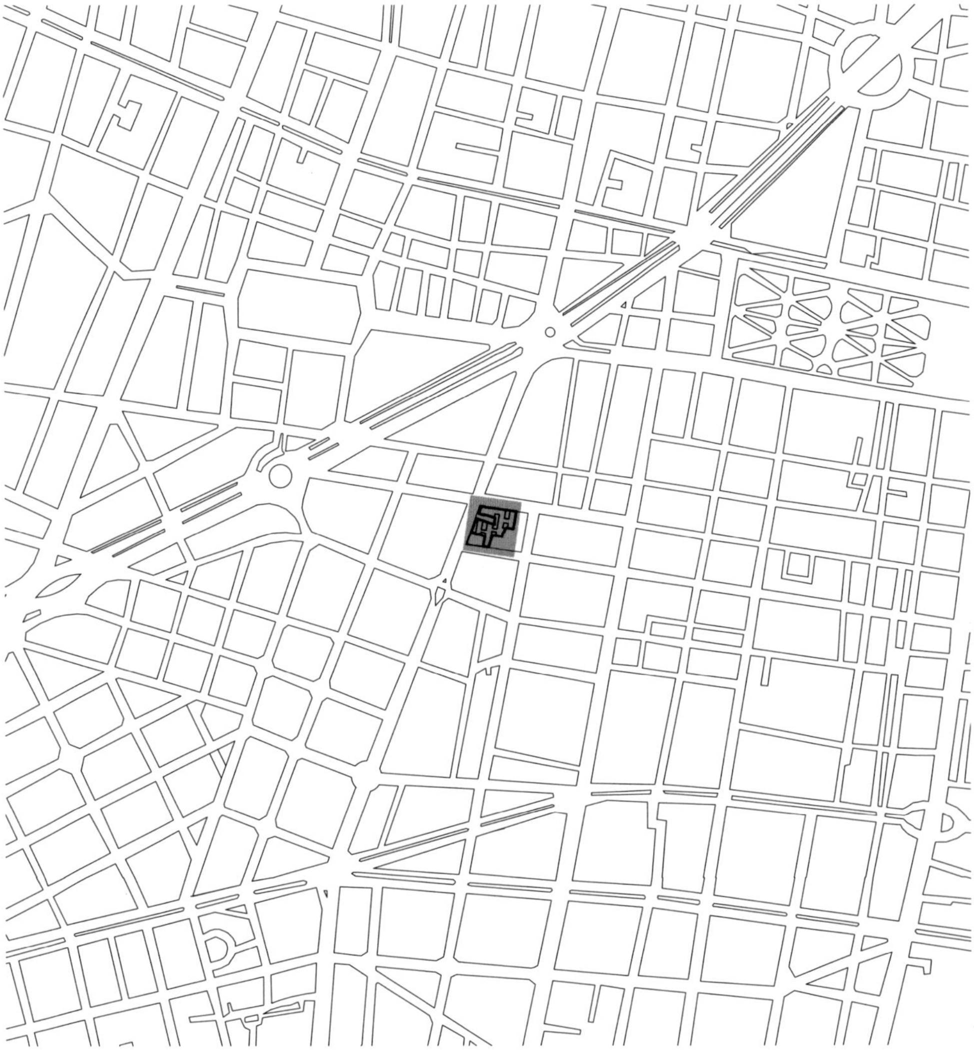

2014, Bucareli, Juan Herreros

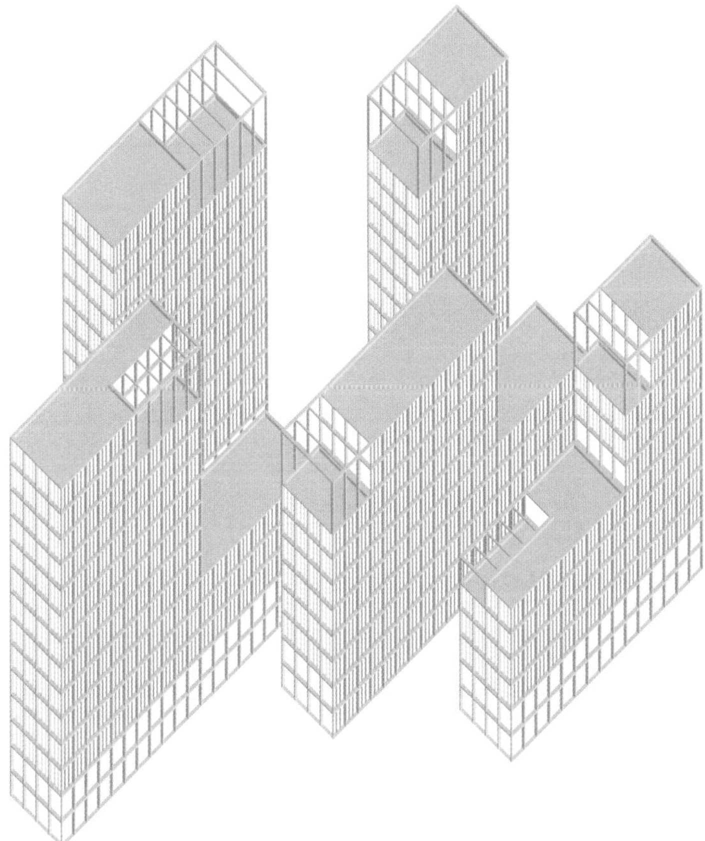

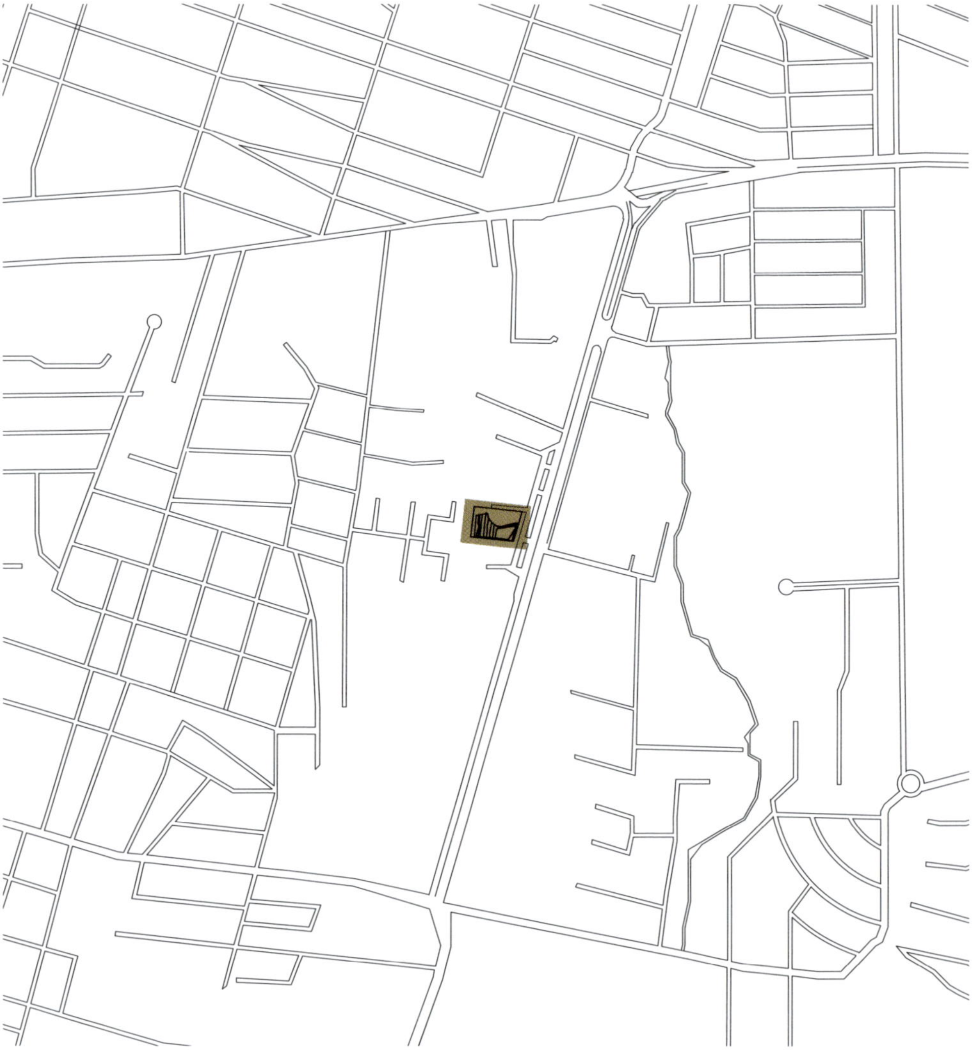

2015, High Park, Michel Rojkind

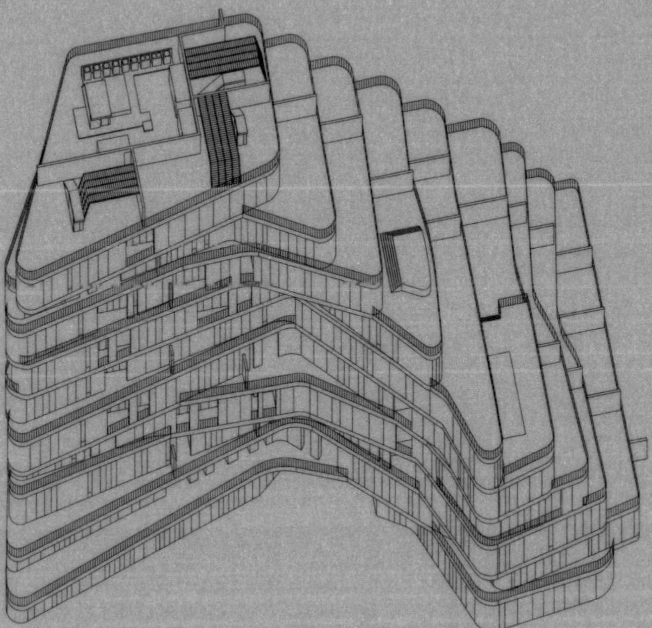

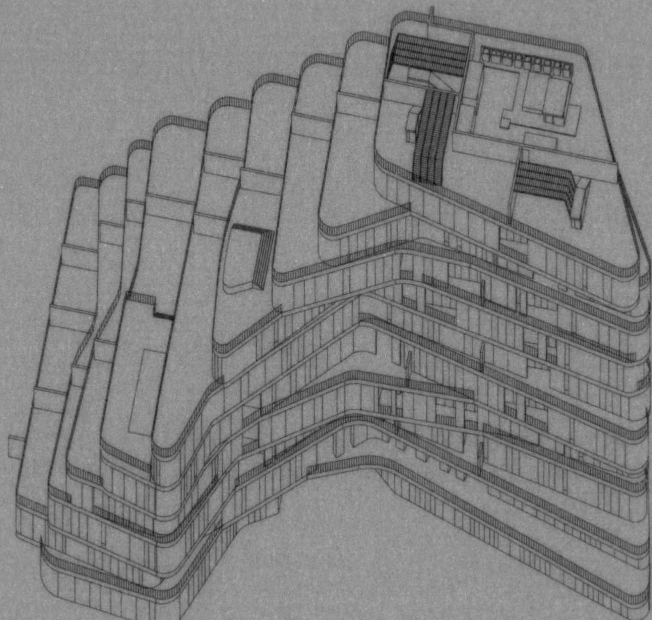

"It's a shame that the highly successful housing units created between the 1950s and 1970s, which produced integrated communities, are no longer being built."[109]

Agustín Landa, 2014

"Until about twenty-five years ago, there were precise zoning regulations that established the ratios of various necessary land uses, according to the number of homes and building density, trying to achieve a reasonable diversity of uses."[110]

Gustavo López Padilla, 2015

"In France, the [housing] sector's net profits are between 1 and 2%, while in Mexico they are between 30 and 35%. They build cheap and sell expensive."[111]

Tatiana Bilbao, 2015

"Those little houses we see piled on the city outskirts like garbage."[112]

Alberto Kalach, 2016

"98% of construction is not designed by architects. The developers and mortgage banks, using the same housing model, have run the business for years. The DIY homes that people build themselves are actually more effective."[113]

Francisco Pardo, 2016

"Trees should be included in the cost of housing."[114]

Alberto Kalach, 2016

109 Interview with Agustín Landa, July 22, 2014.

110 "Pasado memorable, incierto futuro. Navegando la arquitectura. Crítica y reflexiones en torno a la arquitectura y las ciudades", May 12, 2015; available at: https://navegandolaarquitectura.wordpress.com, accessed July 25, 2015.

111 Inder Bugarin, "Critican lucro con la vivienda 'cajón'", in *Reforma,* May 20, 2015, 20.

112 Alberto Kalach, lecture given at Mextrópoli, teatro Metropólitan, Mexico City, March 8, 2016.

113 Alejandro Hernández Gálvez (ed.), *Habitar la ciudad: la obligación de la arquitectura,* Mexico City: Arquine, 2016, 46.

114 Alberto Kalach, op. cit..

2015, Rinconada Margaritas, Luis Aldrete

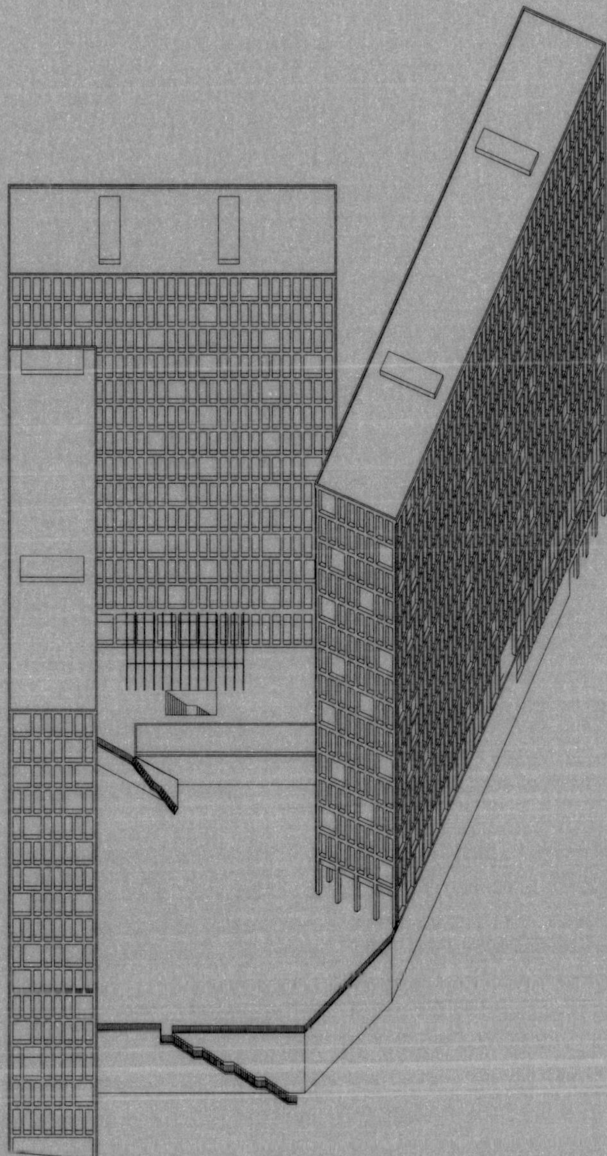

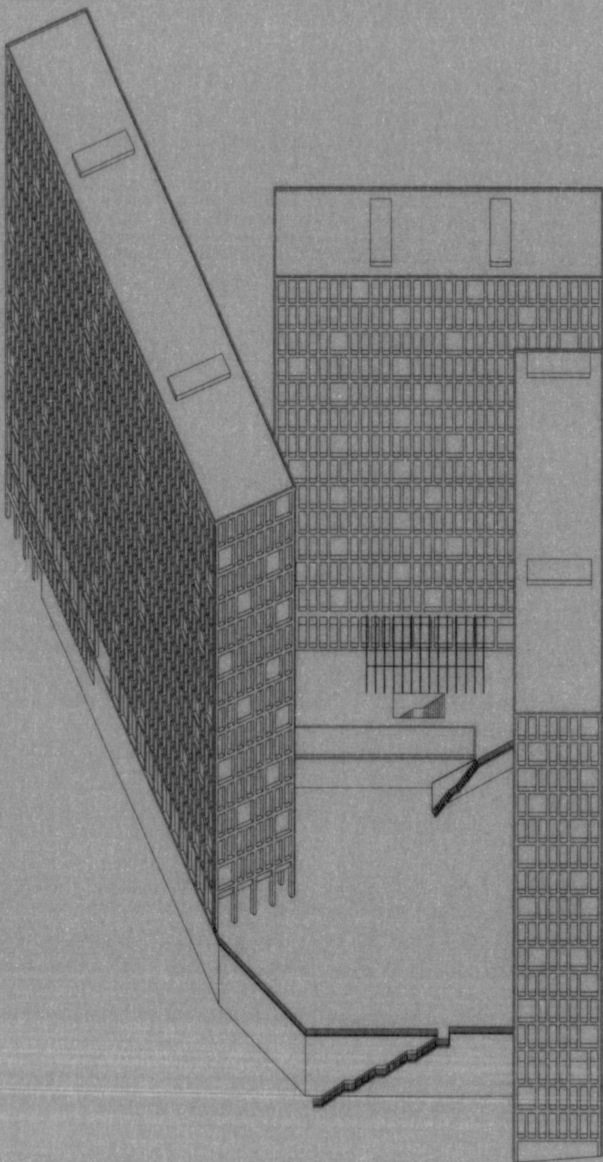

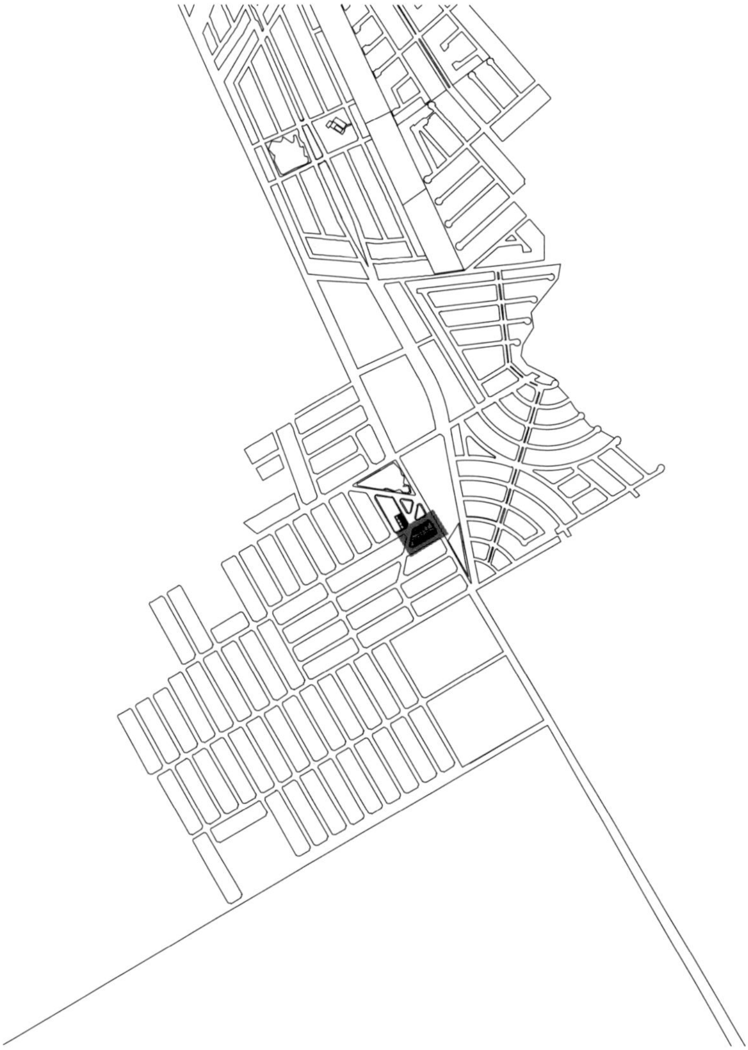

2015, Sustainable Housing, Tatiana Bilbao

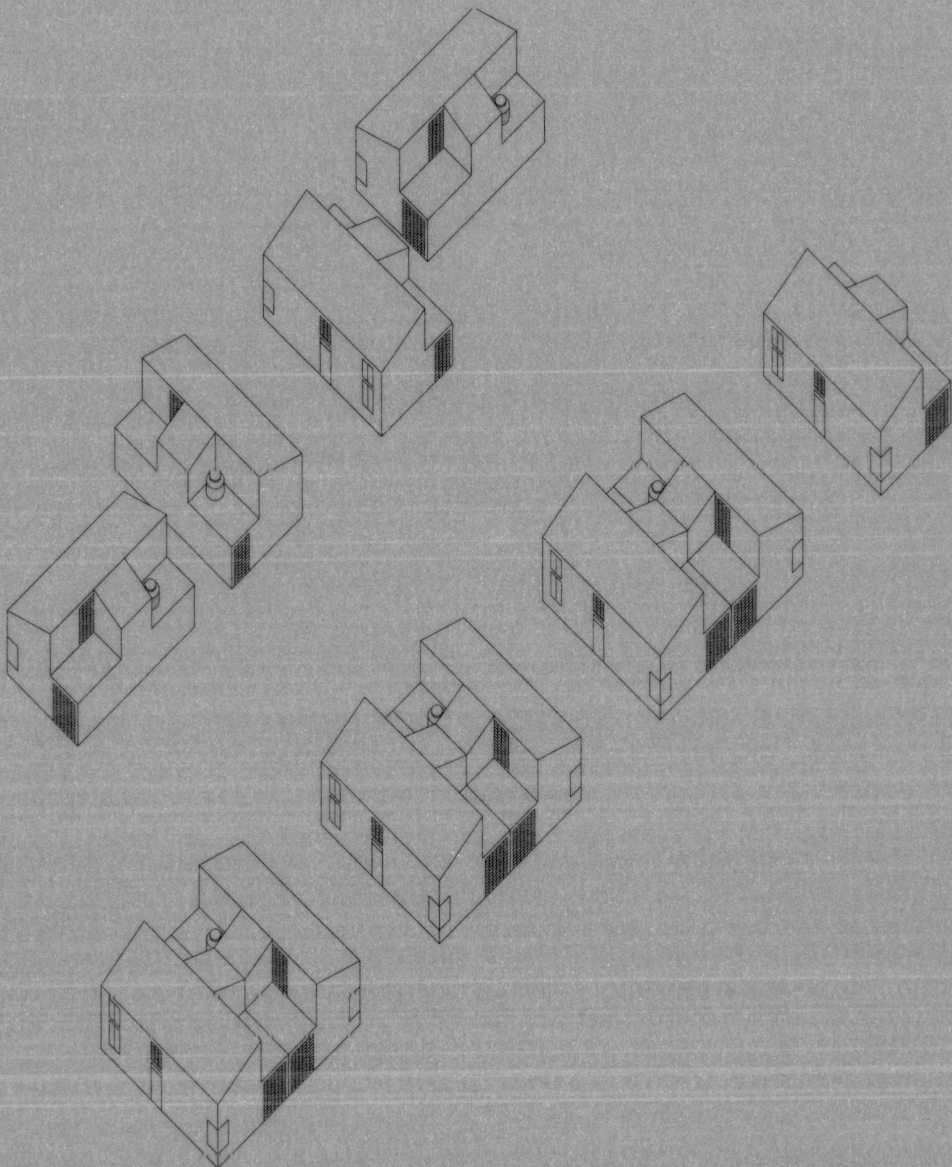

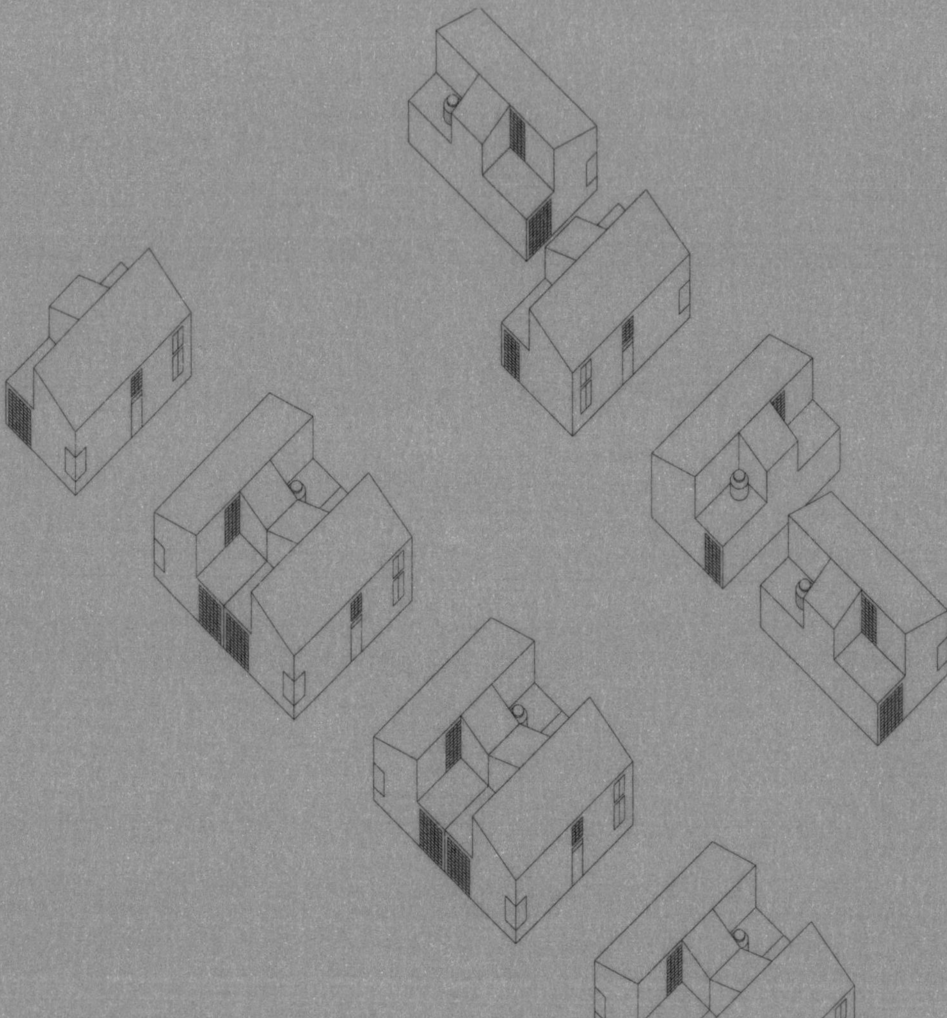

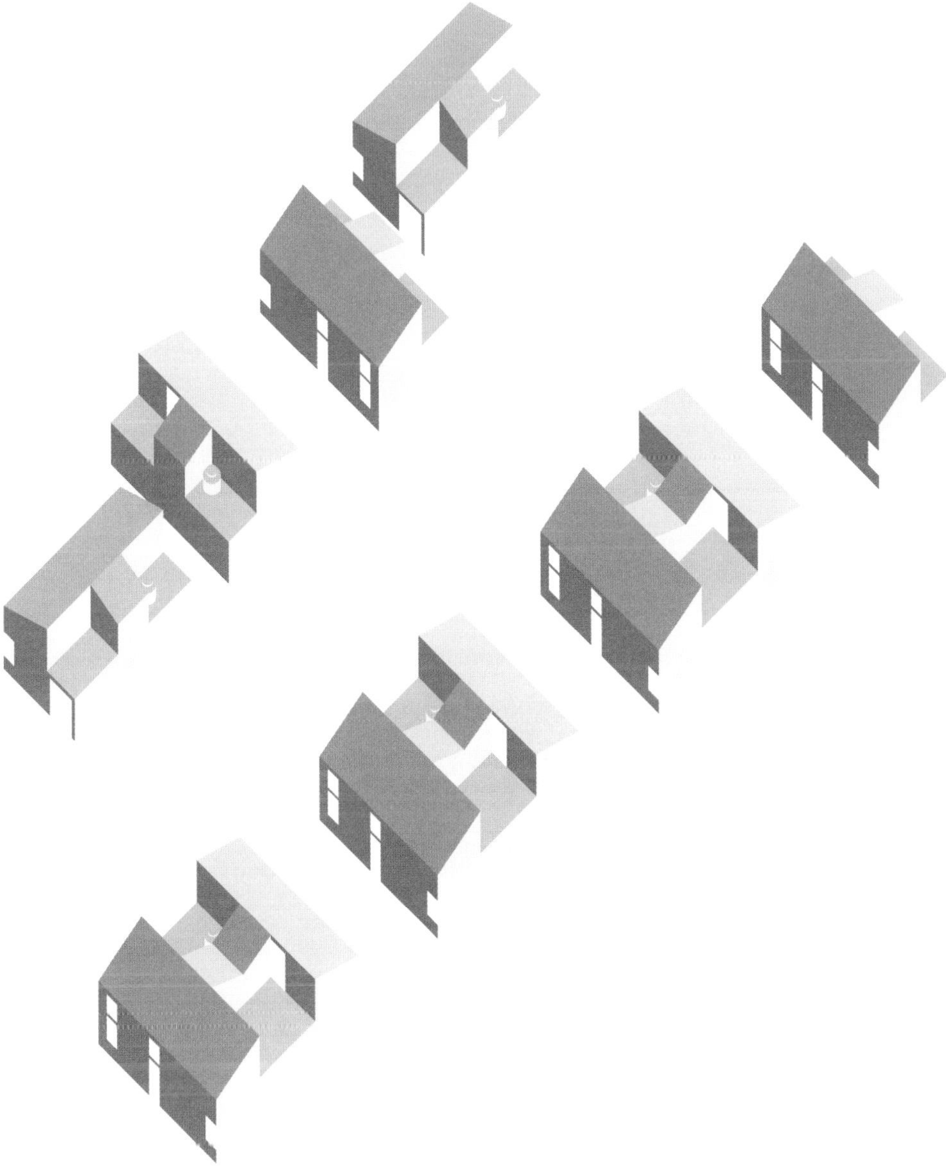

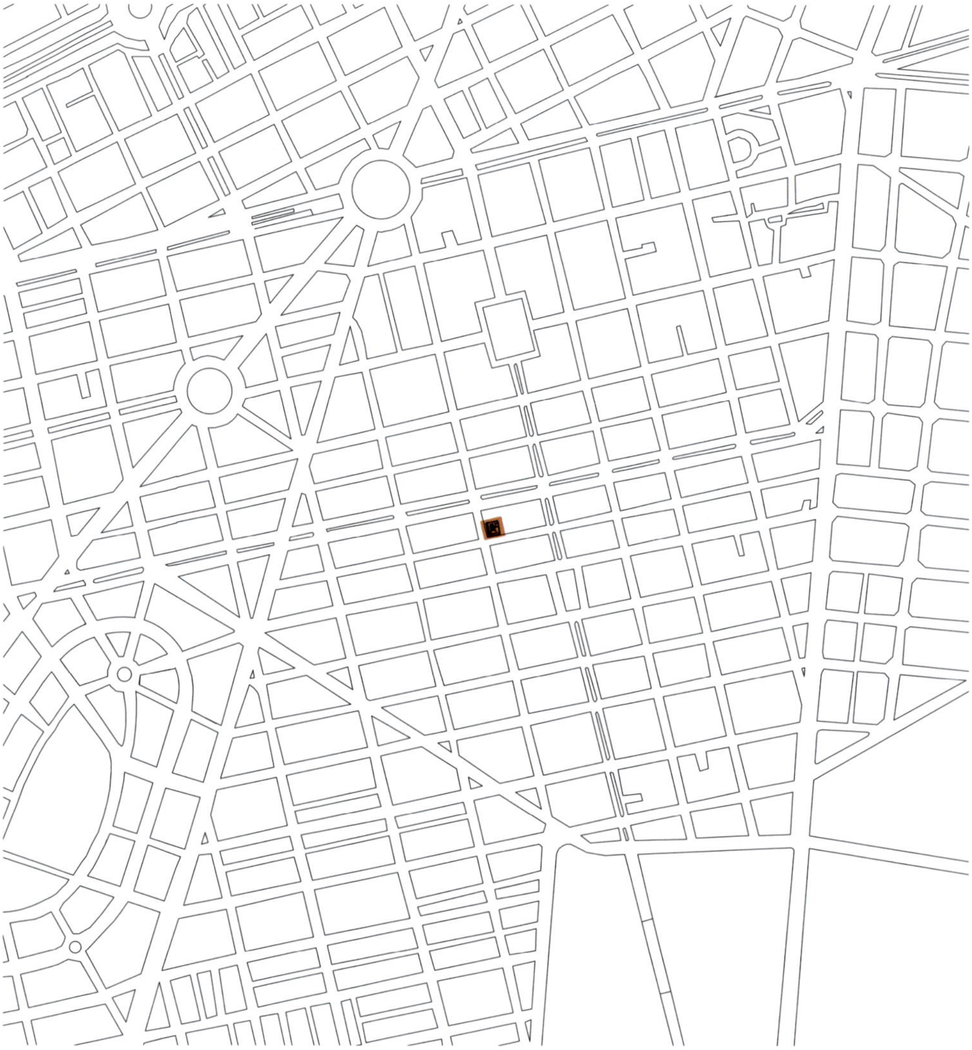

2015, CH-ReUrbano, Cadaval & Solà-Morales

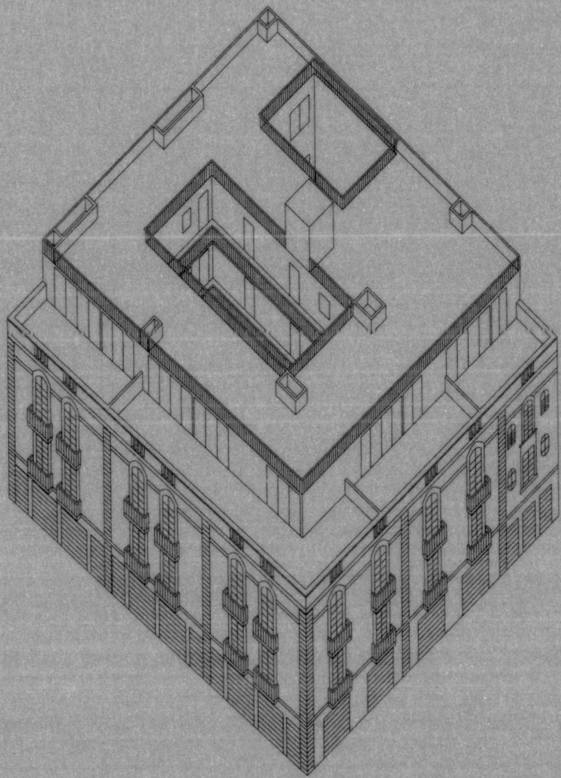

"That mix of street and home goes beyond the ideal combination that Le Corbusier imagined in his unité d'habitation: a building that barely touches the ground but features an interior street, where the 'home' is accompanied by the store, school, and gym. Though the building dreams it is independent –a dream which is often mere illusion or, worse, a nightmare– its own logic is determined by conditions too complex to imagine that these should be the sole responsibility of the private sphere."[115]

Alejandro Hernández Gálvez, 2016

"Why is the government determined to make every Mexican a homeowner, regardless of the home's quality, situation, or proximity of services? The buyer is not the one who profits. We know very well who does."[116]

Francisco Pardo, 2017

"Housing developers have saved so much that they have forgotten to think."[117]

Alberto Kalach, 2016

"The very nature of social welfare housing ought to encourage a sense of belonging, rootedness, pride, and dignity."[118]

Jorge Ambrosi and Gabriela Etchegaray, 2017

"Houses comprise 70% of cities. If we improve housing, we improve the city."[119]

Carlos Zedillo, 2016

115 Alejandro Hernandez Gálvez (ed.), Habitar la ciudad: la obligación de la arquitectura, Mexico City: Arquine, 2016, 8.
116 Francisco Pardo, "¿Dónde vivo?", in Apuntes sobre la vivienda social, Mexico City: Arquine/Instituto del Fondo Nacional de la Vivienda para los Trabajadores, Infonavit, 2017, 106.
117 Alberto Kalach, lecture given at the Housing masters degree program, In Centro, Centro de Diseño, Cine y Televisión, Mexico City, April 13, 2016.
118 Jorge Ambrosi and Gabriela Etchegaray, "Ensayo sobre el espacio para la vivienda social", Apuntes sobre la vivienda social, Mexico City: Arquine/Instituto del Fondo Nacional de la Vivienda para los Trabajadores, Infonavit, 2017, 41.
119 Carlos Zedillo, El reto de la vivienda en México, Mexico City: Instituto del Fondo Nacional de la Vivienda para los Trabajadores, Infonavit, 2016, 5.

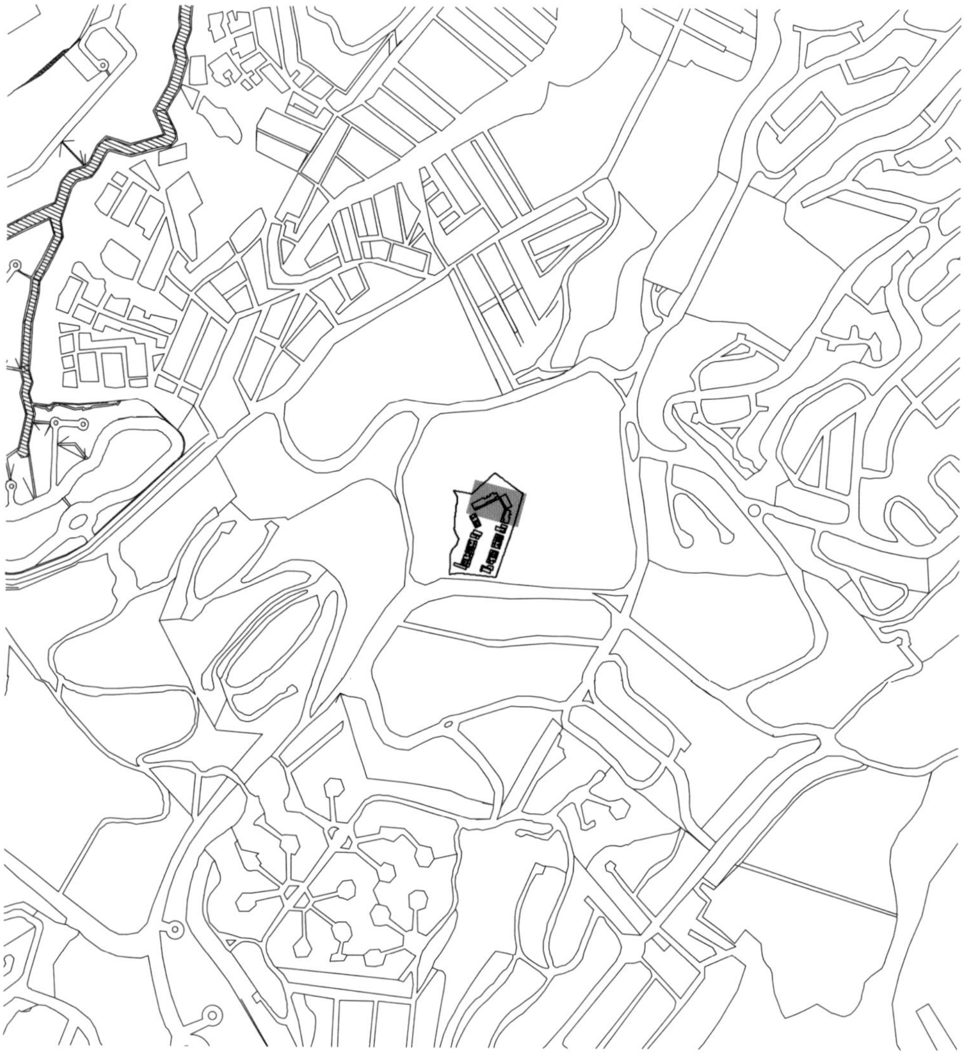

2016, Central Park Interlomas, Migdal Arquitectos

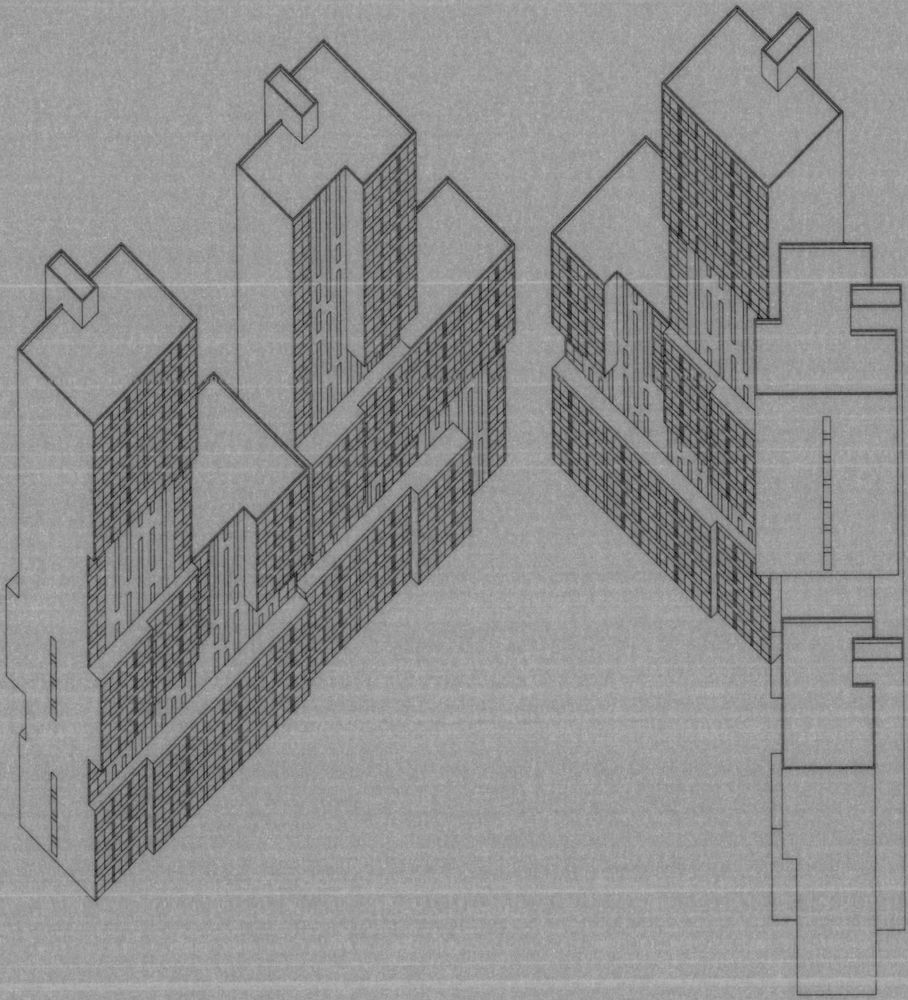

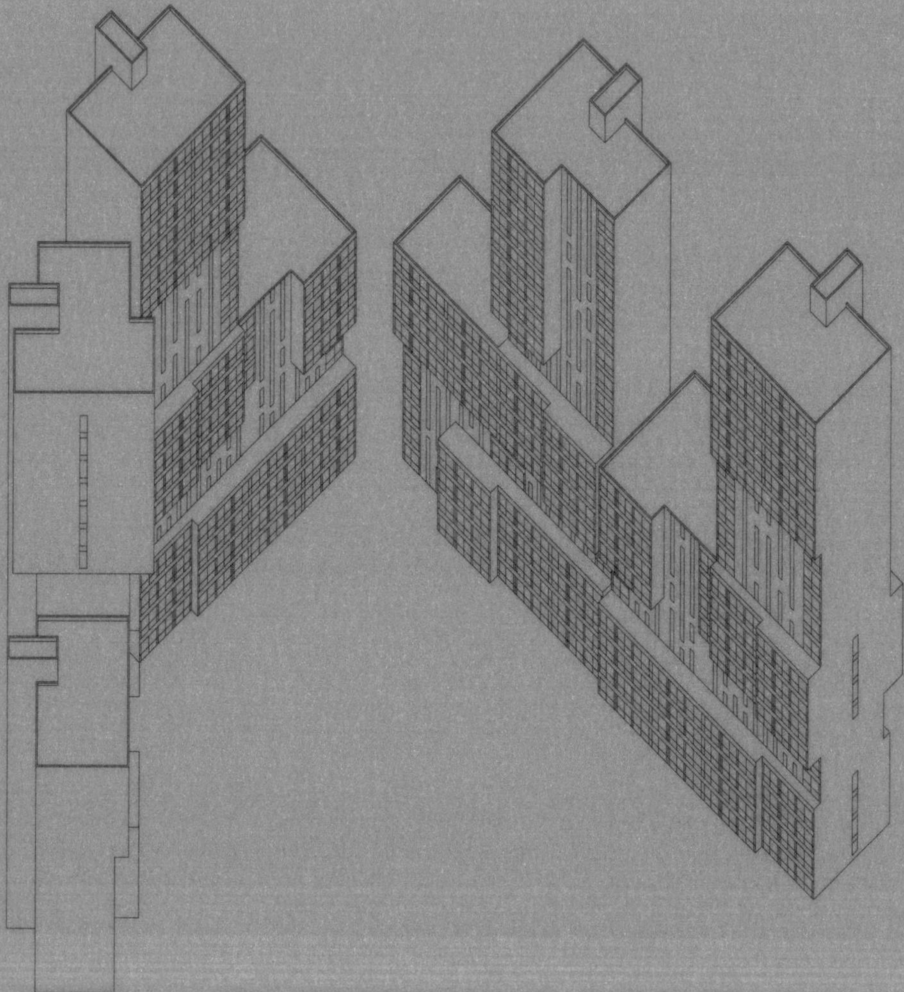

2016, Un Cuarto Más, Rozana Montiel

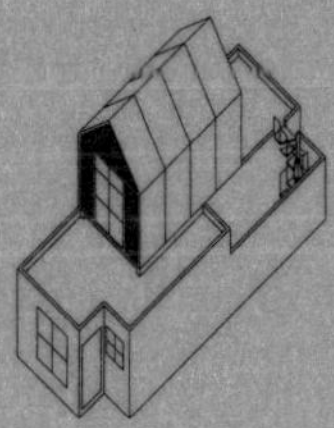

"To rethink that increasingly ephemeral, global, and less social machine for dwelling."[120]

Mauricio Rocha y Gabriela Carrillo, 2017

"Considering that the useful life of a work completed with federal funds must be at least twenty-five years to justify the investment, why are houses or developments constructed largely with tax incentives or public financing only required to work properly for one year?"[121]

Bernardo Gómez Pimienta, 2017

"Every house has similar spaces but different desires, and those desires warrant a response."[122]

Juan Carlos Cano y Paloma Vera, 2017

"We see the process of creating housing as a concerted effort, a combination of various people's labor, knowledge, and talent."[123]

S-AR, 2017

"Homes are built to the smallest legally permissible dimensions, condemning families to spend their entire lives cramped in a few square feet."[124]

Manuel Cervantes, 2017

"Collective housing weaves the fabric that fills the gaps in the mesh of the city."[125]

Miquel Adrià, 2017

120 Mauricio Rocha and Gabriela Carrillo, "De la cantera a la vivienda: Xaltocan", in *Apuntes sobre la vivienda social,* Mexico City: Arquine/Instituto del Fondo Nacional de la Vivienda para los Trabajadores, Infonavit, 2017, 184.

121 Bernardo Gómez Pimienta, "¿Por qué recuperar los conjuntos habitacionales abandonados?", in *Apuntes sobre la vivienda social,* Mexico City: Arquine/Instituto del Fondo Nacional de la Vivienda para los Trabajadores, Infonavit, 2017, op. cit., 57.

122 Juan Carlos Cano and Paloma Vera, "Vivienda Social: partimos del hecho de que toda vivienda es social", in *Apuntes sobre la vivienda social,* Mexico City: Arquine/Instituto del Fondo Nacional de la Vivienda para los Trabajadores, Infonavit, 2017, op. cit., 67.

123 Interview with César Guerrero and Ana Cecilia Garza, Tijuana, September 2, 2017.

124 Manuel Cervantes, "México y la vivienda", in Apuntes sobre la vivienda social, Mexico City: Arquine/Instituto del Fondo Nacional de la Vivienda para los Trabajadores, Infonavit, 2017, op. cit., 71.

125 Miquel Adrià, "Sobre la vivienda social", in *Apuntes sobre la vivienda social,* Mexico City: Arquine/Instituto del Fondo Nacional de la Vivienda para los Trabajadores, Infonavit, 2017, op. cit., 34.

2016, Del Territorio al Habitante, Alberto Kalach + TAX

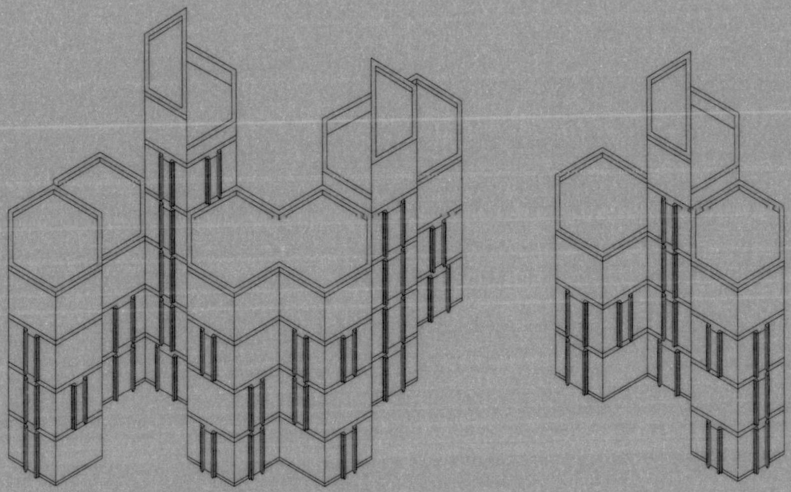

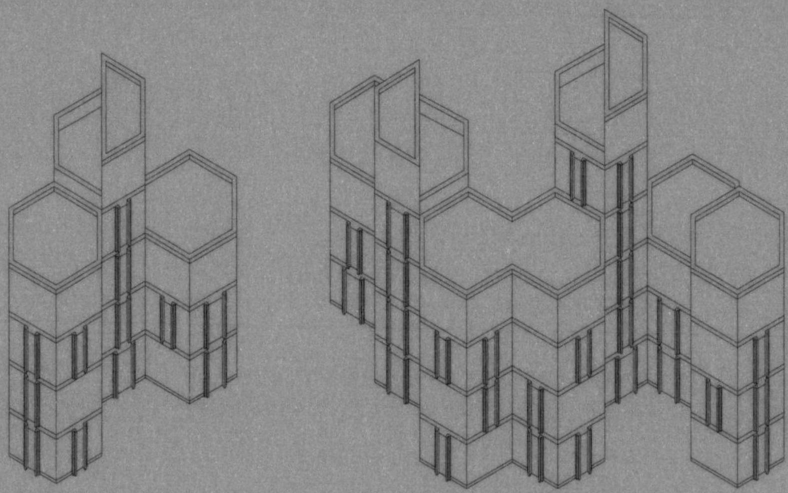

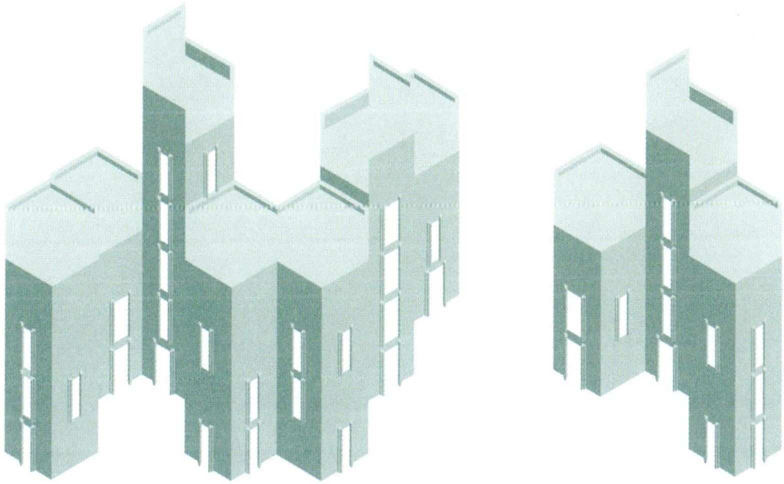

2017, Productive House, Fernanda Canales

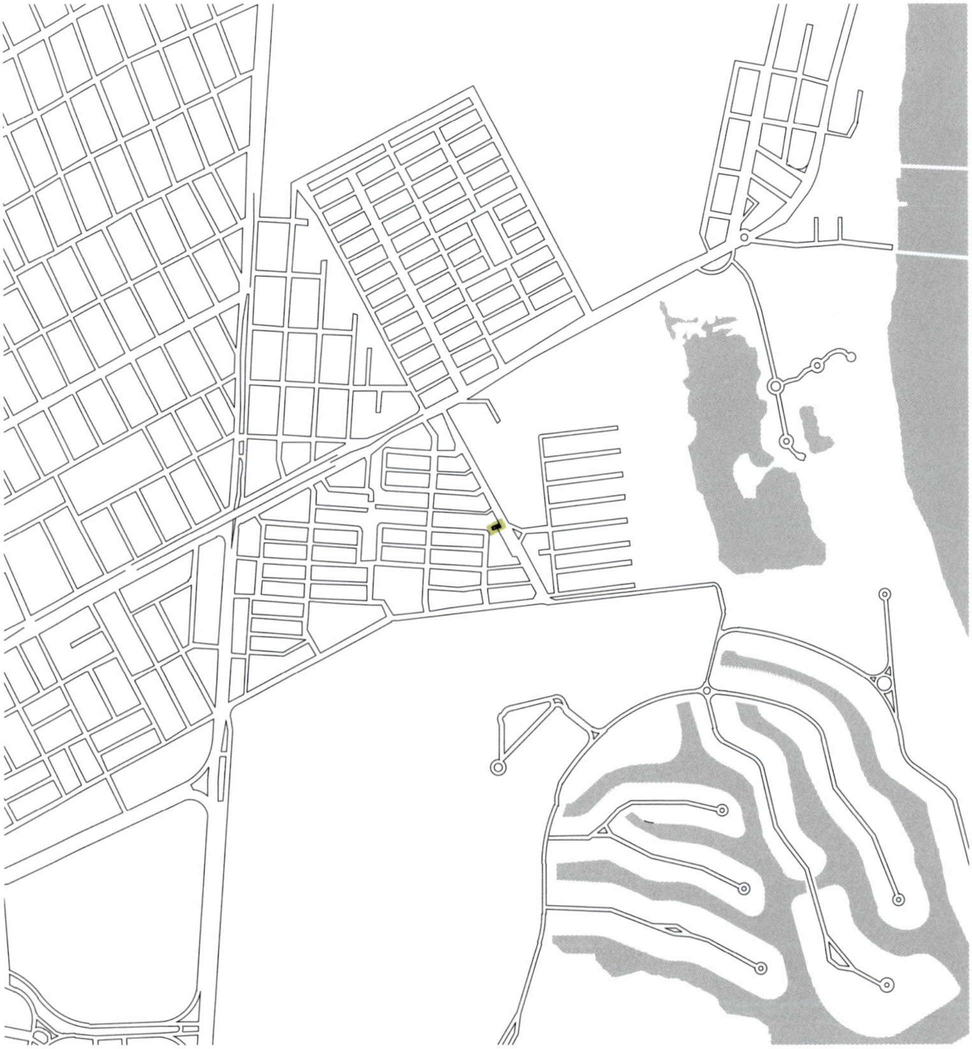

2017, Donceles Studios, Juan Carral

"The manner of constructing social welfare housing, at least in Mexico and Latin America, has not introduced any improvements in spatial quality; not only has it not improved, but the value of the land and the zeal for profit have made social welfare housing narrower and more dehumanized every day [...] the design of common areas, large terraces, and purposeful spaces has been lost."[126]

Mauricio Rocha and Gabriela Carrillo, 2017

"And if home is where your information and your data is –if home is where your cell phone is– then is design perhaps less important than appearance?"[127]

Alejandro Hernández Gálvez, 2017

"Social welfare housing: we need to accept the premise that all housing is social."[128]

Juan Carlos Cano y Paloma Vera, 2017

"Let's stop to think about the more than 9.4 million loans granted by Infonavit thus far, and about the kind of housing that has proliferated and the cities that have taken shape."[129]

Carlos Zedillo, 2017

"The current housing model in Mexico is anti-constitutional. The house is not enjoyed but suffered, not decent but appalling, and not respectable but shameful."[130]

Francisco Pardo, 2017

126 Mauricio Rocha and Gabriela Carrillo, "De la cantera a la vivienda: Xaltocan", in *Apuntes sobre la vivienda social,* Mexico City: Arquine/Instituto del Fondo Nacional de la Vivienda para los Trabajadores (Infonavit), 2017, 184.
127 Alejandro Hernández Gálvez, "Home Is Where Your Heart Cellphone Is", in *Arquine*, no. 79 (Spring 2017), 23.
128 Juan Carlos Cano and Paloma Vera, "Vivienda Social: partimos del hecho de que toda vivienda es social", in *Apuntes sobre la vivienda social,* Mexico City: Arquine/Instituto del Fondo Nacional de la Vivienda para los Trabajadores (Infonavit), 2017, 67.
129 Carlos Zedillo, op. cit., 20.
130 Francisco Pardo, op. cit., 105.

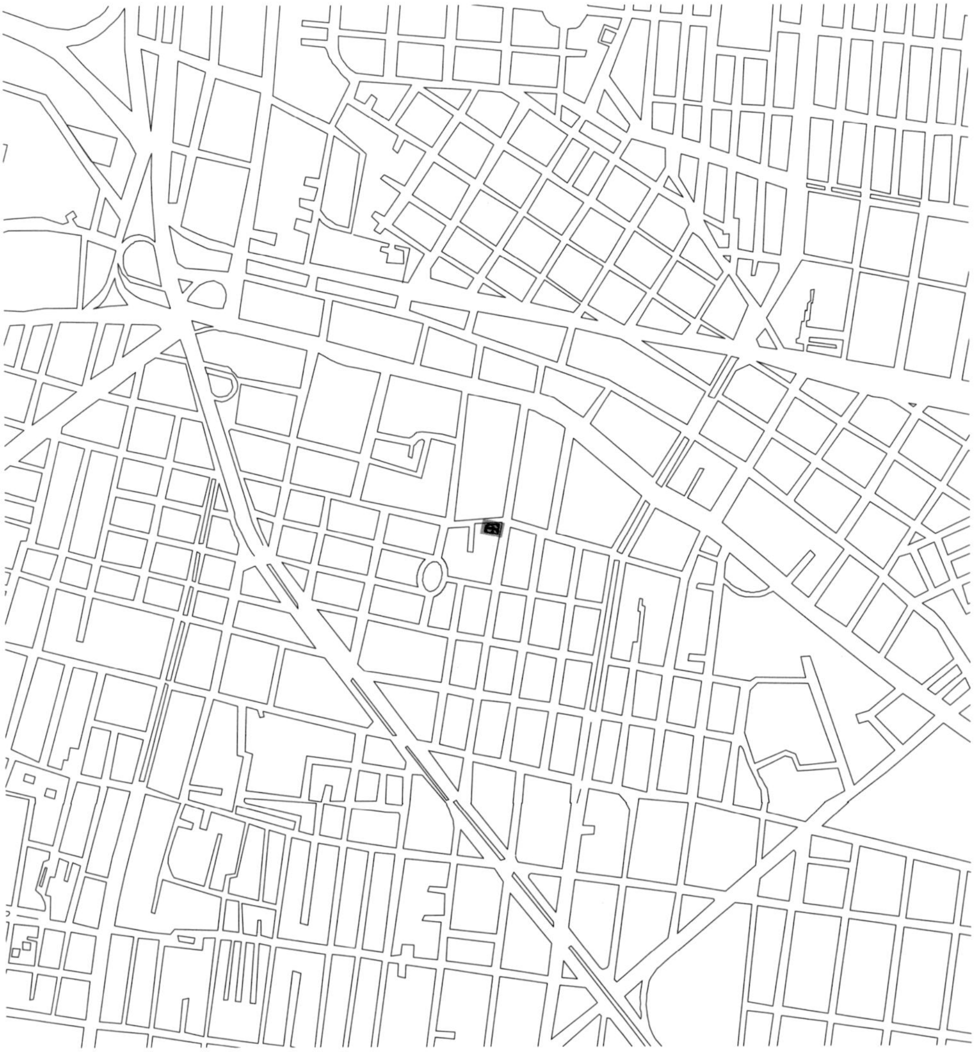

2017, Mar Tirreno, Frida Escobedo

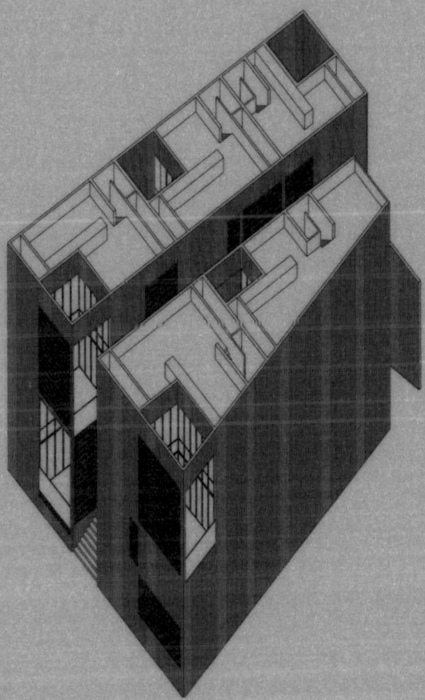

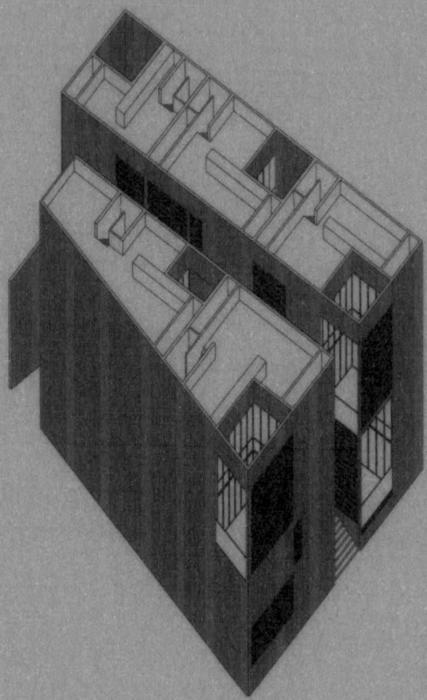

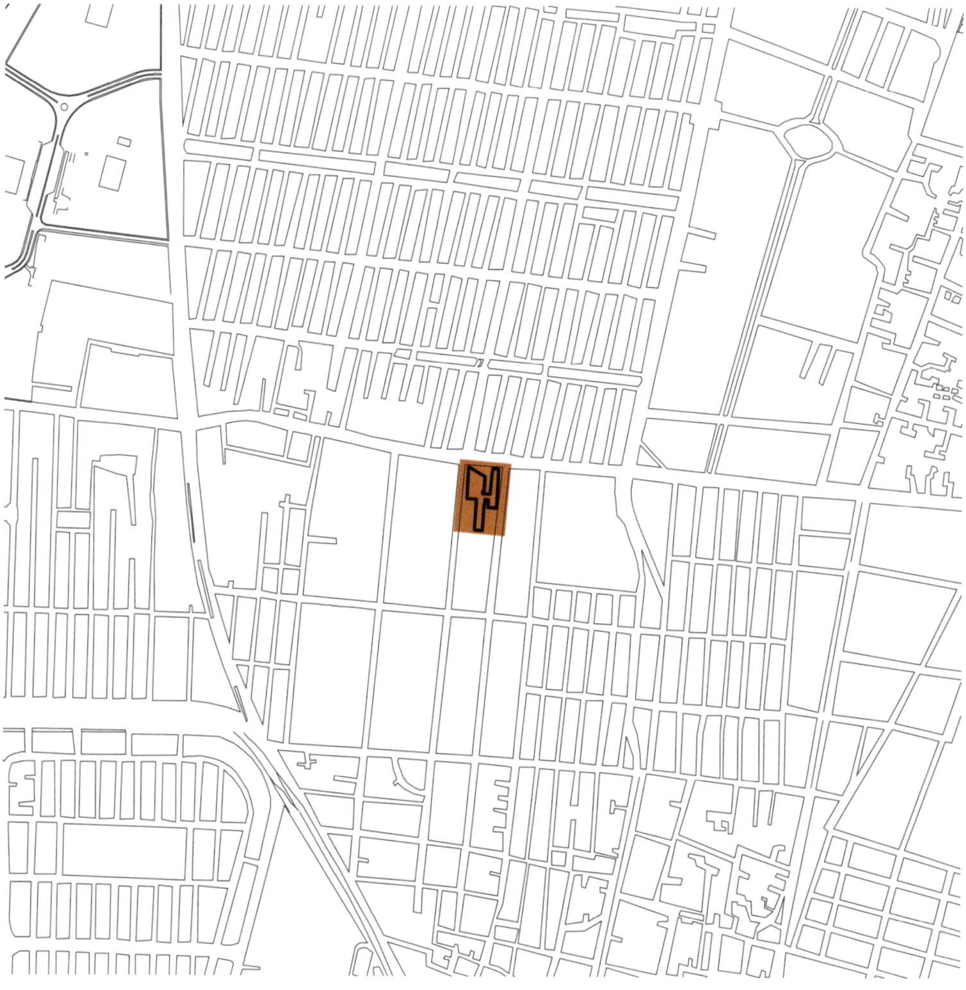

2017, Ermita Iztapalapa Building, Manuel Cervantes

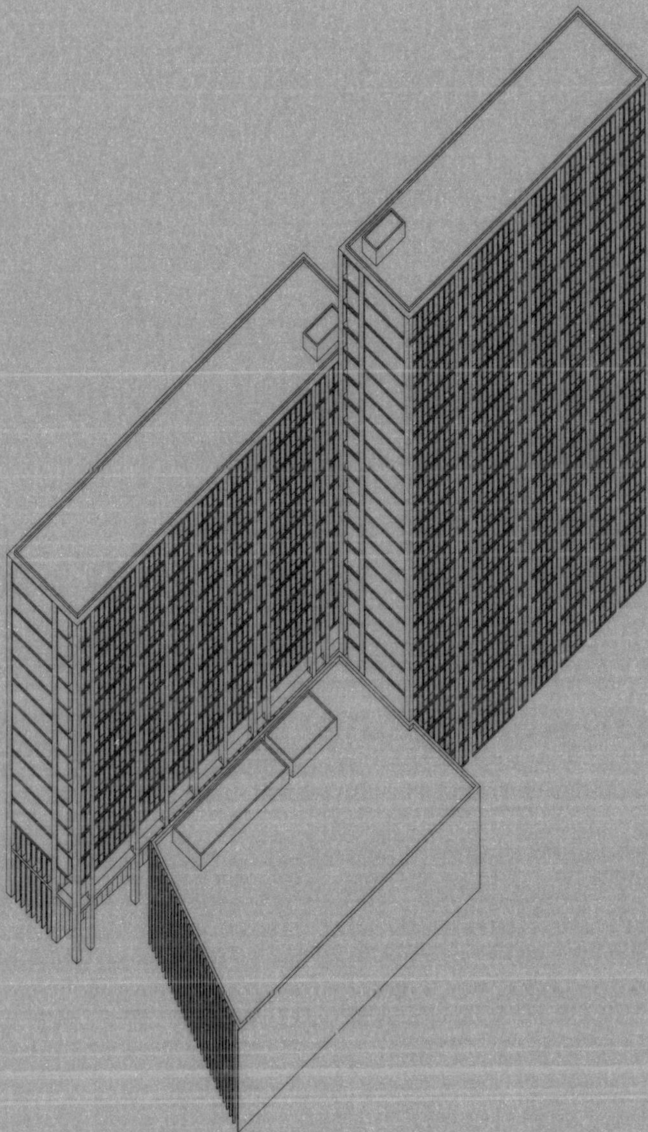

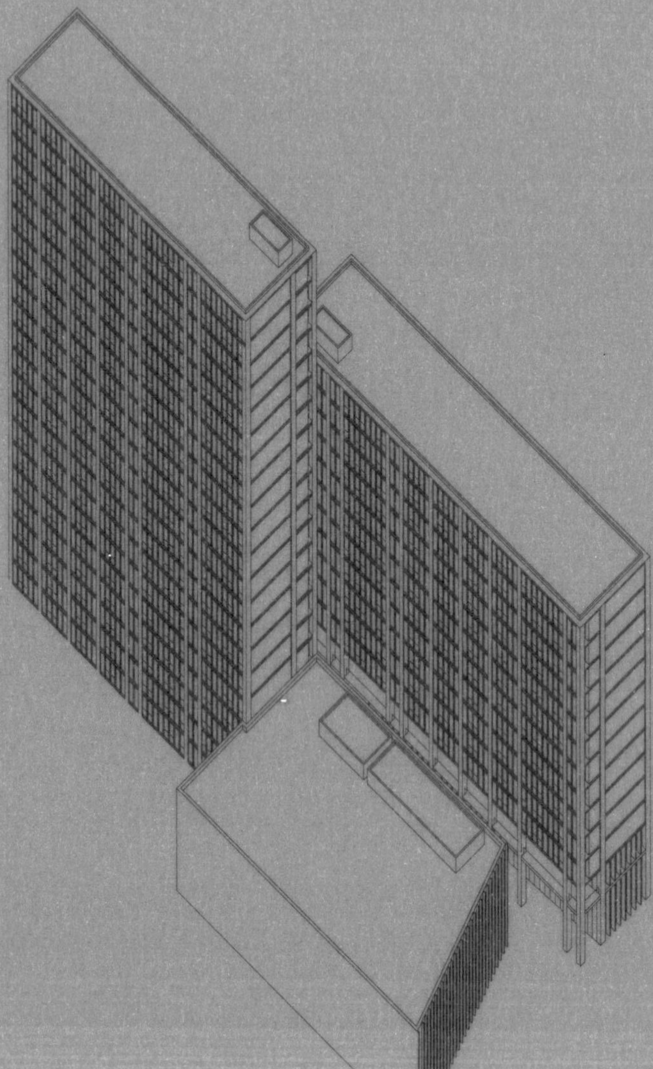

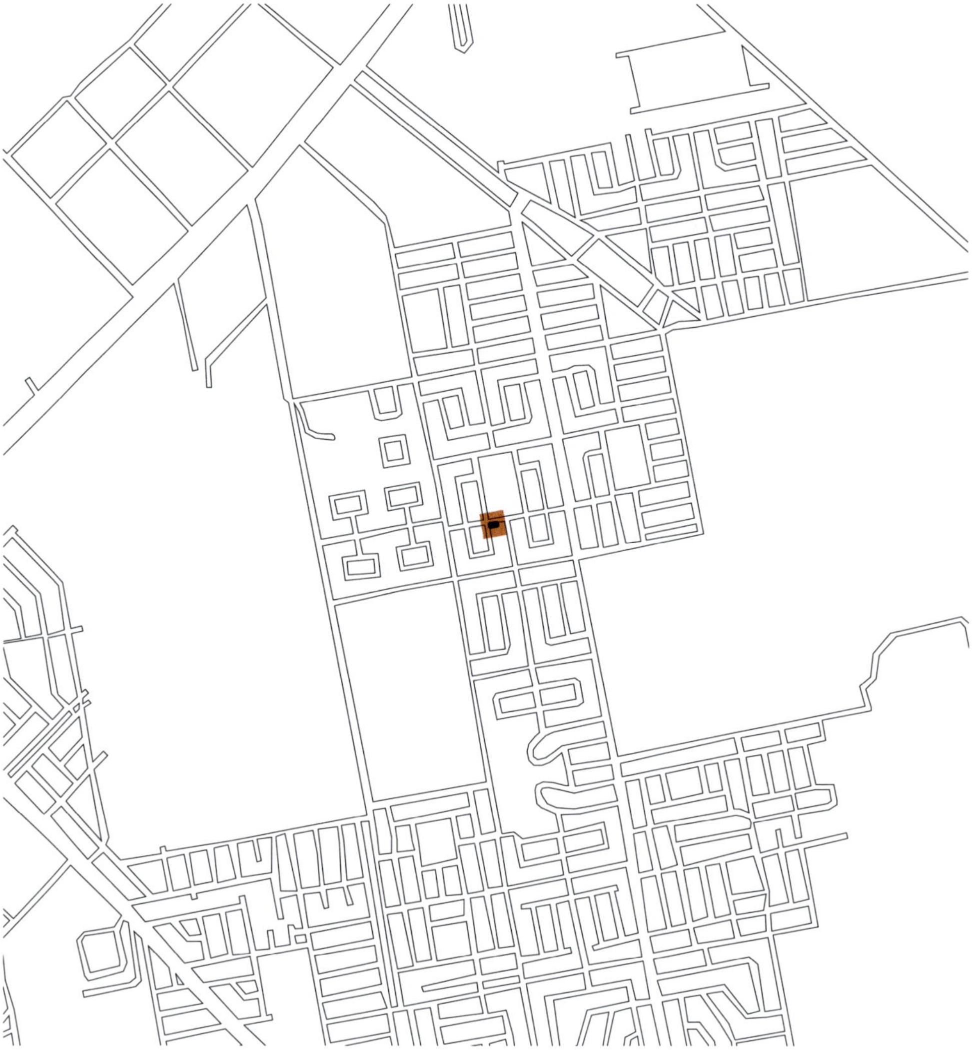

2017, Torre Roja, Zeller & Moye

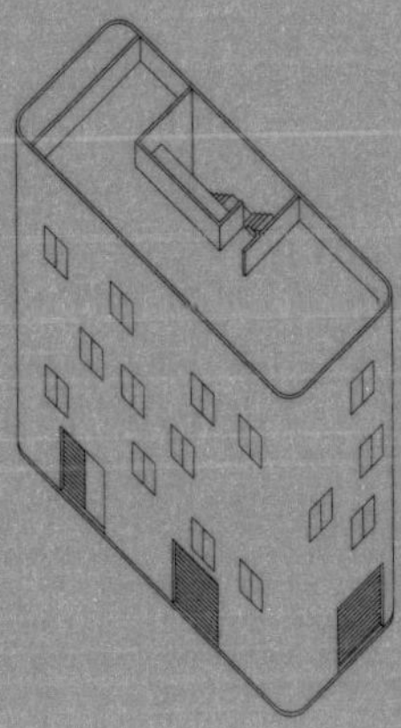

2017, Monte Albán Building, Fernanda Canales

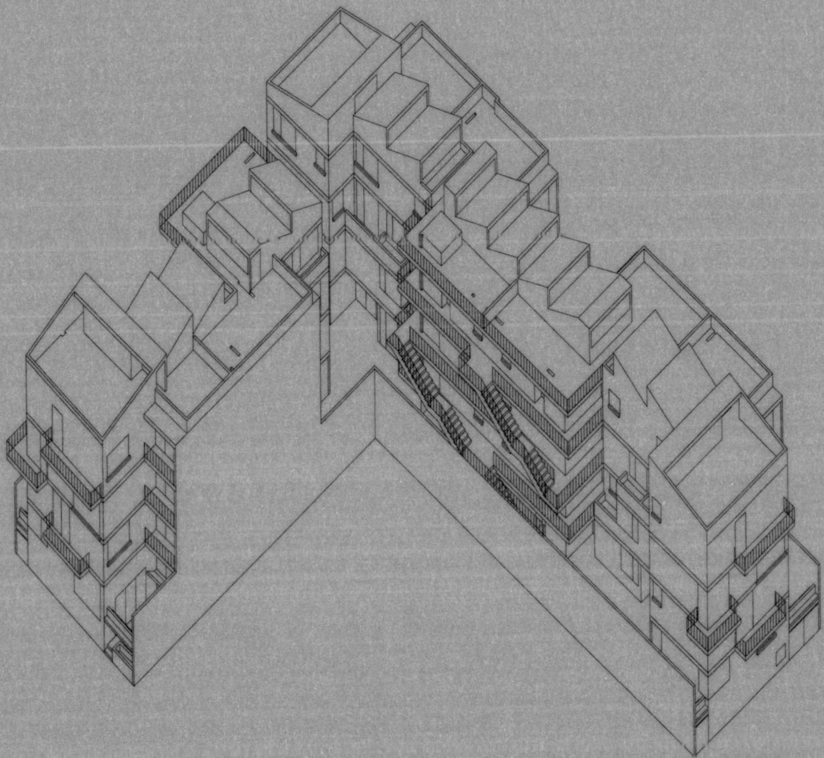

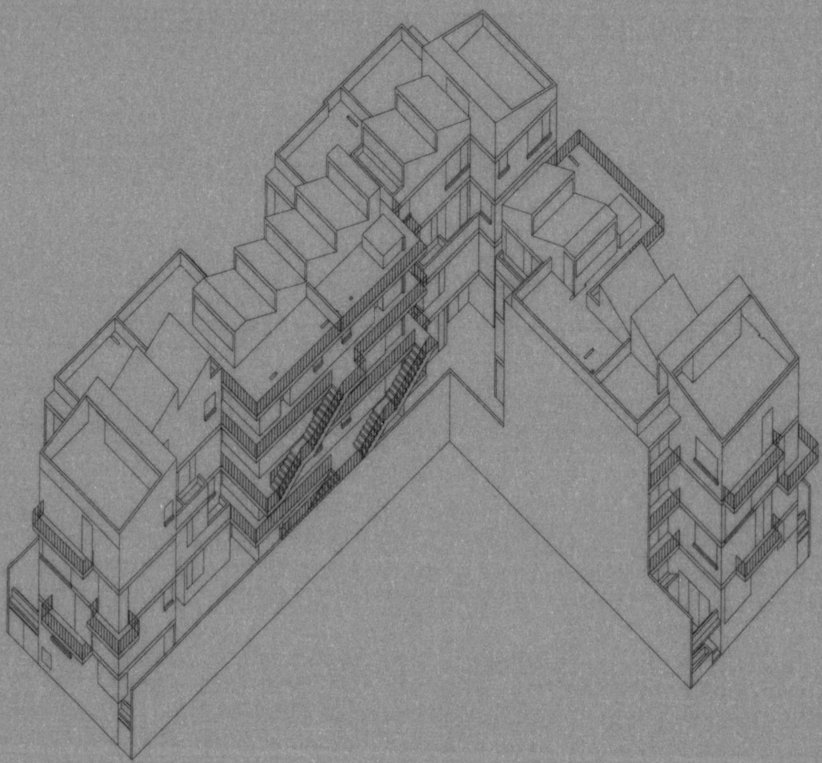

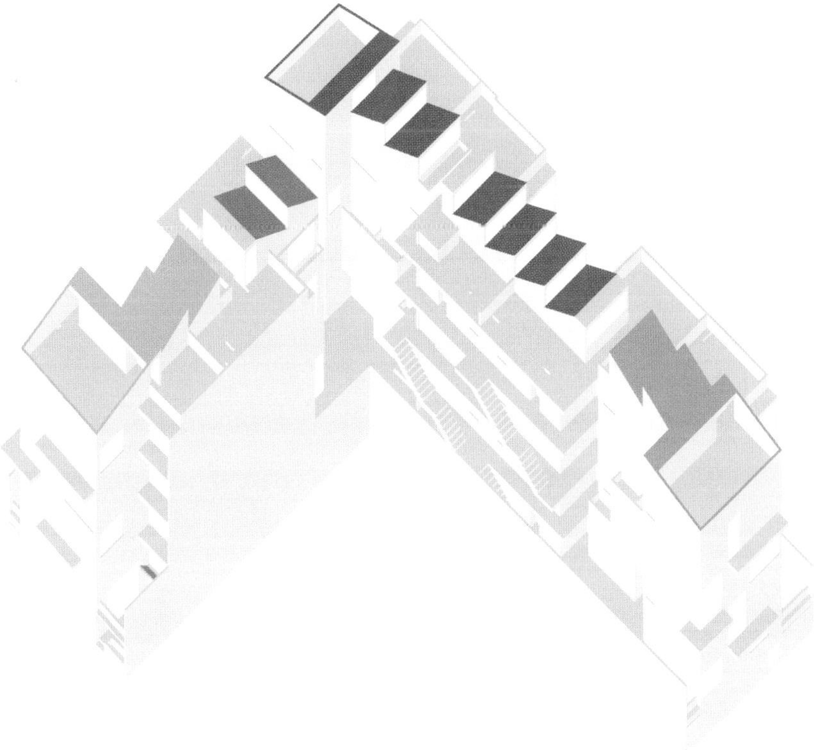

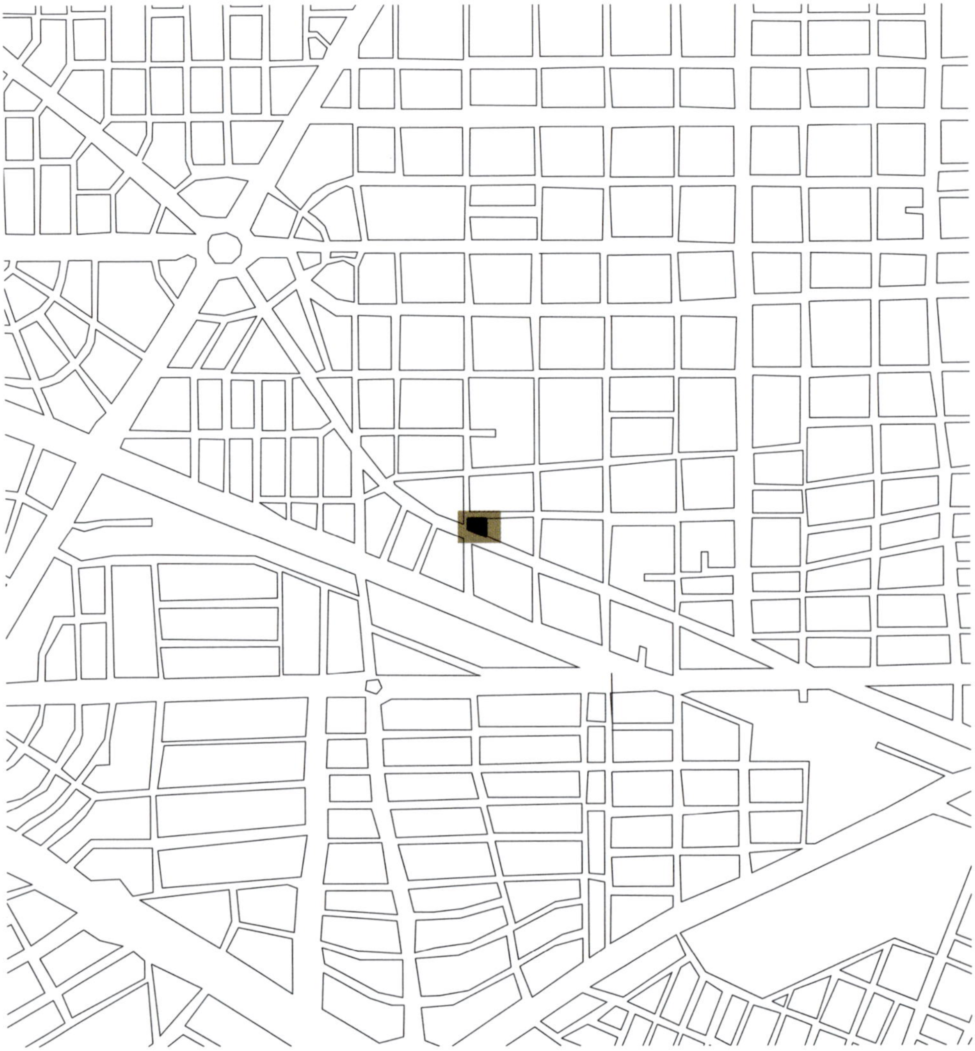

2017, MAJI Building, Salvador Macías and Magui Peredo

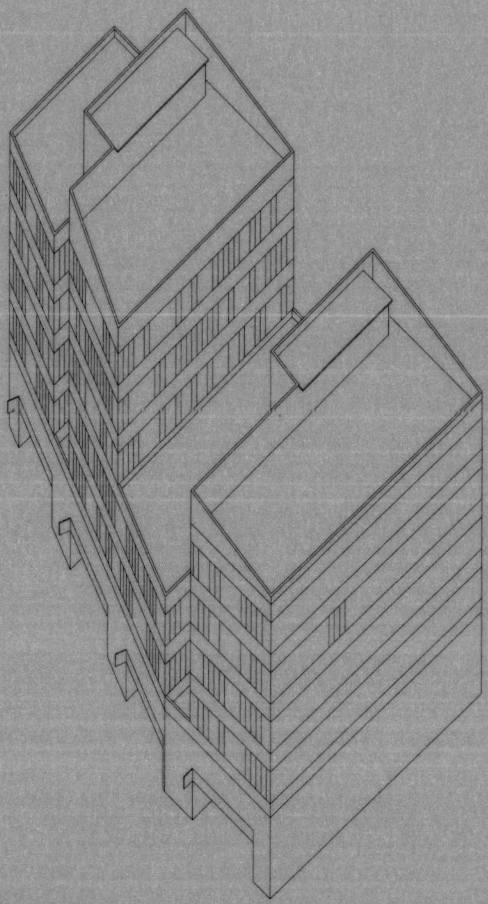

70 projects, addresses

1917 Condesa complex - Juan de la Barrera (between Mazatlán and Pachuca), colonia Condesa, Mexico City

1929 Behn-Zöllinger Houses - San Borja 733, colonia Del Valle, Mexico City (demolished)

ca. 1929 Houses for workers - Mexico City (project)

1930 Elorduy Minimal House - Ernesto Elorduy 8, colonia Exhipódromo de Peralvillo, Mexico City

1931 Ermita Building - Avenida Revolución 23, colonia Tacubaya, Mexico City

1931 Jardín complex - Sindicalismo 87, colonia Escandón, Mexico City

1932 Minimal Worker's House - Avenida del Taller (between Torno and Eje 2 Oriente Congreso de la Unión), colonia Aarón Sáenz, Mexico City

1934 Martí Building - José Martí 251, colonia Escandón, Mexico City

1939 Polanco Passway - Avenida Presidente Masaryk 360, colonia Polanco, Mexico City

1939 Garza Building - Plaza Melchor Ocampo 40, colonia Cuauhtémoc, Mexico City

1940 Tropical Rural House - Papaloapan, Veracruz

1941 Building for artists - Plaza Melchor Ocampo 38, colonia Cuauhtémoc, Mexico City

1942 Basurto Building - Avenida México 197, colonia Hipódromo, Mexico City

ca. 1947 Unidad Modelo complex - Eje 8 Sur (between Río Churubusco and Eje 2 Oriente), colonia Modelo, Mexico City

1949 Centro Urbano Presidente Alemán (CUPA) - Félix Cuevas (between Adolfo Prieto and Avenida Coyoacán), colonia Del Valle, Mexico City

1949 Ala Minimal House - (project)

1953 Fundición Building - Campos Elíseos 45, colonia Rincón del Bosque, Mexico City (demolished)

1956 Reforma Condominium - Río Guadalquivir 109, colonia Cuauhtémoc, Mexico City

1958 La Nacional Insurance Building - Orozco y Berra (between Eje 1 Poniente Guerrero), colonia Buenavista, Mexico City

1958 Barra de Navidad - La Huerta-Barra de Navidad and Nueva España, Pueblo Nuevo, Barra de Navidad, Jalisco (project)

1960 Unidad Independencia complex - Bulevar Adolfo López Mateos (between San Bernabé and Avenida San Jerónimo), colonia Independencia Batán Norte y Sur, Mexico City

1964 Conjunto Urbano Presidente López Mateos de Nonoalco-Tlatelolco - Ricardo Flores Magón (between Avenida Insurgentes and Paseo de la Reforma), colonia Tlatelolco, Mexico City

1964 Railway Workers complex - Héroes Ferrocarrileros (between Calle 2), Ferrocarril, Guadalajara, Jalisco

1968 Mixcoac Towers - Bulevar Adolfo López Mateos 1661, colonia Lomas de Plateros, Mexico City

1968 Olympic Villa - Avenida Insurgentes Sur 3493, colonia Villa Olímpica, Mexico City

1969 Kalikosmia - Acapulco, Guerrero and San Pedro Mártir, Baja California

1973 Unidad Iztacalco complex - Avenida Canal de Apatlaco (between Río Churubusco and Eje 3 Oriente Francisco del Paso y Troncoso), colonia Infonavit Iztacalco, Mexico City

1976 Mexicali Housing - Nueva Zelanda, Conjunto Urbano Orizaba, Mexicali, Baja California

1977 CTM-Atemajac Housing complex - Manuel de Mimbela (between Mezquitán and J. Jesús Ortiz), Fidel Velázquez, Guadalajara, Jalisco

1977 Ricardo Flores Magón Housing complex - Periférico Norte Manuel Gómez Morín (between Celerino Navarro and Teodoro Flores), Ricardo Flores Magón, Guadalajara, Jalisco

1978 Integración Latinoamericana - Eje 10 Sur Copilco (between Cerro del Agua), colonia Integración Latinoamericana, Mexico City

1986 Fuentes Brotantes (II) - Avenida Fuentes Brotantes (between San Juan del Río and Sor Juana Inés de la Cruz), colonia Fuentes Brotantes, Mexico City

1991 Las Crucesitas - Ahome, Sinaloa

1992 Brasil 75 - República de Brasil 75, colonia Centro Histórico, Mexico City

1994 Tláloc complex - Avenida Ricardo Flores Magón 130, colonia Buenavista, Mexico City

1996 Veracruz complex - Veracruz 79, 81, 83, 85 y 91, colonia Condesa, Mexico City

1998 Portal Bretaña - Calle Laboristas 140, colonia San Andrés Tetepilco, Mexico City

1999 Stacked housing - Ayuntamiento 512, Triana La Salud, Aguascalientes, Aguascalientes

2000 Ámsterdam Building - Ámsterdam 18, colonia Hipódromo, Mexico City

2001 Housing for artists - Colima 315, colonia Roma Norte, Mexico City

2003 AR58 - Alfonso Reyes 58, colonia Hipódromo Condesa, Mexico City

2004 13 de Septiembre - 13 de Septiembre 42, colonia Escandón, Mexico City

2008 FR43 - General Francisco Ramírez 43, colonia Ampliación Daniel Garza, Mexico City

2009 Atrio de San Francisco Apartments - Atrio de San Francisco 9, colonia San Francisco, Mexico City

2010 Tlacolula 11H - Lambityeco S/N, Tlacolula de Matamoros, Oaxaca (project)

2010 Elemental Monterrey - Paseo de los Geranios (between aseo de los Lirios), Las Anacuas, Santa Catarina, Nuevo León

2010 Lisboa 7 - Lisboa 7, colonia Juárez, Mexico City

2012 Alfonso Reyes 200 - Alfonso Reyes 200, colonia Hipódromo Condesa, Mexico City

2012 Liverpool 61 - Liverpool 61, colonia Juárez, Mexico City

2012 Reforma 27 - Reforma 27, colonia Tabacalera, Mexico City

2014 Casa Caja - General Zuazua, Nuevo León

2014 Modular house - Xuxcab, Yucatán

2014 Regional single housing - Bosco Residencial, Avenida Jesús Siqueiros, Sahuaro Municipal, Hermosillo, Sonora (project)

2014 Bosco Housing - Jesús Siqueiros (between Juan José Aguirre and Luis Orci), El Llanito/Sahuaro Municipal, Hermosillo, Sonora

2014 Antonio Sola - Antonio Sola 70, colonia Condesa, Mexico City

2014 Complejo Híbrido Bucareli - Bucareli (between Avenida Morelos, Enrico Martínez and Ayuntamiento) colonia Centro, Mexico City (project)

2015 High Park - Avenida Manuel Gómez Morín 922, Zona Santa Bárbara, San Pedro Garza García, Nuevo León

2015 Rinconada Margaritas - Juan Palomar y Arias 705, Prados Providencia, Guadalajara, Jalisco

2015 Sustainable Housing-Acuña - Fraccionamiento Los Altos de Santa Teresa, Ciudad Acuña, Coahuila de Zaragoza

2015 CH-ReUrbano - Chihuahua 139, colonia Roma Norte, Mexico City

2016 Central Park Interlomas - Vía Magna 6, Interlomas, Huixquilucan, Estado de México

2016 Un Cuarto Más - Privada Río Verde 17, Campo Verde Etapa 5, Temixco, Morelos

2016 Del Territorio al Habitante - 1er Calle El Mirador, San Miguel del Arco, Apan, Hidalgo

2017 Productive House - 1er Calle El Mirador, San Miguel del Arco, Apan, Hidalgo

2017 Donceles Studios - Avenida Independencia 59, Donceles, Cancún, Quintana Roo

2017 Mar Tirreno - Mar Tirreno 86, colonia Popotla, Mexico City

2017 Ermita Iztapalapa Building - Ermita Iztapalapa 621, colonia Granjas San Antonio, Mexico City

2017 Red Tower - Siria 828, Villas del Guadiana, Durango, Durango

2017 Monte Albán Building - Concepción Béistegui 1812, colonia Narvarte Oriente, Mexico City

2018 MAJI Building - Agustín Yáñez 2580, Arcos Vallarta, Guadalajara, Jalisco

Bibliography

Aburto, Álvaro, Raúl Cacho, Ricardo Rivas and Luis Cuevas, "El problema de la arquitectura y el urbanismo en México", *Edificación*, no. 1, January-February 1937.

Adrià, Miquel, "Vivienda colectiva", *Arquine*, no. 64, summer 2013.

—— "Sobre la vivienda social", in *Apuntes sobre la vivienda social*, Mexico City: Arquine/Instituto del Fondo Nacional de la Vivienda para los Trabajadores (Infonavit), 2017.

Aldrete-Haas, José, *La deconstrucción del Estado mexicano: políticas de vivienda, 1917-1988*, Mexico City: Alianza, 1991.

Alva Martínez, Ernesto, *Vivienda en edificios de apartamentos y conjuntos horizontales de arquitectos en México*, Mexico City: Comex, 1999.

—— "La vivienda como política", *Arquine*, no. 64, summer 2013.

Ambasz, Emilio, *The Architecture of Luis Barragan*, New York: Museum of Modern Art, 1976.

Ambrosi, Jorge, and Gabriela Etchegaray, "Ensayo sobre el espacio para la vivienda social", *Apuntes sobre la vivienda social*, Mexico City: Arquine/Instituto del Fondo Nacional de la Vivienda para los Trabajadores (Infonavit), 2017.

Anda, Enrique X. de, *Vivienda colectiva de la modernidad en México: los multifamiliares durante el periodo presidencial de Miguel Alemán (1946-1952)*, Mexico City: Instituto de Investigaciones Estéticas-Universidad Nacional Autónoma de México, 2008.

Apuntes sobre la vivienda social, Mexico City: Arquine/Instituto del Fondo Nacional de la Vivienda para los Trabajadores (Infonavit), 2017.

Arai, Alberto T., *La raíz humana de la distribución arquitectónica*, Mexico City: Ediciones Mexicanas, 1950.

—— "La casa mexicana", Sociedad de Arquitectos Mexicanos, June 5, 1956, in *Ciclo de conferencias sobre vivienda popular*, Mexico City: Sociedad de Arquitectos Mexicanos/El Colegio Nacional de Arquitectos Mexicanos, n. d.

—— Raúl Cacho, Enrique Guerrero and Balbino Hernández, "Memoria del proyecto de la Ciudad Obrera de México", in *Arquitectura y Decoración*, no. 11, September 1938.

Arquitectura México, vol. XII, no. 53, March 1956; vol. XIV, no. 61, March 1958.

Attoe, Wayne (ed.), *The Architecture of Ricardo Legorreta*, Austin: University of Texas Press, 1990.

Ayala Alonso, Enrique, "Tres décadas de modernización de la Ciudad de México", in Carlos Sambricio (ed.), *Ciudad y vivienda en América Latina, 1930-1960*, Madrid: Lampreave, 2012.

Barragán, Luis, "Apuntes de Nueva York. Ideas sobre jardines" [1931], in Antonio Riggen, *Luis Barragán: escritos y conversaciones*, Mexico City: El Croquis Editorial, 2000.

—— "Reflexiones sobre la arquitectura moderna en México, DF, y EEUU□ [1938], in Antonio Riggen, *Luis Barragán: escritos y conversaciones*, Madrid: El Croquis Editorial, 2000.

—— "Gardens For Environment: Jardines de El Pedregal", lecture given in California on 6 October 1951, printed in Antonio Riggen, *Luis Barragán: escritos y conversaciones*, Madrid: El Croquis Editorial, 2000.

—— "Cómo deben desarrollarse las grandes ciudades modernas: el crecimiento de la Ciudad de México", in *Zócalo*, October 12, 1959.

Bugarin, Inder, "Critican lucro con la vivienda ´cajón´", in *Reforma*, May 20, 2015.

Burdett, Ricky, *Diseñando la democracia urbana: densidades*, Mexico City: Arquine, 2015.

—— and Philipp Rode, "The Urban Age Project", in *Living in the Endless City: The Urban Age Project by The London School of Economics and Deutsche Bank's Alfred Herrhausen Society*, London: Phaidon, 2011.

—— and Deyan Sudjic (eds.), *Living in the Endless City: The Urban Age Project by The London School of Economics and Deutsche Bank's Alfred Herrhausen Society*, London: Phaidon, 2011.

Cacho, Raúl, *La vivienda. México: 50 años de Revolución*, Mexico City: Fondo de Cultura Económica, 1963.

Calderón, Bernardo, and Juan Galindo, "1925 será el año de la casa popular", *Excélsior*, December 28, 1924.

Canales, Fernanda, *Architecture in Mexico 1900-2010, The Construction of Modernity*, Mexico City: Fomento Cultural Banamex/Arquine, 2013.

Canales, Fernanda, *Vivienda colectiva en México, El derecho a la arquitectura*, Barcelona: Gustavo Gili, 2017.

Cano, Juan Carlos, and Paloma Vera, "Vivienda Social: partimos del hecho de que toda vivienda es social", in *Apuntes sobre la vivienda social*, Mexico City: Arquine/Instituto del Fondo Nacional de la Vivienda para los Trabajadores (Infonavit), 2017.

Caviar, Space (ed.), *SQM: The Quantified Home. Biennale Interieur*, Brussels: Lars Müller, 2014.

Censo de Población y Vivienda 2010 [2010 Population and Housing Census], Instituto Nacional de Estadística, Geografía e Informática (INEGI), Mexico City, 2010.

Cervantes, Manuel, "México y la vivienda", *Apuntes sobre la vivienda social*, Mexico City: Arquine/Instituto del Fondo Nacional de la Vivienda para los Trabajadores (Infonavit), 2017.

Colle, Marie-Pierre, "Luis Barragán: 'La buena arquitectura es bella'", *House and Garden*, New York, September 1981.

Contreras, Carlos, "¿Qué cosa es la planificación de ciudades y regiones?", *Planificación*, no. 1, September 1927.

Delgado, Álvaro, "Derroche al estilo García Luna", *Proceso*, April 20, 2013.

Dömer, Klaus, Hans Drexler and Joachim Schultz-Granberg (eds.), *Affordable Living: Housing for Everyone*, Berlin: Jovis Verlag GmbH, 2004.

El Arquitecto. Órgano de la Sociedad de Arquitectos Mexicanos, special memorial issue devoted to the architect Juan Legarreta, October 1934.

Estadísticas sociales del Porfiriato, 1877-1910, Mexico City: Secretaría de Economía/Dirección General de Estadística/Talleres Gráficos de la Unión, 1956.

Fariña Tojo, José, "Una ciudad más próxima: el futuro de las ciudades", *El País*, June 28, 2015.

Gaeta, Julio, "Fábrica: una conversación con Javier Sánchez", *Higuera + Sánchez*, Mexico City: Arquine/RM, 2005.

García Ramos, Domingo, "La planificación de la habitación popular", lecture given to the Society of Mexican Architects, July 24, 1956, printed in *Ciclo de conferencias sobre vivienda popular*, Mexico City: Sociedad de Arquitectos Mexicanos/El Colegio Nacional de Arquitectos Mexicanos, n. d.

—— *Definiciones y conceptos generales: iniciación al urbanismo*, Mexico City: Escuela Nacional de Arquitectura-Universidad Nacional Autónoma de México, 1961.

Garcés, Marina, *Filosofía inacabada*, Barcelona: Galaxia Gutenberg, 2015.

Garza, Gustavo (ed.), *La Ciudad de México en el fin del segundo milenio*, Mexico City: El Colegio de México, 2000.

Goldberger, Paul, *Por qué importa la arquitectura*, Madrid: Ivorypress, 2012.

Gómez Mayorga, Mauricio, "El problema de la habitación en México: realidad de su solución (una conversación con Mario Pani)", in *Arquitectura México*, no. 27, April 1949.

—— "Notas polémicas", in *Artes de México*, year IX, no. 36: *La arquitectura contemporánea en México*, 1961.

—— *Ensayos críticos de arquitectura*, Guadalajara: Universidad Autónoma de Guadalajara, 1977.

—— *Al rescate de México*, Mexico City: Editores Asociados Mexicanos, 1982.

Gómez Pimienta, Bernardo, "¿Por qué recuperar los conjuntos habitacionales abandonados?", in *Apuntes sobre la vivienda social*, Mexico City: Arquine/Instituto del Fondo Nacional de la Vivienda para los Trabajadores (Infonavit), 2017.

González Gortázar, Fernando, "México y sus alfileres", *La Jornada*, October 12, 1985.

—— *Escritos reunidos*, Cuadernos de Arquitectura, nos. 11-12, Mexico City: Consejo Nacional para la Cultura y las Artes/Instituto Nacional de Bellas Artes, 2004.

González de León, Teodoro, *Retrato de arquitecto con ciudad*, Mexico City: Artes de México, 1996.

González Lobo, Carlos, *Arquitectura en México durante la cuarta década: el Maximato, el cardenismo. Apuntes para la historia y crítica de la arquitectura mexicana del siglo XX, 1900-1980*, vol. II, Cuadernos de Arquitectura y

Conservación del Patrimonio Artístico, nos. 22 and 23, Mexico City: Secretaría de Educación Pública/Instituto Nacional de Bellas Artes, 1982.

Gouverneur, David, *Planning and Design for Future Informal Settlements: Shaping the Self-Constructed City*, New York: Routledge, 2015.

Granados Roldan, Luz María, *¿Un funcionalista radical? Juan Legarreta*, Architecture BA thesis, Mexico City: Universidad Iberoamericana, 1987.

Guzmán Urbiola, Xavier, *Arquitectura mexicana: vivienda, escuela y hospitales*, Mexico City: Consejo Nacional para la Cultura y las Artes, 2008.

Hagerman, Óscar, *Arquitectura y diseño*, Mexico City: Arquine, 2014.

Hannes Meyer, pensamiento, Cuadernos de Arquitectura, no. 5, Mexico City: Dirección de Arquitectura y Conservación del Patrimonio Artístico Inmueble/ Consejo Nacional para la Cultura y las Artes/Instituto Nacional de Bellas Artes, 2002.

Hernández, Mirtha, "Habitan 7.4 millones en zonas de riesgo", *Reforma*, September 18, 2015.

Hernández Gálvez, Alejandro (ed.), *Densidades*, Mexico City: Arquine, 2015.

—— (ed.), *Habitar la ciudad: la obligación de la arquitectura*, Mexico City: Arquine, 2016.

—— "Home Is Where Your Heart Cellphone Is", in *Arquine*, no. 79, spring 2017.

Herreros, Juan (ed.), *Vivienda y espacio doméstico en el siglo XXI*, Madrid: La Casa Encendida, 2008.

Hill, Dan, "The Commodification of Everything: On Restaurant Day and Airbnb", in S. Caviar (ed.), *SQM: The Quantified Home. Biennale Interieur*, Brussels: Lars Müller, 2014.

Ingersoll, Richard, "La mirada del marciano. Rem Koolhaas, a Reporter of Globalization", in *Arquitectura Viva*, no. 188, Madrid, October 2016.

Jiménez Gálvez, J., "Amnistía acusa a España: "Incumple las obligaciones sobre vivienda"", *El País*, Madrid, June 23, 2015

Kalach Alberto, and Fernando Fernández (eds.), *Croquis: los dibujos de Carlos Mijares*, Mexico City: Consejo Nacional para la Cultura y las Artes/Contornos, 2015.

Kandell, Jonathan, *La Capital: The Biography of Mexico City*, New York: Henry Holt and Company, 1988.

Katzman, Israel, *Arquitectura contemporánea Mexicana*, Mexico City: Instituto Nacional de Antropología e Historia/Secretaría de Educación Pública, 1963.

Klein, Alexander, *Vivienda mínima, 1906-1957*, Barcelona: Gustavo Gili, 1980.

Kotkin, Joel, "Megacities and the Density Delusion: Why More People Doesn't Equal More Wealth", in *Forbes*, April 16, 2013.

Larrosa, Manuel, *Mario Pani, arquitecto de su época*, Universidad Nacional Autónoma de México, 1985.

Larrosa, Manuel, "Vivienda en renta: congelación y deshielo", in *Periodismo arquitectónico*, Cuadernos de Arquitectura, no. 13, Mexico City: Consejo Nacional para la Cultura y las Artes/Instituto Nacional de Bellas Artes, 2006.

—— "La vivienda enajenante. Cultura sin casas", in *Periodismo arquitectónico*, Cuadernos de Arquitectura no. 13, Mexico City: Consejo Nacional para la Cultura y las Artes/Instituto Nacional de Bellas Artes, 2006.

Leal, Jesús, "Segregación social y mercados de vivienda en las grandes ciudades", *Revista Española de Sociología*, no. 2, Madrid, 2002.

Legarreta, Juan, "Pláticas sobre arquitectura", lecture given in Mexico City in 1933, printed in *Raíces. Documentos para la Historia de la Arquitectura Mexicana*, Mexico City: Universidad Autónoma Metropolitana-Azcapotzalco, 2001, p. 39; first edition, Mexico City: Sociedad de Arquitectos Mexicanos, 1934.

Linde, Pablo, "Los alcaldes de las grandes ciudades piden más peso en la escena mundial", *El País*, October 18, 2016.

Martin, Reinhold, Jacob Moore and Susanne Schindler (eds.), *The Art of Inequality: Architecture, Housing and Real State: A Provisional Report*, New York: The Trustees of Columbia University in the City of New York, 2015.

Mariscal, Federico, *La patria y la arquitectura nacional*, Mexico City: Imprenta Stephan y Torres, 1915.

—— "El estilo de la casa mexicana debe ser el que mejor cuadre", in *Excélsior*, March 16, 1924.

McGuirk, Justin, "Understanding the Numbers", in Ricky Burdett and Deyan Sudjic (eds.), *Living in the Endless City: The Urban Age Project by The London School of Economics and Deutsche Bank's Alfred Herrhausen Society*, London: Phaidon, 2011.

Medellín, Jorge L., "La habitación frente a la psicología del trabajador", in *Arquitectura y lo Demás*, vol. I, no. 6, October/November 1945.

Medina Ramírez, Salvador, "El alarmante crecimiento de autos", *Nexos*, April 7, 2015.

Meyer, Hannes, "Der Architekt im Klassenkampf", in *Der Rote Aufbau*, no. 13, Hamburg, 1932; Spanish version: *El arquitecto en la lucha de clases*, Havana: Arte y Literatura, 1981.

—— "La Ciudad de México: fragmentos de un estudio urbanístico", *Arquitectura México*, no. 12, April 1943

Mijares, Carlos, "El fenómeno arquitectónico", *Calli*, no. 1, July/August 1960.

—— *Tránsitos y demoras: esbozos sobre el quehacer arquitectónico*, Mexico City: Universidad Nacional Autónoma de México, 2008.

Monkkonen, Paavo, "La segregación residencial en el México urbano: niveles y patrones", in *Revista de Estudios Urbano-Regionales*, vol. 38, no. 114, Santiago de Chile, May 2012.

Montaner, Josep Maria, *La arquitectura de la vivienda colectiva: políticas y proyectos de la ciudad contemporánea*, Colección Estudios Universitarios de Arquitectura, no. 26, Barcelona: Reverté, 2015.

—— and Zaida Muxí, *Arquitectura y política: ensayos para mundos alternativos*, Barcelona: Gustavo Gili, 2011.

Neira, Eduardo, *El desarrollo sustentable y las metrópolis latinoamericanas*, Mexico City: Red Latinoamericana de Estudios Ambientales Urbanos/El Colegio de México, 1996.

OECD *Urban Policy Reviews: Mexico, Transforming Urban Policy and Housing Finance*, Organization for Economic Cooperation and Development (OCDE), Paris, 2015.

O'Gorman, Juan, "Pláticas sobre arquitectura", lecture given in Mexico City in 1933, printed in Cuadernos de Arquitectura, Mexico City: Dirección de Arquitectura y Conservación del Patrimonio Artístico Inmueble/Consejo Nacional para la Cultura y las Artes/Instituto Nacional de Bellas Artes, 2001.

—— "Crítica a la arquitectura mexicana contemporánea", Academia de Artes, Mexico City, December 9, 1952, in *La palabra de Juan O'Gorman*, Mexico City: Universidad Nacional Autónoma de México, 1983.

—— "En torno a la integración plástica", in *Espacios*, Mexico City, July 16, 1953, n. d.

—— "Más allá del funcionalismo", lecture given at Unidad Profesional Zacatenco ca. 1957, printed in Ida Rodríguez Prampolini, *Juan O'Gorman: arquitecto y pintor*, Mexico City: Universidad Nacional Autónoma de México, 1982.

—— "Acerca de la arquitectura en México", lecture given at Academia de Artes, Mexico City, November 1967, printed in *La palabra de Juan O'Gorman*, Mexico City: Universidad Nacional Autónoma de México, 1983.

Obregón Santacilia, Carlos, *50 años de arquitectura mexicana, 1900-1950*, Mexico City: Patria, 1952.

Olvera Camacho Roberto (ed.), *Reinaldo Pérez Rayón: ideas y obras*, Mexico City: Roc, 1990.

Orozco, Gabriel, *Materia escrita: cuadernos de trabajo, 1992-2012*, Mexico City: Era, 2014.

Pallares, Alfonso, "¿Cómo habita el pueblo mexicano y cómo debía habitar?", *Excélsior*, November 23, 1924.

Pani, Mario, "Habitaciones colectivas", *Calli*, no. 1, July/August 1960.

Pardo, Francisco, "¿Dónde vivo?", in *Apuntes sobre la vivienda social*, Mexico City: Arquine/Instituto del Fondo Nacional de la Vivienda para los Trabajadores (Infonavit), 2017.

Paz, Octavio, *Sor Juana Inés de la Cruz o las trampas de la fe*, Mexico City: Fondo de Cultura Económica, 1982.

Pérez Rayón, Reinaldo, "La enseñanza del funcionalismo en la ESIA. 30 años de funcionalismo en la ESIA. 25 años del IPN", in Cuadernos de Arquitectura, no. 6., Departamento de Arquitectura-Instituto Nacional de Bellas Artes, July 1962.

Prieto y Souza, Luis, "Problemas del momento material y económico de las clases sociales", *El Universal*, September 26, 1926.

Quintero, Pablo (ed.), *Modernidad en la arquitectura mexicana: 18 protagonistas*, Mexico City: Universidad Autónoma Metropolitana-Xochimilco, 1990.

Ramírez Vázquez, Pedro, "Arquitectura para la vivienda", *Arquitectura: Pedro Ramírez Vázquez*, Mexico City: Porrúa, 2013.

Rex, John, and Robert Samuel Moore, *Race, Community and Conflict*, London: Institute of Race Relations, 1967.

Ricalde, Humberto, and Gustavo López Padilla, "Arquitectura en México, 1960-1980", in *Apuntes para la historia y crítica de la arquitectura Mexicana del siglo XX: 1900-1980*, vol. 2, Cuadernos de Arquitectura y Conservación del Patrimonio Artístico, nos. 22-23, Mexico City: Secretaría de Educación Pública/Instituto Nacional de Bellas Artes, 1982.

Riggen, Antonio, *Luis Barragán: escritos y conversaciones*, Madrid: El Croquis Editorial, 2000.

Rocha, Mauricio, and Gabriela Carrillo, "De la cantera a la vivienda: Xaltocan", *Apuntes sobre la vivienda social*, Mexico City: Arquine/Instituto del Fondo Nacional de la Vivienda para los Trabajadores (Infonavit), 2017.

Rodman, Selden, *Mexican Journal: The Conquerors Conquered*, New York: The Devin-Adair Co., 1958, pp. 96-97; Spanish version: Antonio Riggen, *Luis Barragán: escritos y conversaciones*, Madrid: El Croquis Editorial, 2000.

Rodríguez Prampolini, Ida, *Juan O'Gorman: arquitecto y pintor*, Mexico City: Universidad Nacional Autónoma de México, 1982.

Rosa, Marcos L., and Ute E. Weiland (eds.), *Handmade Urbanism: From Community Initiatives to Participatory Models*, Berlin: Jovis Verlag GmbH, 2013.

Rossi, Aldo, *L'architettura della città*, Padua: Marsilio, 1966; Spanish edition: *La arquitectura de la ciudad*, Barcelona: Gustavo Gili, 1971.

Sambricio, Carlos (ed.), *Ciudad y vivienda en América Latina, 1930-1960*, Madrid: Lampreave, 2012.

Sánchez, Félix, "La realidad mexicana y las nuevas concepciones arquitectónicas urbanísticas en materia de habitación popular", in *Estudios*, no. 1, January 1952.

—— "Aspectos del problema de la casa habitación en México", lecture given to the Society of Mexican Architects, July 3, 1956, printed in *Ciclo de conferencias sobre vivienda popular*, Mexico City: Sociedad de Arquitectos Mexicanos/El Colegio Nacional de Arquitectos Mexicanos, n. d.

—— *Vivienda adentro: la arquitectura (no) importa*, Mexico City: Arquine, 2013.

Sánchez Corral, Javier, "Vivienda social: factores que influyen en la producción de la vivienda en México. Primer informe de trabajo del Sistema Nacional de Creadores de Arte, emisión 2008", Mexico City, August 2009-2010.

Sennet, Richard, *Juntos: rituales, placeres y políticas de cooperación*, Barcelona: Anagrama, 2012.

Señudo Gavaldón, Andrés, "Garantía de estacionamiento: ¿beneficio público?", *Nexos*, November 1, 2015.

Smith, Clive Bamford, *Builders in the Sun: Five Mexican Architects*, New York: Architectural Book Publishing, 1967.

Suárez Pareyón, Alejandro, "La situación habitacional", in Gustavo Garza (ed.), *La Ciudad de México en el fin del segundo milenio*, Mexico City: El Colegio de México, 2000.

Testimonios vivos, Cuadernos de Arquitectura y Conservación del Patrimonio Artístico, nos. 15-16, Mexico City: Secretaría de Educación Pública/Instituto Nacional de Bellas Artes, 1981.

Torres, Yuridia, "Deshabitadas 14% de las viviendas en México", *El Economista*, March 20, 2013.

Trejo, Sergio, "En 70 años creció 700 veces la mancha urbana", *La Razón*, July 6, 2013.

Trueblood, Beatrice (ed.), *Ramírez Vázquez en el urbanismo: conversaciones con José Antonio Aguilar Narváez*, Mexico City: Studio, 1995.

Vargas Salguero, Ramón, and J. Víctor Arias Montes (eds.), *Ideario de los arquitectos mexicanos*, vol. II: *Los olvidados*, Mexico City: Instituto Nacional de Bellas Artes, 2010.

Urrutia, Óscar, "Veinticinco años de arquitectura moderna en México", *Arquitectura México*, year XXV, vol. XX, no. 83, September 1963.

Villagrán García, José, course on "Estructura teórica del programa arquitectónico", El Colegio Nacional, August 1963, printed in Ramón Vargas Salguero and J. Víctor Arias Montes (eds.), *Ideario de los arquitectos mexicanos*, vol. II: *Los olvidados*, Mexico City: Instituto Nacional de Bellas Artes, 2010.

vivienda comunitaria en México, La, Mexico City: Instituto del Fondo Nacional de la Vivienda para los Trabajadores (Infonavit), 1988.

Yáñez, Enrique, *Del funcionalismo al post-racionalismo: ensayo sobre la arquitectura contemporánea en México*, Mexico City: Limusa, 1990.

—— *Arquitectura, teoría, diseño, contexto*, Mexico City: Limusa, 2006.

Zárraga, Guillermo, "La habitación barata", *Arquitectura y lo Demás*, vol. I, no. 6, October/November 1945.

Zedillo, Carlos, *El reto de la vivienda en México*, Mexico City: Instituto del Fondo Nacional de la Vivienda para los Trabajadores (Infonavit), 2016.

—— "Introducción", in *Apuntes sobre la vivienda social*, Mexico City: Arquine/Instituto del Fondo Nacional de la Vivienda para los Trabajadores (Infonavit), 2017.

Zohn, Alejandro, *Entorno e identidad*, Mexico City: Menhir, 1997.

Online references

Colomer, Jordi, *Avenida Ixtapaluca (houses for México)*; available at http://www.archdaily.mx/271308/video-avenida-ixtapaluca-houses-for-mexico-jordi-colomer/, accessed July 2017.

"CDMX, la ciudad con más tráfico a nivel mundial"; available at www.elfinanciero.com.mx, accessed March 23, 2016.

Hernández Gálvez, Alejandro, "Ubi? Quo? Unde? Qua?", June 8, 2011; available at otrootroblog.blogspot.mx, accessed December 13, 2015.

http://imco.org.mx/competitividad/el-peso-de-los-estacionamientos/, accessed June 27, 2017.

http://www.ine.es/censos2011_datos/cen11_datos_inicio.htm, accessed May 18, 2016.

"Pasado memorable, incierto futuro. Navegando la arquitectura. Crítica y reflexiones en torno a la arquitectura y las ciudades", May 12, 2015; available at https://navegandolaarquitectura.wordpress.com, accessed July 25, 2015.

Acknowledgements

Writing a book is, in a way, an act of giving thanks: to the readers, to those who believed in the project, to the people who helped make it a reality, and to those who followed through the process. It is also an expression of gratitude to other books and authors who paved the way.

I especially want to thank Carlos, my children, María and Francisco, and my sisters, Lorea and Jimena.

This book was made possible thanks to Carlos Zedillo, head of the Infonavit Research Center for Sustainable Development and primary instigator of this project, to Alberto Kritzler and Rodrigo Rivero Borrell from Reurbano, and to the Fundación Jumex Arte Contemporáneo.

I am also grateful to Iñaki Ábalos for his lessons and for writing the foreword; to Isabel Abascal and Alessandro Arienzo at LANZA Atelier, who collaborated in the creation of the axonometric drawings; to Ricardo Devesa and Ramon Prat at Actar; to Adela García-Herrera for editing and correcting the texts; to the translation agency Polisemia and Luis E. Carranza and Gabriel Amor for their support in the English version.

Finally, I would like to thank Ana Yumbé, Gustavo Rojas Paredes and Virginia Ruano, and all the architects who generously provided documentary material on their projects and to all who have contributed to rethink the house.

1917-2017

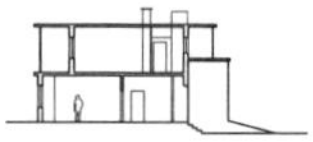
2, 1929

4, 1930

11, 1940

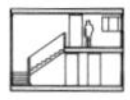
12, 1941

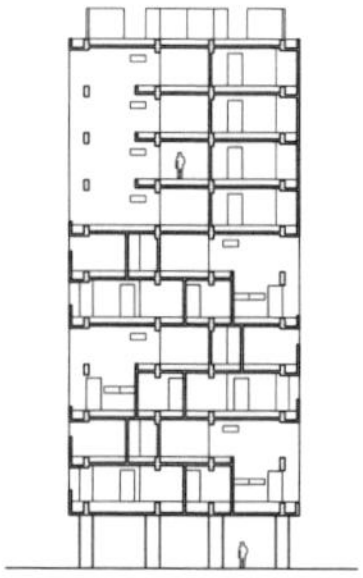
14, c. 1947

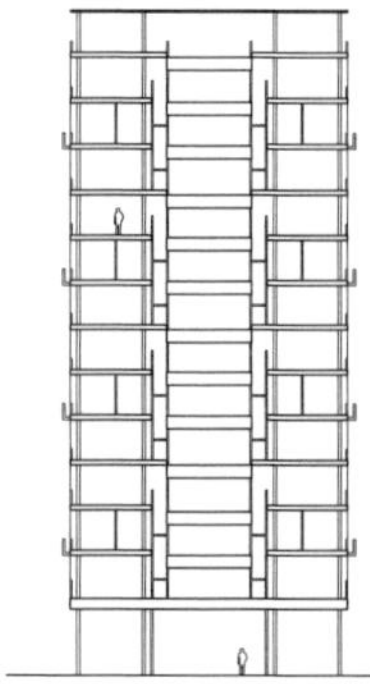
15, 1949

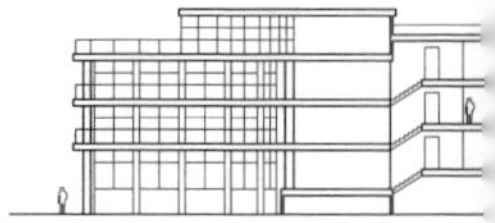
17, 19…

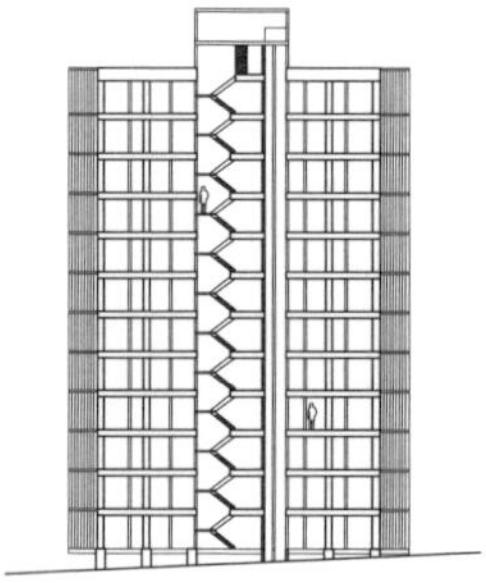
24, 1968

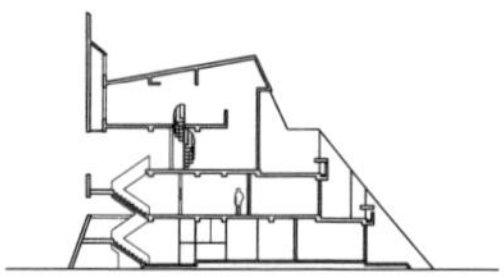
27, 1973

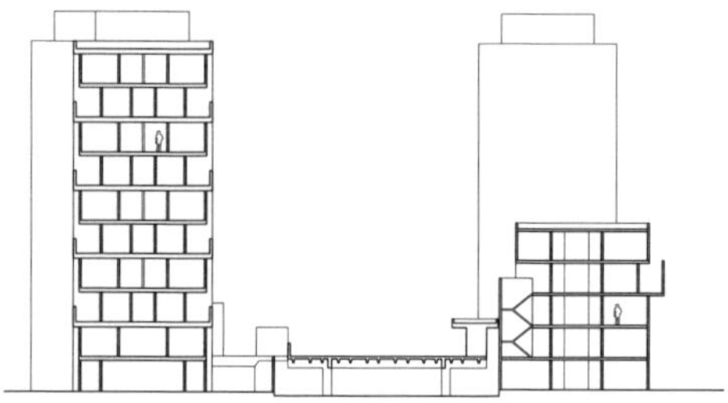
31, 1978

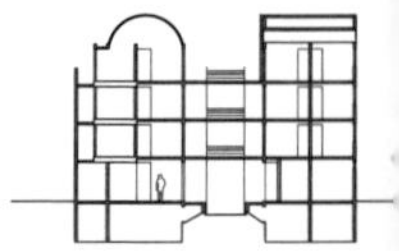
34, 19…

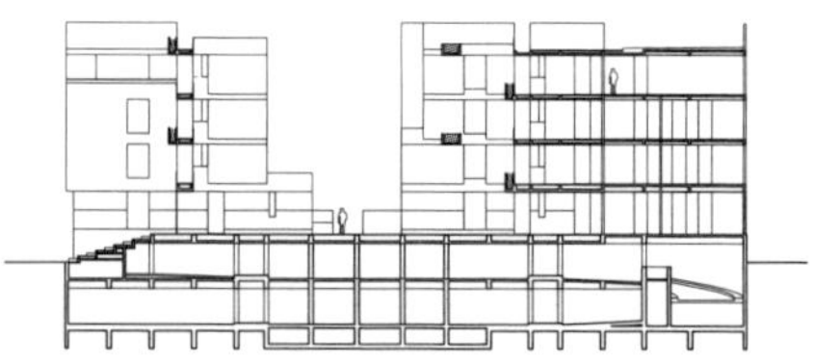
49, 2012

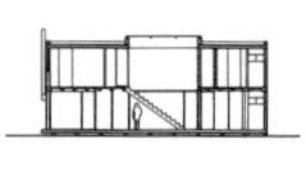
51, 2014

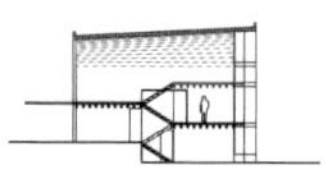
53, 2014

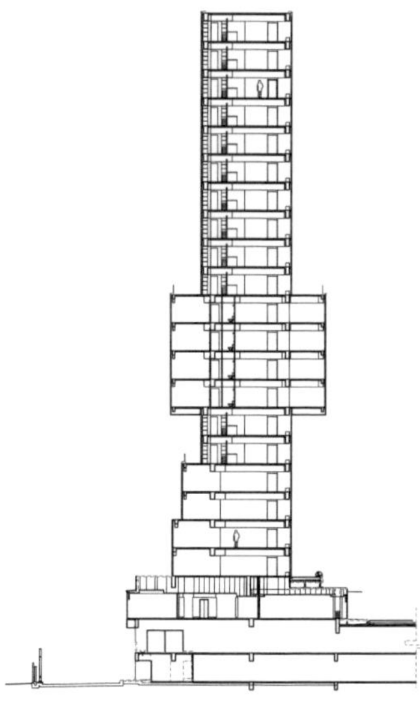
61, 2016

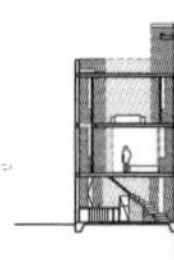
63, 20…

 # Project, Year

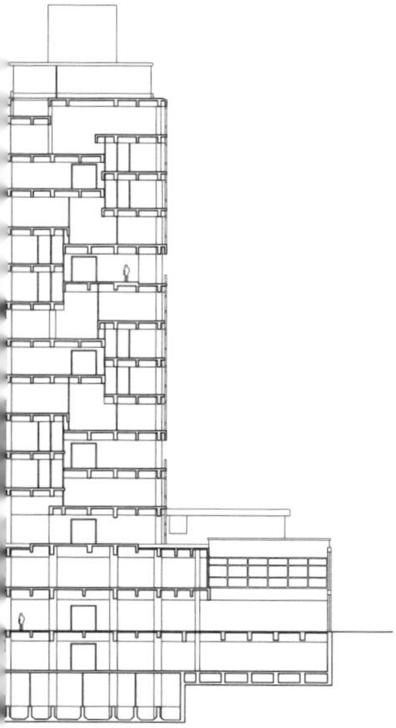

18, 1956

19, 1958

20, 1958

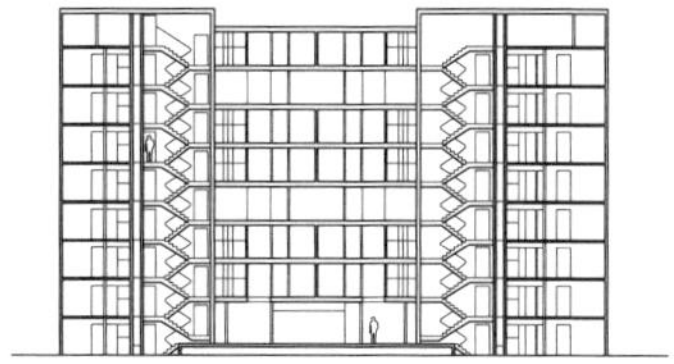

22, 1964

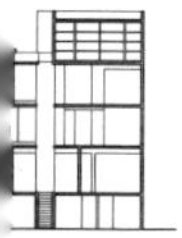

39, 2000

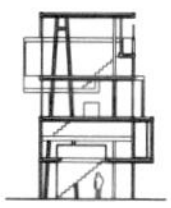

40, 2001

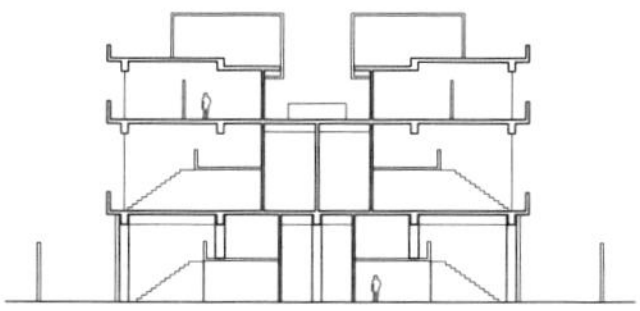

42, 2004

43, 2008

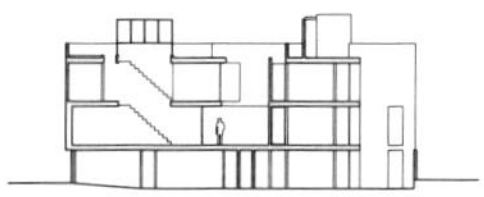

44, 2009

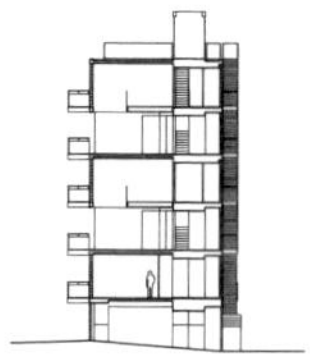

48, 2012

2017

66, 2017

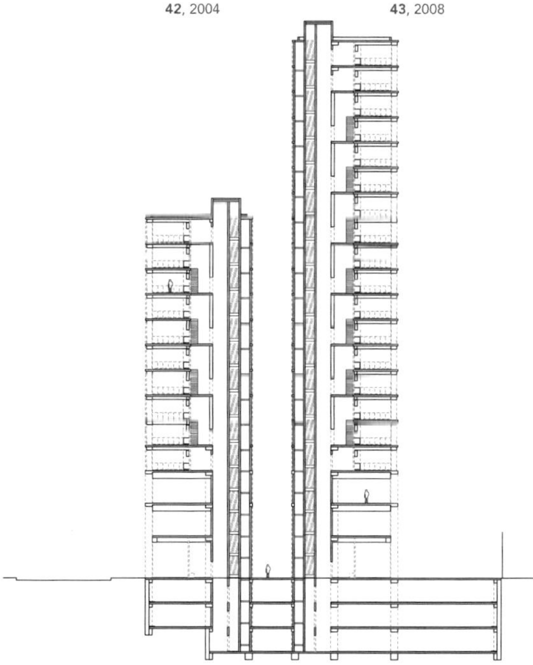

67, 2017

70, 2017

Fernanda Canales is a practicing architect and author of *Vivienda Colectiva en México: El derecho a la arquitectura* (Gustavo Gili, 2017) and *Architecture in Mexico 1900-2010: The Construction of Modernity* (Arquine, 2013). She holds a PhD in Architecture (ETSAM, Madrid), and has been visiting faculty member at Yale School of Architecture and invited speaker at the Architectural Association School in London, Edinburgh School of Architecture and Landscape Architecture, and Columbia University in New York. Her work has been distinguished with several international awards, such as the Emerging Voices Award from The Architectural League of New York and widely exhibited, among other venues, at the Royal Academy of Arts in London, ifa-Gallery in Stuttgart and at the Venice Biennale of Architecture.

"Civilization is primarily urbanism; by that I mean, more than a vision of world and men, a civilization is a vision of men in the world and men as a world: an order, a social architecture."[1]

Octavio Paz

1 Octavio Paz, *Sor Juana, or, The Traps of Faith*, Margaret Sayers Peden (trans.), Cambridge, MA: Harvard University Press, 1988.

Shared Structures,
Private Spaces
Housing in Mexico

Fernanda Canales

Published by
Actar Publishers, New York, Barcelona
www.actar.com

Edited by
Fernanda Canales
Ricardo Devesa

Drawings: Fernanda Canales
Axonometric drawings: Fernanda Canales
+ LANZA Atelier
Texts: Fernanda Canales
Foreword: Iñaki Ábalos

Graphic design review
Ramon Prat, Marga Gibert

Copy editing and proofreading:
Adela García-Herrera
Anna Tetas

Translation to English:
Polisemia

Priting and binding:
Tiger Printing, Hong Kong

Distribution
Actar D, Inc. New York, Barcelona.

New York
440 Park Avenue South, 17th Floor
New York, NY 10016, USA
T +1 2129662207
salesnewyork@actar-d.com

Barcelona
Roca i Batlle 2
08023 Barcelona, Spain
T +34 933 282 183
eurosales@actar-d.com

Indexing
English ISBN: 978-1-945150-88-3
PCN: Library of Congress Control
Number: 2017960644

Printed in China

Publication date: 2020

Con la colaboración de:

FUNDACIÓN JUMEX
ARTE CONTEMPORÁNEO

INFONAVIT

REURBANO